AF304894

THE DEPARTMENT OF REVENGE

How Trump Took Control of American Justice

DEVLIN BARRETT

SIMON & SCHUSTER

NEW YORK   AMSTERDAM/ANTWERP   LONDON
TORONTO   SYDNEY/MELBOURNE   NEW DELHI

Simon & Schuster
1230 Avenue of the Americas
New York, NY 10020

For more than 100 years, Simon & Schuster has championed authors and the stories they create. By respecting the copyright of an author's intellectual property, you enable Simon & Schuster and the author to continue publishing exceptional books for years to come. We thank you for supporting the author's copyright by purchasing an authorized edition of this book.

First Simon & Schuster hardcover edition June 2026

SIMON & SCHUSTER and colophon are registered trademarks of Simon & Schuster, LLC

Simon & Schuster strongly believes in freedom of expression and stands against censorship in all its forms. For more information, visit BooksBelong.com.

For information about special discounts for bulk purchases, please contact Simon & Schuster Special Sales at 1-866-506-1949 or business@simonandschuster.com.

The Simon & Schuster Speakers Bureau can bring authors to your live event. For more information or to book an event, contact the Simon & Schuster Speakers Bureau at 1-866-248-3049 or visit our website at www.simonspeakers.com.

Interior design by Carly Loman

Manufactured in the United States of America

1   3   5   7   9   10   8   6   4   2

Library of Congress Control Number: 2026938264

ISBN 978-1-6680-6512-9
ISBN 978-1-6680-6514-3 (ebook)

Scan here to get book recommendations, exclusive offers, and more delivered to your inbox.

For my father and my stepmother

Contents

Prologue

W e own the doors to the courtroom," a senior Justice Department official declared in mid-2025. "And we are going to take back the streets."

Every week, the senior official, Aakash Singh, convened a video conference call with top federal prosecutors around the country. The most experienced lawyers in U.S. attorney offices would gather to listen to the new marching orders from Justice Department headquarters.

Singh had been tapped to deliver those orders on behalf of his boss, Deputy Attorney General Todd Blanche.

At thirty-three years old, Singh had been a low-level federal prosecutor for only a handful of years, but what he lacked in experience he made up for in swagger and bravado. Singh was part of a group of senior advisors in the administration that some Justice Department veterans derisively called "Blanche's bros." Singh's weekly calls from Washington, DC, tended to be awkward pep talks in which the younger lawyer exhorted his older, more sophisticated subordinates to carry out the drastic changes President Trump wanted to see at the Justice Department.

In the calls, Singh sometimes referred to Trump as the Justice Department's "chief client," which grated on a generation of Justice Department lawyers who had taken an oath to uphold the country's laws and principles, not to serve the whims of a particular person, even if that person was the president.

Singh's video speeches could be comical but also frightening; for all the bluster, his directives underscored to many veteran government lawyers that one of the most important principles of the Justice Department, prosecutorial discretion, was dying at the hands of the Trump administration. In 2025, prosecutorial discretion would be replaced by an entirely different principle: presidential discretion.

We own the doors to the courtroom. Singh's point in that call and others was that federal prosecutors had tremendous power to decide whom to charge with crimes, and he implied that federal judges had little authority to stop them. His message was simple: Federal prosecutors should be charging more people with more serious crimes. When he talked that way, people on the video conference thought he came off as oblivious—ignorant of how some federal criminal laws worked. As part of the new Trump administration, Singh frequently urged the legal army underneath him to get more aggressive and to charge more serious crimes for conduct that would previously have merited lesser charges or no charges at all. Someone who loans a car to a drug dealer should be charged with material support for terrorism, he urged in one call. Minnesota officials who criticized immigration crackdowns should be investigated for possibly impeding law enforcement, he declared in another.

Many of the lawyers on the calls found Singh's commands a waste of time, particularly when he rattled off statutes as if reading from a menu. But like it or not, Singh spoke for Blanche and the other Trump appointees running the department, and those appointees frequently made the job of enforcing federal law in the United States chaotic.

Justice Department lawyers are trained to obsessively follow the rules, of which there are many, particularly the *Principles of Federal Prosecution,* a 23,000-word set of instructions designed to ensure "the fair, even-handed administration of the federal criminal laws." Those guidelines are meant to restrain prosecutors from pursuing cases because they like particular people, or dislike others, or because pursuing a case might advance the prosecutor's career.

The guidebook for prosecutorial discretion preaches restraint in a system with so many federal criminal laws that every violation can't possibly be investigated and prosecuted. The job of federal prosecutors is to pursue the cases that matter the most in their communities and to do so in a way that builds public trust that the government's vast law enforcement powers are being used reasonably, carefully, and fairly.

As Blanche, Attorney General Pam Bondi, FBI Director Kash Patel, and the rest of Trump's team took control of the Justice Department in 2025, federal prosecutors saw the old principles of prosecutorial discretion discarded. Instead, they would operate under new rules, based on personal connections to power, the political agenda of the administration, and a deep-seated desire by the president for revenge against the department that had tried and failed to convict him of crimes.

In 2025, prosecutorial discretion crumbled under the force of presidential decree.

"I was the hunted," Trump told reporters in June 2025. "And now I'm the hunter. It's a big difference."

CHAPTER I

Day One

The people chosen to run Trump's Justice Department in his second term came into the job vowing to rid law enforcement institutions not just of the people who had investigated President Trump and his allies between 2021 and 2025, but also of any people who might seriously consider investigating him or his allies in the future. The personnel purges they oversaw didn't affect every law enforcement official or every case, because much of the Justice Department's work has no meaningful connection to politics. But the intensely political focus of the department's leaders was felt almost everywhere in 2025, and many lawyers and agents came to dread being assigned a case that might draw a malevolent eye from their leaders.

I've covered federal law enforcement for a quarter century, a time span that has included stints at the Associated Press, the *New York Post*, *The Washington Post*, *The Wall Street Journal*, and now *The New York Times*. In that period, there has never been a year like 2025, because there has never been this kind of all-out battle within the department or the FBI: a fight over the mission itself.

In Trump's first White House stint, the president cursed and complained when the people he had picked to run the Justice Department and the FBI failed to do what he wanted. Those individuals often refused to accede to his demands, or they tried to appease him with half measures and vague assurances of future satisfaction.

In his second term, Trump and the members of his inner circle were far shrewder about how to get what they wanted, and far more demanding. In many ways, Trump's second term has been defined by his four years out of office. In those years, Trump's home was raided by the FBI, and some of his aides were turned into witnesses against him. In those years, two federal grand juries handed up indictments against him that carried the potential for decades of prison time. In those years, local grand juries in Atlanta and Manhattan also indicted him, piling up the legal risks of what Trump and his allies called "lawfare," a term he used to mean deploying the legal system as a political cudgel against him.

Trump campaigned explicitly in 2024 on the promise of revenge for those things. That revenge would come first to people who worked at the Justice Department. A second wave of revenge would be delivered by the Justice Department against others. Revenge against the people who had investigated and prosecuted him and his supporters. Revenge against an entire legal system that had once been poised to ruin not just his career but also his business and his life. And ultimately, revenge against the parts of America he despised.

The people tapped to run the department in his second term reflected that change in mindset. No longer would the people in the Attorney General's Office, on the fifth floor of Justice Department headquarters, or the Deputy Attorney General's Office, on the fourth floor, seek to protect career prosecutors from a president who viewed them as his mortal enemies.

In the first Trump term, there were huge fights within his administration about the independence of the department and the FBI, but those battles were largely waged along Pennsylvania Avenue, from the White House on one end to the Justice Department and FBI buildings six blocks away. The fights were predominantly between different parts of the government—clashes between institutions and between their powerful leaders.

The second Trump term saw those battles move inside those buildings, from office to office and floor to floor, as career officials pushed to maintain rules and standards meant to ensure that no one was above the law, even if they worked in the White House or Congress or at major corporations.

Over time, judges and juries started to reject some of the cases demanded by Donald Trump and his senior advisor Stephen Miller, but the arsenal of federal law enforcement power was largely the president's and Miller's to deploy. In the eyes of many of the people receiving those directions, the White House badly misused the law and the department for political ends. Gone was the long-standing tradition in which decisions about how and when to prosecute individuals were left to law enforcement professionals.

Gone, too, according to many veteran agents, was the FBI as it had existed since the Watergate era. As the nation's premier investigative agency, the FBI in 2025 continued to pursue a vast array of criminal investigations, many of which were of little interest to the country's political leaders. But when it came to subjects Trump and Miller cared about, their demands were clear and unbending—hunt the people and institutions they reviled, punish the left for what they considered its cardinal sins against conservatives, and amass within the office of the president far more power over law enforcement operations.

Donald J. Trump was sworn into office as the forty-seventh president of the United States at approximately 12:02 p.m. on January 20, 2025. As one of his last acts in office that morning, President Joe Biden preemptively pardoned his two brothers and his sister, to shield them from what he feared would be politically motivated investigations by the Trump administration.

Earlier in the day, Biden had pardoned a slew of former officials he thought might also be targeted by Trump, including Dr. Anthony Fauci, the retired U.S. Army General Mark Milley, and members and staff of the House committee that had investigated the January 6, 2021, pro-Trump riot at the Capitol Building.

In a statement, Biden made clear that the pardons came from a place of fear—fear of what Trump might do to those people if they were not protected by a federal pardon. "The issuance of these pardons should not be mistaken as an acknowledgment that any individual engaged in wrongdoing, nor should acceptance be misconstrued as an admission of guilt for any offense," Biden said. "Our nation owes these public servants a debt of gratitude for their tireless commitment to our country."

At the Justice Department, where Attorney General Merrick Garland and his deputy, Lisa Monaco, had experienced a series of legal setbacks in 2024, the pardons landed like another grim thud, a fresh measure of just how much faith the outgoing Democratic president had lost in the future independence and judgment of the department.

Justice Department headquarters, a seven-story stone building in downtown Washington, DC, opened in 1934. The department outgrew the original 1.2-million-square-foot building decades ago, and what the DOJ employees call "Main Justice" now encompasses a constellation of office buildings scattered around Washington. The main building, named after Robert F. Kennedy, remains the organization's head, where the attorney general and top staffers meet and make decisions. In the center of the building, protected from the noise of city traffic, is a quiet and often empty courtyard. At the center of the courtyard sits a giant fountain ringed by a circular driveway of pink and beige cobblestones.

Visitors to the courtyard tend to arrive in black SUVs, delivered by stern security details. Cabinet secretaries and foreign dignitaries are whisked in, rarely pausing to look around as they hurry to reach the inner sanctum of the nation's top law enforcement agency. If they did look up, they still might easily miss the figures carved high on the courtyard walls. Boreas, a bearded, muscular figure, blows the north wind. East, west, and south compass points are staffed by Eurus, Zephyrus, and Notus. The four Greek gods of wind appear to be flying, their robes billowing around them as they blow justice to the four corners of the country.

The Justice Department, which has long sought to serve as a moral compass for the nation, has a physical compass built into its walls. Close examination of the little-noticed carvings reveals a dirty secret: Boreas, the north wind, is off-kilter, pointing more northwest than true north.

The Depression-era sculptors did not build a perfect compass, and since the Justice Department's creation after the Civil War, it has never been a perfect institution. Like the building's white marble veined with blue, our justice system has always been streaked with human errors, misjudgment, and instances of shameful wrongdoing.

In the post-9/11 era, Justice Department lawyers wrote legal opinions greenlighting waterboarding and other forms of abuse against terrorism suspects. One 2002 Justice Department memo said the only abuse of prisoners that could constitute torture were actions causing organ failure or death. In 1995, an FBI agent in Boston tipped off mobster Whitey Bulger to his impending indictment—the last act of betrayal in a long-corrupt relationship. In the twentieth century, J. Edgar Hoover's FBI repeatedly violated the rights of protesters, activists, and subversives under investigation and even sent an anonymous letter to Martin Luther King Jr. decrying his "immoral conduct lower than that of a beast." The letter warned ominously, "King, there is only one thing left for you to do. You know what it is."

The capacity for horrible conduct highlights how important the Justice Department is to the functioning of the country. A Justice Department and an FBI without rules, without good judgment, and without a moral compass represent a massive danger not just to Americans' constitutionally guaranteed rights and freedoms but also to the nation's stability and safety.

Most Americans can remember the start of the Preamble to the Constitution, the one that begins, "We the people of the United States, in Order to form a more perfect Union . . ." But for many, the classroom memory fades just before the next stated reason for creating America: to "establish Justice."

From the start, this country's founders sought a shared moral sense of true north—agreed-upon definitions of right and wrong. The path to justice is not drawn with the certainty of GPS positioning. Real-life justice is like navigating by the stars, and the way forward must adapt and adjust to changes in conditions. Hoover long dismissed the threat posed by the Mafia, preferring to focus on spies, subversives, and Communist sympathizers. Later, a new generation of Justice Department and FBI leaders used federal law to end the Mob's stranglehold on many industries, unions, and cities.

As Bondi, Blanche, and Associate Deputy Attorney General Emil Bove radically reshaped the Justice Department in 2025, lawyers and Democrats sharply criticized what they saw as the death of the department's independence in matters of criminal investigations and prosecutions. President Trump and his administration defended their actions as a necessary counter to the decisions made by the Biden administration to investigate and prosecute him, and he tended to angrily brush aside any rebuttal suggesting that the Trump cases, whatever their flaws, had been built on evidence gathered and measured by career law enforcement officials.

Much of the public debate about the politicization and "weaponization" of the Justice Department glosses over the dual nature of the department's work. After Watergate, key safeguards were put in place by successive administrations to prevent White House meddling with prosecutorial and investigative decisions, but the department and the attorney general still took some direction from political leaders. The Justice Department and the FBI have been independent from the White House in some ways and obedient in others. In 1999, President Bill Clinton used his State of the Union speech to announce that the Justice Department would launch a civil investigation of tobacco companies, and months later, the DOJ sued those companies.

What changed in 2025 was not that there were suddenly politics in the sacrosanct halls of justice, but that Trump's campaign of revenge became the most important work in the building, overpowering long-standing department traditions forged by Republicans and Democrats to insulate criminal prosecutions from manipulation and misuse.

How Trump's triumvirate of Bondi, Blanche, and Bove carried out his wishes, and the effect it had on the department and the country, is a story of right and wrong, of courage and cowardice. Obscure government lawyers were frequently forced to choose between standing up or submitting, or between speaking out or shutting up. This didn't mean that speaking out was always a sign of bravery, or that silence always meant capitulation. Inside the Justice Department in 2025, courage was sometimes quiet, and cowards sometimes bellowed.

The real takeover of the Justice Department began at 3 p.m. on the day of Trump's inauguration, and it came via email.

Four senior officials overseeing the nation's immigration courts received emails from the Justice Management Division, the human resources office of the department, notifying them they were being fired. Little understood by most Americans, the nation's immigration courts are actually a part of the Justice Department. The first-day firings showed just how fast the administration would move to crack down on immigration, starting with the people who guided asylum and deportation decisions.

Simultaneously, seven of the most senior career officials in the Justice Department received similarly shocking 3 p.m. emails. The messages said they had been reassigned to something called the Sanctuary Cities Enforcement Working Group, an office that no one had ever heard of because it didn't exist yet.

More than one of the recipients of these emails initially thought it must have been a mistake. The people targeted within hours of the new administration's tenure served in some of the most senior and sensitive career positions in the department.

Bruce Swartz was a deputy assistant attorney general, the kind of Justice Department job title that came with too many nouns to be descriptive. But Swartz was an uncommon voice of authority inside the building, having held the job for twenty-five years. As a senior law enforcement official, he often did a significant amount of diplomatic work, negotiating the most difficult cases of extradition and negotiations with foreign law enforcement agencies.

George Toscas held the same nondescript title and played a similarly huge role at the department's National Security Division, where he had overseen espionage and terrorism cases for nearly two decades.

Eun Young Choi, who was much younger than Toscas, oversaw the department's rapidly expanding portfolio of cryptocurrency investigations.

At the Antitrust Division, Manish Kumar also received an immediate reassignment to the Sanctuary Cities Enforcement Working Group. Stephanie Hinds, a senior official with thirty years at the Department, received one of the notices.

The most senior lawyer targeted for removal that first day was Bradley Weinsheimer, who served as the top career official in the department. In that role, Weinsheimer had overseen special counsel investigations not just of Trump, but also of President Biden and his son Hunter.

Corey Amundson, the head of the department's Public Integrity Section, was among the lower-ranking officials targeted that first day, but his rank did not reflect the importance of the office he ran. The Public Integrity Section, referred to as "PIN" by lawyers, and sometimes as "piss" by disgruntled FBI agents, was a critical chokepoint in the chain of command when it came to corruption investigations.

As shocked and upset as the lawyers were to be effectively demoted, some of them had feared or expected it. Toscas had played a key role in the Biden investigations, but also in several Trump investigations, and in the 2015 and 2016 investigation of Hillary Clinton's use of a private email server. Swartz, too, had touched past Trump cases. Amundson, as the head of PIN, was arguably a frequent flyer in Trump's angry orbit. He had weighed in on a raft of legal issues related to Trump or his allies. Others, like Kumar, were hard to connect to any case or issue Trump's inner circle might care about. In one strategic swipe, the new administration removed many of the key players who carried clout inside the organization. Without those people and the personal authority they brought to their positions, the department was newly vulnerable.

About 4 p.m., Amundson and others had a meeting with their new boss, Emil Bove, to talk about a delicate issue for the incoming administration. Tom Homan, who was about to become President Trump's "border czar," had been a subject in a secret corruption investigation in Texas the previous year.

According to people familiar with the investigation, undercover FBI agents posing as contractors had been investigating a Texas businessman, a federal contractor who worked near the southern border, when that man suggested in 2023 that Homan could help the undercovers win federal contracts for border security work. The businessman suggested that a payment of a million dollars to Homan could get them contracts worth much more.

That initial conversation in 2023 led to further discussions and, eventually, to a September meeting in a hotel room, where the undercover agents allegedly gave Homan a bag from the Cava food chain containing fifty thousand dollars in cash. Homan's friend who had first suggested the meeting also got paid, to the tune of ten thousand dollars.

"We both know there's no Cava in that bag," one of the undercovers said to Homan, according to a person familiar with the investigation. Homan indicated that he understood, and he told the agents that if they wanted to pass requests to him, to do it through his businessman friend, according to people familiar with the discussion. He left the hotel room with the bag.

When Trump won the election less than two months later, federal investigators realized they now had a bigger headache on their hands. The senior prosecutors in Texas were wary of proceeding, as was the FBI. The next logical investigative step would have been to reconnect with Homan or his friend in December and find out if their plan of paying for contracts would proceed. But that didn't happen, because the decision-makers overseeing the case were not particularly eager that it do so.

In December 2024, about a month before Trump's inauguration, the Justice Department gave the Trump team a vague heads-up that there was an investigation related to Homan. To law enforcement officials, it seemed like a potentially awkward but necessary move to deal with the incoming administration in good faith. Neither the department nor the FBI wanted to be accused, once Trump's team was in power, of having sandbagged them or kept them in the dark about the case.

So, on the very first day of the new administration, Emil Bove walked into the Justice Department as the "principal associate deputy attorney general"—another noun-heavy job title, one that insiders called "the PAY-DAG." He was also the acting deputy attorney general, which meant he held tremendous decision-making authority in the department, at least until Bondi and Blanche were confirmed by the Senate.

The late-afternoon meeting about the Homan case began oddly, with Bove at first joining remotely by phone, but later he appeared in the room to finish the discussion in person.

Handing an incoming public official a bag of cash is the kind of evidence many corruption prosecutors dream of, but Bove said little in the meeting about his views of the case. A former supervisor in the Manhattan federal prosecutor's office, where he had a reputation as a bully with a bad temper, Bove would later tell Justice Department lawyers that he thought the Homan case seemed like weaponization of law enforcement against a Trump ally.

Bove, who had worked feverishly throughout 2024 to defend Trump in court, still sounded like a defense lawyer. Meanwhile, the reassigned senior department lawyers were starting to realize who else had been targeted, and it became clear that the administration had decided to do immediate housecleaning of some of the most respected and influential officials in the building.

Among the lawyers fired or sidelined that day, some wept for the end of careers they loved and didn't want to leave. Others tried to be philosophical about it, reasoning that if the Trump administration wanted to chop off some heads, it was good to get it out of the way early, so that the building could restabilize as quickly as possible. Those who tried to be optimistic did not want to consider the reality that it was just the start of what Trump planned to do to the department and the FBI.

That evening, Trump pardoned or commuted the sentences of everyone convicted or charged in connection with the January 6, 2021, riot at the U.S. Capitol, where a pro-Trump mob briefly delayed the certification of Biden's electoral victory.

The decision to grant sweeping clemency to more than 1,500 people caught many of Trump's own deputies by surprise. Just days earlier at her confirmation hearing, Bondi had suggested to senators that Trump would not pardon people convicted of assaulting police officers.

Elizabeth Oyer, the Justice Department's pardon attorney, struggled to explain to the incoming administration that federal prisons couldn't simply throw their doors open in a matter of hours and let hundreds of people walk out that night. The bureaucratic process of freeing many hundreds of inmates would take at least a day.

Nevertheless, the federal Bureau of Prisons tried hard to please the new administration. In Colorado, federal prison officials released Andrew Taake, a Texas man serving a six-year prison sentence after pleading guilty to assaulting police officers with bear spray and a whip made of braided metal cable, sometimes called a stinger. Taake was released from custody despite pending charges against him in Houston, Texas, for online solicitation of a minor. Five days earlier, the Houston District Attorney's Office had specifically flagged to prison officials that Taake should not be released. He was released anyway. It took law enforcement authorities more than two weeks to find the fugitive.

Paul Ingrassia was sworn in that afternoon as the White House liaison to the Justice Department. After Trump signed the January 6 pardons, Ingrassia rushed to the DC jail to join pro-Trump protesters demanding the release of the few remaining January 6 defendants there. Shortly after midnight, jail officials relented and released two brothers who had been charged with assaulting police officers during the riot at the Capitol Building.

Ingrassia hadn't waited until day one to start flexing his power at the department and the FBI. Four days earlier, in his role as a Trump transition official, he phoned Brian Driscoll, the FBI's special agent in charge of the Newark field office.

Drizz, as he was known inside the Bureau, was something of a legend. For years he had worked on the Hostage Rescue Team, a kind of supercharged SWAT program designed to tackle the most difficult counterterrorism and hostage situations. Driscoll had excelled in the role, receiving a Medal of Valor for his work raiding an ISIS operative's home in Syria. He'd also worked on a mission that rescued a kidnapped kindergartener in Alabama, and another that neutralized a mass shooter in Upstate New York.

In the conformist culture of the FBI, Driscoll stood out. He wore his curly hair long and had a mustache that hung over the ends of his mouth, and colleagues compared him to the fictional pirate Jack Sparrow. For much of his career, he had stayed out of the traditional command structure, preferring to operate in the FBI's equivalent of special forces.

Driscoll had gotten a heads-up from other FBI officials, including Paul Abbate, the acting director, that he and Robert Kissane, the senior counterterrorism official in the FBI's New York office, were being considered for temporary roles at FBI headquarters, though it was unclear what the roles were exactly.

Ingrassia's first call with Driscoll, on the Friday before Trump's inauguration, did not go well. Ingrassia asked two relatively straightforward questions about the organizational structure of the FBI and about threats to the United States. Then he asked Driscoll whom he had voted for. Offended, Driscoll refused to answer, and said asking those kind of questions were a violation of federal law—specifically, the Hatch Act.

Ingrassia then asked if Driscoll agreed that the FBI agents who had "stormed" Trump's home in Mar-a-Lago should be held "accountable" for what they'd done.

No, Driscoll replied, because they were doing their job based on a properly premised investigation and a warrant approved by a judge.

Ingrassia then asked when Driscoll had started supporting President Trump.

Shocked that he had even been asked the question, Driscoll refused to answer. Like all FBI agents and Justice Department career employees, he had been trained, tested, hired, and promoted in a culture that sought to studiously avoid bringing politics into their work. It's not that prosecutors or agents were ideological eunuchs or prudes—FBI agents overall tended to run conservative, while Justice Department lawyers, like lawyers generally, often leaned more liberal.

A core principle of federal civil service was that people did not carry their political baggage into work decisions. In such large organizations, there were some people who violated the rules and some people who tried to bend them, but the overwhelming majority of Justice Department employees followed them and understood that they existed for good reason. Generations of law enforcement officials had sought to make a professional class of government lawyers and investigators, a work culture that demanded high standards not just in court or at crime scenes, but in every facet of their work.

None of that seemed to matter to Ingrassia.

He asked Driscoll if he had voted for a Democrat in the last five elections.

Driscoll refused to answer. With that, Ingrassia cut the interview short. The whole exchange had been bizarre. An aggressive young Trump staffer with no law enforcement or even White House experience had grilled a veteran FBI agent with a series of highly inappropriate questions about his political loyalty. Driscoll found it alarming and insulting.

Later that night, Bove called Driscoll and told him he had "failed" the interview. Driscoll, Ingrassia had told others, was not "based out" enough—not willing to declare his allegiance to the president's agenda.

Bove still wanted Driscoll in the job and told him he had worked to "flip" Ingrassia's negative review. Driscoll asked what job he was even up for, and Bove told him it was the deputy director position—the number two job at the FBI, an incredibly important and demanding role that is akin to the chief operating officer of the Bureau.

Driscoll told Bove he would serve only if someone above him in the chain of command asked him to do so. Bove explained that the administration planned to make Kissane the acting director and Driscoll the acting deputy director. If either of them refused, Bove added, the president would probably appoint someone from outside the FBI to run the Bureau temporarily while awaiting the confirmation of Trump's choice for director, Kash Patel. Implicit in Bove's description was a carrot and stick for two men who had made the FBI their life and wanted to protect it: *If you guys don't do this, we will find someone worse.*

Driscoll arrived at FBI headquarters around 1 p.m. Monday, about an hour after Trump became president of the United States for the second time. The FBI director's conference room features a large table and two special chairs, one reserved for the director and the other for the deputy director. Kissane took the director's chair, and Driscoll took a seat in the deputy's chair.

As they sat in the conference room discussing the huge task ahead of them, a senior aide came in with a copy of the White House directive for their assignments. Somehow the paperwork had produced a mix-up in the job assignments and described Driscoll as the acting director and Kissane as his deputy. Confused, Kissane called Bove to explain why the announcement was wrong. Bove, now serving as the acting number two official at the Justice Department, told Kissane that it was a simple clerical error.

But, rather than admit the error, the White House said that Kissane and Driscoll should just take the jobs as described on paper.

Awkwardly, Driscoll got up out of the deputy director's chair and sat instead in the director's chair. Kissane, in turn, took a seat in the deputy chair where Driscoll had been sitting. The FBI's first accidental director then got to work.

At the Justice Department and FBI, day one of the new administration was a blur of sweeping pardons, chaotic promotions, and the sudden ouster of senior career officials who served critical roles in upholding law enforcement standards. Those actions would set the tone for everything that happened next, and they were a warning of just how fast all the president's men and women would pursue his revenge.

CHAPTER 2

The Worst Lawyers Money Can Buy

On March 3, 2025, John Giordano raised his hand and swore an oath to the Constitution to become the sixty-fourth U.S. attorney for the state of New Jersey. He had previously worked, briefly, as a federal prosecutor in Virginia, before taking jobs at Justice Department headquarters and, later, in the New Jersey state government. A Villanova Law School graduate, Giordano had clerked for a federal judge in New Jersey.

He was also a loyal Trump supporter, having worked for the president's transition team. The day he got the U.S. attorney job, he called it the "honor of a lifetime." That honor lasted all of three weeks, when Giordano was suddenly replaced by Alina Habba, President Trump's personal lawyer. Dumped from a job he had just started, Giordano received as a consolation prize a posting as ambassador to Namibia.

Habba's professional path to become the top federal prosecutor in the Garden State was much different from Giordano's. A lithe brunette who favored high heels and short skirts, she cheerfully agreed that much of her success had been due to her looks. "Somebody said to me, 'Alina, would you rather be smart or pretty?'" she said in a 2024 podcast. "I said, 'Oh, easy—pretty. I can fake being smart.'"

Habba then proceeded to test that theory, with disastrous results.

That year, she represented Trump in two civil trials. One was a defamation case brought by E. Jean Carroll, a writer who said Trump had sexually assaulted her decades earlier during a chance encounter at Bergdorf Goodman, a high-end Manhattan department store. Carroll sued him in federal court over statements he had made when he denied her accusations.

For Trump and Habba, the January 2024 trial was a debacle from start to finish.

The judge, Lewis Kaplan, had zero patience for Habba's unfamiliarity with basic courtroom procedure or for Trump's penchant for audible, angry outbursts. By the end of the trial, Judge Kaplan was so fed up with Habba's conduct in court that he threatened to send her to jail. "You are on the verge of spending some time in the lockup. Now sit down," he told her. She immediately complied.

Trump was far less restrained than his lawyer. Judge Kaplan became so upset over Trump's commentary during Carroll's testimony that he threatened to have the former president removed from the courtroom. "I understand you are probably very eager for me to do that," the judge said.

At that, Trump threw up his arms and said, "I would love it, I would love it!"

"I know you would, because you can't control yourself in this circumstance. You just can't," Kaplan said.

Trump also lost his temper on the day he testified at the trial. The former president was furious that the judge sharply limited what he could say to the jury. Fuming as he walked out of the courtroom, Trump repeatedly declared, "This is not America."

While Trump and Habba complained that the judge's rulings made it impossible for them to defend themselves, the verdict suggested that their belligerent behavior had badly alienated the jury.

In late January, the panel awarded Carroll $83 million of Trump's money. A month later, in another case argued by Habba, a state court judge in Manhattan ruled that Trump and his companies had to pay $355 million (and growing, with interest) in a civil judgment for having inflated the value of assets. While that judgment was later set aside on appeal, Habba had managed, in a two-month span in early 2024, to lose her boss more than $400 million in legal judgments.

Those verdicts, plus a criminal conviction in May for business records fraud in state court in Manhattan, became key parts of Trump's ever-growing grievances against the entire legal system.

Habba was proud to represent Trump, and she shared his outrage when judges and juries ruled against him. She, Trump, and his legal team used the term *lawfare* to describe how judges like Kaplan wouldn't let them enter the kind of evidence they wanted to. Habba also counted New York's attorney general, Letitia James, as among the worst "lawfare" offenders, because she campaigned on the explicit promise to investigate Trump and then, after winning office, filed lawsuits against him and his companies. Such arguments often went nowhere in court, but plenty of his supporters agreed with Trump that such cases seemed like overkill, a way of trying to hurt him in court because his political appeal was undiminished.

Habba was fully committed to defending Trump aggressively in such cases, but her representation came at a steep cost. In 2023, a federal judge in Florida ordered her and Trump to pay nearly a million dollars and sanctioned her for having filed a far-ranging lawsuit against a host of Trump targets, including Hillary Clinton.

"Here, we are confronted with a lawsuit that should never have been filed, which was completely frivolous, both factually and legally, and which was brought in bad faith for an improper purpose," Judge Donald Middlebrooks wrote. "Mr. Trump is a prolific and sophisticated litigant who is repeatedly using the courts to seek revenge on political adversaries. He is the mastermind of strategic abuse of the judicial process, and he cannot be seen as a litigant blindly following the advice of a lawyer. He knew full well the impact of his actions."

The judge called the lawsuit a "shotgun pleading," meaning it had been a wild mess of unrelated and unsubstantiated allegations. "The deliberate use of a shotgun pleading is an abusive litigation tactic which amounts to obstruction of justice," Middlebrooks wrote. A federal appeals court later unanimously upheld his decision.

Sigal Chattah had a big idea and was not afraid to pitch it to the top of the Justice Department. In July 2025, the failed GOP candidate turned interim U.S. attorney in the state of Nevada reached out to Deputy Attorney General Todd Blanche and a few of his senior aides.

Chattah had first assumed the role of Nevada's top federal prosecutor on April 1, acting in an interim capacity while, in theory, the administration prepared a Senate nomination for someone to take the job permanently. Under federal law and long-respected government practice, Chattah had only 120 days in such an appointment. So, by late July, she was, in theory at least, running out of time.

That's when she made her pitch to Todd Blanche, the second-highest official in the Justice Department. Earlier in his life, Blanche had worked as a federal prosecutor in New York, then later as a criminal defense lawyer. In both jobs, he was generally regarded by colleagues as a good lawyer, a reasonable man, and a decent person. In 2023, Trump hired Blanche to represent him, a choice that would have profound consequences for both men, the Justice Department, and the legal system.

When Trump hired Blanche, the ex-president was facing a seemingly insurmountable problem—no fewer than four criminal cases barreling toward indictment and potential trials. Many Republicans feared that the cases would derail not just Trump's political comeback but the GOP itself. Some Republicans fervently embraced Trump's argument that Democrats had engaged in "lawfare" to use the legal system to defeat a populist politician. Other Republicans were ready to put Trump and the Make America Great Again movement behind them but felt powerless to resist the political tide propelling Trump forward. Many Democrats, in turn, hoped Trump's criminal cases would send him to prison before he got anywhere near the White House.

With Blanche at his side, Trump had gone on trial in the spring of 2024 and been convicted in a Manhattan courtroom of all thirty-four counts against him for falsifying business records—a legally sanitized way of describing the company paperwork used to cover up hush money payments made to a porn star around the time of his 2016 campaign.

Blanche had been Trump's lead attorney throughout that trial. There are few bonding experiences more intense than working together through a long, high-profile criminal trial, and for all the pummeling Blanche received from the jury, from the judge, and sometimes behind closed doors from Trump himself, there was a rare degree of trust and understanding between the two. They also had made a strange kind of history together, collaborating in the first criminal trial of a former American president.

Outside the Manhattan courtroom, Blanche also led Trump's legal effort to delay the other criminal cases against him until after the election. Thanks in no small part to the Supreme Court, he succeeded.

Blanche's reward for that largely successful rope-a-dope strategy was to be named the deputy attorney general—or DAG, as department lawyers call it. The second most powerful position in the department, the deputy attorney general runs the day-to-day operations of the Justice Department. With more than ten thousand lawyers, the DOJ is the largest law office on earth, which means there is endless opportunity for internal disagreements. Because intractable disputes and thorny issues often land on the desk of the deputy attorney general, the job is sometimes referred to as the "bad cop" of the department.

While Trump had been Blanche's client in his private practice, the Justice Department's client is the United States—its people and its government. In some cases, that means the department defends the interests of the office of the presidency, but in the modern era, the department has never tried to be a law firm that works for only one person—until, that is, Trump was sworn into office in January 2025.

In the new architecture of the Trump administration, Pam Bondi was the attorney general. She quickly declared that all employees must zealously work for the president's agenda—a decree that stunned much of her workforce, particularly given how many people at the department had worked through the first Trump administration and not experienced such sweeping and consequential changes in direction, personnel, or purpose.

Blanche answered to Bondi but had a special role in the department and with the president's inner circle. While Bondi went on Fox News from the White House Lawn to talk about deporting immigrants, fighting Democrats, and criticizing judges, Blanche set out to rebuild the engine of American justice according to Trump's specifications.

So, in late July 2025, it was Blanche whom Sigal Chattah reached out to with a proposal that was as aggressive as it was strange. Chattah proposed that the Justice Department and her office take a series of steps, many of them with baldly political motives. In essence, she proposed a freewheeling investigation of spurious right-wing claims of mass illegal voting by undocumented immigrants in Nevada. Such claims had been made in 2020 to try to undo the narrow victory Joe Biden had won in that state, and those claims had been repeatedly rejected by experts in voting procedure as based on meaningless or misleading data.

Now Chattah envisioned repurposing that debunked data to do something incredible: reallocate census numbers to redraw the state's map of congressional districts. She also wanted to use the data to launch an investigation of the Culinary Workers Union, the largest union in Nevada, one that had long supported Democrats.

That same data, she argued, should be used to launch an investigation of Mi Familia Vota, a nationwide group that promotes Latino voting, including in Nevada. Chattah envisioned nothing less than a takedown of those groups like the one carried out years before by conservative activists against ACORN, an umbrella group that advocated for low-income people. After ACORN workers were caught on undercover videos in 2009 making embarrassing and alarming statements about how to evade taxes and avoid arrest for prostitution, the group lost funding and eventually shut down.

That wasn't all Chattah wanted. The same data, she argued, should spur a Justice Department investigation of ActBlue, a political action committee that functioned as a key arm of Democratic fundraising, raising billions of dollars for candidates.

Finally, Chattah wanted the federal investigation to exonerate a group of Republicans known as the Nevada Six. The Nevada Six were "alternate electors" from the 2020 post-election scrum launched by then-President Trump to try to forestall his Electoral College defeat to Biden. The six Republicans, including the state GOP Chairman Michael J. McDonald, had been charged in December 2023 by the Clark County district attorney with felony crimes involving offering a false instrument and uttering a forged instrument, a legal term for using a false document.

Alternate electors were one of the 2020 Trump campaign's key means of trying to fight Biden's victory. By claiming they had their own slate of electors, often based on false or unfounded assertions of mass voter fraud in states like Nevada, Michigan, and Pennsylvania, they tried to present an alternate reality of a Trump victory in those states.

In some states like Pennsylvania, the alternates made clear that they were stepping forward as electors only if Trump were found to be the real winner. But in Nevada, the declarations of the alternates had no such caveat—they simply declared themselves to be the rightful electors, and Trump the true victor.

Six months after the Nevada Six were indicted, a Clark County judge dismissed the case, saying prosecutors had filed it in the wrong jurisdiction and suggesting that it might have been more properly brought in the state capital of Carson City. Prosecutors appealed that decision, hoping to revive the criminal charges. At the time Chattah reached out to Blanche, Nevada's supreme court had not ruled on the question.

Chattah's attempt to use her role as U.S. attorney to exonerate the Nevada Six was a brazen gambit, given that she had only recently stopped representing one of the defendants, Shawn Meehan. Any first-year law student, and many people who had never studied the law, understood the ethical conflict of a lawyer trying to use her powerful government position to kill a case against a former client. Chattah, however, was not just any lawyer, and she was proposing to the number two official at the Justice Department that she could use her government authority to help her former client and his co-defendants escape the charges against them.

Chattah was just as aggressive a U.S. attorney as she had been a private lawyer and GOP operative. In 2022, she had run for state attorney general in a campaign that led to revelations that she had once texted about her Democratic rival for the job, Aaron Ford, "This guy should be hanging from a fucking crane." Ford, the incumbent, is Black, and the comment sounded to many Nevadans like a racist callback to the days of lynching. In an interview with *Nevada Newsmakers*, a show about state politics, Chattah denied that this was what she meant. Defending the comment, she said it was an expression from her Yemeni Jewish heritage, though she also said the remark was "not necessarily tongue-in-cheek."

Chattah lost that election but remained an angry voice in Nevada Republican circles, and her legal work often served as an extension of her politics.

In July, as her time as the top federal prosecutor in the state seemed like it might be running out, she sought to convince Blanche and his aides to approve a host of investigations to punish Democrats, take away a congressional seat, and exonerate a former client of hers.

In another administration, either Democratic or Republican, such an overture might have led to an investigation, discipline, or even dismissal. Not this one. Within twenty-four hours after making her pitch in writing, Chattah got a meeting with members of Blanche's staff. Days later, the Justice Department made a series of procedural moves to keep her in the job indefinitely as the acting U.S. attorney for Nevada.

She had passed her audition for Donald Trump's Justice Department.

Around the nation, ninety-three U.S. attorneys served in such offices. Every administration ends up with, in the words of one former U.S. attorney, "a few clunkers"—people who get these important jobs primarily for their political connections rather than for their lawyerly experience or good judgment, or people who have the right kind of experience but who, once they take a top job, seem to lose their good judgment and become an unexpected embarrassment to the administration.

Chattah would never be confused with one of those clunkers. She was hired because of, not despite, her obsession with accusing Democrats of crimes and for launching far-reaching investigations whose stated purpose was not simply to harm or destroy groups supporting Democrats, but also to exonerate Republicans charged with crimes, including one of her former clients. And at the Justice Department in 2025, she was not an exception. She was the rule.

Shortly after her private pitch to use the Justice Department to redefine the political math of a key swing state, and shortly after being made acting U.S. attorney, Chattah gave an interview to KLAS, the local CBS news station in Las Vegas, where she talked more like a mobster than a prosecutor.

Her unusual appointment was constitutional, "not done in a nefarious manner, and there's nothing that politicians can do about it," she declared. "I know that they're scared because I know where a lot of bodies are buried, because I come from the defense world," she said. "So without saying too much about my previous experience as a defense attorney, but when you play that side, you know where all the bodies are buried, sometimes you even choose the location to bury them."

She also said she was working on a big investigation related to voting.

Many Americans, including members of Congress, don't grasp how cases are built inside the Justice Department. People often assume the department functions like most other government agencies—that the top leaders issue orders and instructions, and the lawyers and employees under them follow those instructions. That is true up to a point, but it is not true when it comes to how most criminal cases are launched and investigated.

Yes, the chain of command flows from top to bottom, but the chain of evidence typically flows from the bottom up—meaning agents or prosecutors get information and follow the evidence where it leads. To use some investigative techniques requires the approval of supervisors and, as in the case of search warrants, judges. The more sensitive or important the case, the higher up they need to go for such approvals, but typically, senior officials have been on the receiving end of such requests.

Donald Trump and his senior aides learned to their great frustration in his first term how much low-level prosecutors, managers, and senior career officials could thwart their desires for specific people to be investigated or charged with crimes. A single U.S. attorney could, and sometimes did, refuse instructions in politically sensitive cases that the career prosecutors felt were not properly grounded in the law and in the known facts or were simply unwise.

Trump was determined not to let that happen again. In January 2025, just before the president's inauguration, Stephen Miller held a meeting at Mar-a-Lago with a number of Trump lawyers expected to join the administration and made explicit what many of them had already expected: Justice Department leaders in the next administration would take orders directly from the White House, and would execute those orders enthusiastically, according to people familiar with the discussion. When it came to cases the White House cared about, the tradition of career prosecutors and agents feeding information up the chain of command would go out the window. Decisions would be made from the top down.

Enter Ed Martin.

"The best way to avoid getting indicted is to be investigated by Ed Martin," said one federal prosecutor who worked for him briefly in early 2025 before quitting in disgust.

Before joining the department, Martin was a Missouri lawyer involved in state politics. The second Trump administration drew heavily from conservative lawyers from the Show Me State. During Trump's long legal battles as an ex-president, one of the lawyers who joined Blanche's team, D. John Sauer, had worked in the Missouri Attorney General's Office.

Sauer could rightly claim to have redefined the constitutional balance of power when he convinced the Supreme Court in 2024 that presidents had immunity for official acts. Sauer had guided Trump's appeal argument that such presidential immunity protected him from the unusual prosecutorial theory pursued by Special Counsel Jack Smith over the January 6, 2021, pro-Trump riot at the U.S. Capitol. Sauer's strategy worked so well that the conservative members of the High Court went even farther than Trump's legal team thought they would, carving out a wide new lane of "presumptive" immunity for ill-defined "official" acts of a president.

The conservative majority created a new category of conduct that not only could not be prosecuted, but likely could not even be investigated. What exactly counted as an official act was left deliberately vague by the Court, though it seemed clear that the Court's decision would cripple and perhaps kill at least one of Special Counsel Jack Smith's cases against Trump. In the end, Trump's election victory ended the cases against him.

The Supreme Court opinion went even farther, suggesting that the president had the authority to direct criminal investigations of the Justice Department. "The president may discuss potential investigations and prosecutions with his Attorney General and other Justice Department officials," the majority ruled, a determination that effectively eradicated a post-Watergate practice of keeping the department's criminal work mostly walled off from political intervention by the White House.

Sauer's Supreme Court victory opened the door to an entirely different kind of relationship between a U.S. president and the Justice Department, and no one tried to rush through that door faster than Ed Martin.

The moment Trump became president again, he moved to take control of the prosecutors' offices the White House cared most about— New York; Washington, DC; and the Eastern District of Virginia. Those offices, and the types of cases they investigated, had been potential weapons pointed at Trump's inner circle, and the president's team was determined to control them as quickly as possible.

So, on Trump's first day back in office, Martin was appointed as the interim U.S. attorney in Washington, DC. His impact on morale was immediate and decisive—his staff overwhelmingly viewed him as a clown, albeit a dangerous one.

After less than a week, many prosecutors in the office marveled at what seemed to be a man on a mission to prove he didn't know how to do his job. In an email written days after his appointment, Martin lashed out at his own staff, complaining about leaks over his decision to launch an internal investigation into the office's charging practices against hundreds of pro-Trump rioters who took part in the January 6, 2021, attack on the U.S. Capitol.

"Wow, what a disappointment to have my email yesterday to you all was leaked almost immediately," he wrote in a grammatically challenged message that was also immediately shared with reporters. "Again, personally insulting and professionally unacceptable." He went on to emphasize that a failure to respond to his demand for information about the old January 6 cases "strikes me as insubordinate."

But it was his correspondence to people outside the office that made staff realize just how strange Martin's concept of his job as a prosecutor was. He sent menacing letters to politicians, to Georgetown University, and to medical journals, including *CHEST Journal,* a relatively obscure medical publication that published technically dense pieces on topics like lung cancer. The lawyers who received such correspondence often found them bizarre—part menace, part emotional appeal, and often devoid of any reference to a legal issue or actual law Martin was claiming to enforce.

What possible interest, or jurisdiction, could the U.S. attorney have in medical journals? The answer was never clear, even to those who worked for him. But Martin's letters seem to come from the same kind of deep suspicion of expertise that guided much of Trump's supporters. The Make America Great Again movement derided experts of all kinds—medical, scientific, legal, diplomatic, and cyber. Trump, after all, was a candidate who had first proved political experts wrong by winning the 2016 election. During the Covid-19 pandemic, he once suggested shining light inside patients' bodies or injecting them with disinfectant to fight the virus. And when he lost the 2020 election, he attacked the experts who repeatedly showed there had been no widespread voter fraud. To some of his staff, Martin's correspondence had the tone of someone who for years had nursed resentments against "elites" and was now getting even.

The letter he sent to *CHEST* in April had many of the hallmarks of a Martin missive. "As United States Attorney for the District of Columbia, I receive frequent requests for information and clarification," he wrote cryptically. "It has been brought to my attention that more and more journals and publications like *CHEST Journal* are conceding that they are partisans in various scientific debates—that is they have a position for which they are advocating either due to advertisement (under postal code) or sponsorship (under relevant fraud regulations)," the letter read.

"The public has certain expectations and you have certain responsibilities," he wrote, never bothering to say what any of those might be or what his job as a prosecutor had to do with either category.

"How do you assess your responsibilities to protect the public from misinformation? How do you clearly articulate to the public when you have certain viewpoints that are influenced by your ongoing relations with supporters, funders, advertisers, and others? Do you accept articles or essays from competing viewpoints?" he wrote.

The letter struck medical experts as bizarre. What point did Martin believe he was making, and what information was he actually looking for? Some of the lawyers who had to review and respond to such missives were dumbstruck as to how a good lawyer could even answer such a letter, and they marveled at how bad a lawyer one had to be to write one.

Martin fired off a number of similar demands to various medical journals, alarming professionals who understandably felt that the government was suddenly taking a factually vague but accusatory approach to the very premise of medical expertise.

When he wasn't hunting medical mysteries, Martin was pushing for cases against Democrats.

Though he'd never been a prosecutor before he became the head of the largest U.S. attorney's office in the country, Martin quickly announced "Operation Whirlwind," ostensibly designed to investigate the growing problem of threats against public officials. In practice, he seemed to care only about possible threats made against Republicans and Elon Musk.

On his first full day on the job, Martin sent a letter to the leader of the Senate Democrats, Chuck Schumer, seeking cooperation in what he said was an investigation into comments the New York lawmaker had made in March 2020 following the Supreme Court decision ending a national right to abortion. In his comments, Schumer had singled out two of the conservative justices, Neil Gorsuch and Brett Kavanaugh: "I want to tell you, Gorsuch. I want to tell you, Kavanaugh. You have released the whirlwind, and you will pay the price. You won't know what hit you if you go forward with these awful decisions," Schumer said.

Schumer retracted his comments the following day, saying he meant the two would face "political consequences" for what they had done. As inappropriate as they may have been, the senator's comments were a far cry from what criminal prosecutors would consider a threat under criminal statutes.

No matter. Martin was determined to plow forward and present evidence to a grand jury.

In a normally functioning Justice Department, an investigation into a political figure, let alone one of the leaders of a chamber of Congress, would be carefully studied and vetted before such a step was taken.

For decades, the Public Integrity Section of the Criminal Division of the Department of Justice had served as a kind of quality control for public corruption cases, an imperfect but serious effort to ensure that elected officials faced the same legal standards regardless of the federal jurisdiction in which they were investigated or the party to which they belonged. Justice Department regulations require that any U.S. attorney consult with the Public Integrity Section before pursuing such a case.

Martin had little patience for such rules. On Friday, February 21, he asked the on-duty PIN lawyer for a consult into the supposed threat made by Schumer. He also wanted to conduct an interview with

Schumer and get the Public Integrity Section's approval for a draft indictment of the minority leader.

The request set off immediate alarm bells within PIN. Barely a month into the job, Martin seemed determined to create a showdown with Congress over a set of old facts, a speech by the minority leader of the Senate, that government lawyers considered not even close to crossing the line of criminal conduct.

Two PIN lawyers had a Friday-afternoon call with Martin, to try to understand the case he thought he had. Martin backed off a little, saying at this time he was only seeking a consultation to open a criminal case and interview the senator. The anti-corruption lawyers told Martin there was probably not sufficient evidence to do either.

That night, hoping to nip this bit of prosecutorial overreach in the bud, PIN lawyers wrote a formal "non-concurrence" for the opening of a criminal case and interviewing Schumer and sent it to the acting head of the Criminal Division, Antoinette "Toni" Bacon.

In their memo to Martin, the PIN lawyers noted what Schumer had said after the "whirlwind" comment: "The bottom line is very simple: We will stand with the American people. We will stand with American women. We will tell President Trump and Senate Republicans who have stacked the Court with right-wing ideologues, that you're gonna be gone in November and you will never be able to do what you're trying to do now, ever, ever again. You hear that over there on the far right? You're gone in November."

Prosecuting someone under federal law 18 USC 1503 requires proof of a true threat, which requires that the person knowingly communicated a serious expression of an intent to commit "an unlawful act of violence" to a specific person.

Schumer's language, the prosecutors noted, had been "ambiguous." It could be understood to mean a potential for violence, but it was not explicit, and was in fact much softer, vaguer language than many other threat cases that had been dismissed by the courts, including one in which a debtor sent a bankruptcy judge a note that read, "Suppose I become homicidal."

The prosecutors also noted that given where Schumer had spoken those words—directly outside the Supreme Court Building—the law was more likely to consider such rhetoric political, rather than threatening, speech.

In a normally functioning Justice Department, the Friday-night freakout probably would have ended there, but it didn't.

Bacon seemed to want to help Martin, and on Saturday morning she requested that PIN lawyers write up draft jury instructions for a case against Schumer. The very notion of creating jury instructions struck some Public Integrity lawyers as dumb, given that they had just advised that there was insufficient evidence even to open an investigation, let alone charge it. But drafting jury instructions can be a helpful legal tool for prosecutors, because it is a way of creating a factual and legal checklist for the case being contemplated. Bacon and Martin seemed determined to build a rationale, however flimsy, to charge Schumer. The career prosecutors, however, saw the jury instruction assignment as another chance to show that the case Martin wanted to build was absurd.

The next day, Bacon and Martin tried to go farther. Now they wanted jury instructions for an additional charge of "aiding and abetting" the underlying threat case. The request pushed Martin's already weak prosecution theory deeper into the realm of farce. Now Martin and Bacon were trying to envision a criminal case in which Schumer had not only threatened Supreme Court justices, but had also aided and abetted . . . someone in the act of threatening them. It wasn't entirely clear who that someone could be, but some in the department suspected Martin was trying to draw a straight line from Schumer's remarks to Sophie Roske, who in 2022 flew from California to Virginia with a gun, zip ties, and burglary tools. As Roske walked through Justice Kavanaugh's neighborhood, she called 911 and essentially turned herself in. Under police questioning, she admitted that her plan had been to kill the judge and then commit suicide.

Mystified, the Public Integrity lawyers nevertheless did as instructed and created a second set of jury instructions for the case against Schumer for "aiding and abetting" the noncrime.

Bacon, a former corruption prosecutor in Ohio who had served in the first Trump administration as the acting U.S. attorney in Albany, New York, was something of an enigma to the Public Integrity prosecutors when she first took the helm of the Criminal Division. She had prosecuted real cases, but in her new role as a senior official in the department's Criminal Division, they found her to be a problem— someone who seemed to want to please higher-ups more than she wanted to tell them the truth or explain the law.

A few days later, Bacon told prosecutors that she had told Justice Department leaders about the PIN lawyers' "non-concurrence" with the Martin effort to investigate and question Schumer.

When Martin's efforts were derailed, rather than learn from his missteps, Martin became furious with the corruption prosecutors who he felt had boxed him in. He complained bitterly to Blanche and Bove that the "deep state" was blocking him from carrying out the president's agenda.

Martin would not let it go. Over the next month, he sent two more letters to Schumer, demanding "clarification" of what he had meant in his speech. "Your cooperation is more important than ever to complete this inquiry <u>before any action is taken</u>."

That third warning was sent February 11, underlining the implication that Schumer could face charges.

Six days later, Trump nominated Ed Martin to assume the job of U.S. attorney on a more permanent basis—assuming Senate Republicans confirmed him for the job. Once again, a lawyer with a spotty track record and questionable ethics had passed the audition for the Trump administration by promoting cases that horrified most other government lawyers who learned of them.

Martin's antics occasionally caught senior Justice Department officials like Blanche and his deputy Emil Bove by surprise. Martin, they thought, often created headaches, but he was doing what the White House wanted: attack, attack, attack. If he had to be reined in occasionally and saved from himself, that was a hassle the administration was willing to live with to have him as a prominent member of Trump's team. And Justice Department officials realized that Martin had his own frequent line of communication not just with the White House but also with the president himself.

To the outside world, Martin often seemed like a singularly strange force inside the Trump Justice Department. On the inside, many of the prosecutors in his office saw him as often oblivious to the havoc he caused. Sometimes, he would approach low-level prosecutors in the U.S. Attorney's Office and slyly suggest he had a special assignment for them, if they were interested. In such moments, according to people who had observed such approaches, he did not say what the case or assignment was, just that it was important.

Eventually, mid-level managers in the office had to instruct their subordinates to come tell them if Martin had made such an overture to them. The managers felt they had to protect their junior people from getting unwittingly sucked into a problematic case that could embarrass the office or derail a young lawyer's career.

When it came time to put him in the job permanently, Martin had to face a Senate confirmation, and that proved to be a problem. In the years after the January 6, 2021, riot at the Capitol, he had represented some January 6 defendants, and once he took over the office that had prosecuted them, he became, if anything, an even more passionate advocate for people convicted in those cases.

Senator Thom Tillis, a North Carolina Republican, was particularly troubled by Martin's positions on the January 6 cases. Tillis disliked the tendency of Trump supporters to act as if January 6 were anything other than rampant lawlessness. And because Tillis was a member of the Senate Judiciary Committee, his disapproval could torpedo Martin's nomination.

In early May, as Martin's chances at confirmation seemed to be fading because a handful of Republican lawmakers saw him as dangerous, he and Tillis met privately to discuss the senator's concerns.

Tillis was unconvinced by the conversation. "I think anybody that breached the perimeter should have been in prison for some period of time, whether it's 30 days or 3 years is debatable, but I have no tolerance for anybody who entered the building on January the 6th, and that's probably where most of the friction was," the senator told reporters.

As a member of the Senate Judiciary Committee, Tillis had more sway than most in deciding whether Martin could be confirmed. But it wasn't just Tillis: A handful of other moderate Republicans also had grave misgivings about Martin's judgment, and eventually the White House conceded and withdrew his nomination.

Failure to be confirmed by a Republican-controlled Senate did not mean the end of a career in Trump's Justice Department; it was in many ways a path to promotion. Trump decided to elevate Martin to the job of pardon attorney at the Justice Department. That job didn't require Senate approval, but in Trump's new Justice Department, it was a powerful perch from which Martin got multiple other assignments, allowing him to ride herd over U.S. attorney offices.

The Trump administration had forced out the prior pardon attorney, Elizabeth Oyer, after a disagreement about whether the right to own and carry firearms should be restored to the actor Mel Gibson, a Trump supporter. Gibson had lost the right to own guns over a domestic violence conviction, and Oyer had balked at providing bureaucratic cover for the effort to give them back for no stated reason other than that he was a friend of the president. She was fired shortly after her refusal to endorse the plan.

As Oyer's successor, Martin saw his job as freeing Trump supporters convicted of crimes. "No MAGA left behind," he posted on social media the month he got his promotion.

But he wouldn't focus solely on undoing criminal convictions or shortening sentences. Trump also put him in charge of what the administration called the Weaponization Working Group, with the "weaponization" billed as an effort to end the deep-state behavior of Justice Department career officials who, Trump, Martin, and others argued, had grossly misused prosecutorial powers to harm Trump and his supporters.

For much of 2025, Justice Department officials held a weekly weaponization meeting, and a biweekly version that wrapped in other federal agencies. The topics that fell under the category of "weaponization" gave away the game, including separate investigations of Environmental Protection Agency grants and the mortgage paperwork of a member of the Federal Reserve Board. It was hard to claim with a straight face that EPA grants or a Fed board member had prosecuted Trump or his allies. But they were important parts of a machinery at the 2025 Justice Department, one that viewed the federal government and its independent agencies as insufficiently compliant with Trump's political goals.

The Trump administration's weaponization work was far-reaching and government wide. Trump's top federal housing official, Bill Pulte, made repeated criminal referrals for mortgage investigations and prosecutions of people Trump despised, like Senator Adam Schiff, a California Democrat. Staffers at the Office of the Director of National Intelligence were also important players in the weaponization work, as Trump aides sought to use intelligence documents to pursue cases against former officials who had investigated Trump.

Even the State Department's inspector general was drafted into the effort, tasked with investigating how the government had paid for Jack Smith's time and travel in late 2022 after his appointment as special counsel.

While *weaponization* was a term most often applied to the Justice Department, it could accurately be applied in 2025 to the various other agencies now feeding Trump's revenge campaign, agencies that previously had had little to nothing to do with criminal prosecutions of politically sensitive subjects.

In the months that followed Martin's appointment, he set out to prove wrong those federal prosecutors who had concluded he was so inept that he couldn't produce an indictment. His efforts were aided by Pulte and others throughout the administration who sought to use weak evidence or fanciful theories of crimes to launch investigations of people the president despised, often over the strenuous objections of the career prosecutors who could scarcely believe some of the instructions they were receiving. These prosecutors were often left to fend for themselves against their own bosses, seeking to hold fast to basic facts and a concept of justice that had guided their work for more than half a century. Martin's letter to Georgetown University's law school, in which he threatened to withhold jobs from its graduates over unspecified concerns about "diversity, equity, and inclusion" in the curriculum, led to an ethics complaint from the disciplinary body for DC lawyers. The Trump administration, however, sought to kneecap any such attempts to punish its lawyers. In early 2026, Bondi, who had fired her own in-house ethics advisor, pushed a plan to stall or stop any local or state bars from conducting ethics investigations of Justice Department lawyers from doing so.

The case that Martin failed to file against Schumer showed that career law enforcement officials could still win individual battles to maintain Justice Department standards for investigations and prosecutions. But Trump's Justice Department put Martin, Chattah, Habba, and many others like them into key jobs around the department, and they would not relent in their quest to bring unfounded cases against Trump's perceived enemies.

Those efforts wouldn't all succeed, but some would soon bear fruit.

CHAPTER 3

Pin Drop

Minutes after the flashing ball of light descended in Times Square to mark the start of 2022, Eric Adams stood on a nearby stage to be sworn in as the New York City mayor.

In a city still recovering from the Covid-19 pandemic and its side effects on society, most of the people onstage with Adams wore masks. The city depended in part on the revenue generated by 1.6 million commuters pouring in every day to earn their daily bread and spend it. But many of those commuters had been slow to return, and partially empty streets had amplified problems of crime, homelessness, and drug addiction.

Adams was a former police officer who turned his job as leader of the group 100 Blacks in Law Enforcement Who Care into a political career, first as a state legislator, then as borough president of Brooklyn, and eventually, as mayor of New York.

In a city dominated by Democrats, Adams had won a crowded primary by letting others tack to the left while he emphasized fighting crime and supporting the city's business community. That victory paved the way for an easy general election win over the Republican candidate, Curtis Sliwa, a longtime anti-crime activist, radio host, and tart-tongued pundit who was generally not considered mayoral material.

Months later, federal investigators launched a corruption investigation into the new mayor. Historically, corruption investigations into City Hall—any city hall—revolved around local issues. A businessman offered a bribe to get approval for a project. A donor demanded special favors in exchange for campaign money. The Adams investigation, however, reflected what many corruption investigators considered a growing trend in American political bribery: mayors, governors, or other officials being courted by foreign officials or businessmen.

All politics may be local, but political corruption was becoming global.

By 2024, it looked increasingly likely that Adams would be charged for his dealings with Turkish government officials and Turkish businessmen. In September of that year, a five-count indictment was unsealed charging him with conspiring to commit wire fraud, solicit campaign contributions from foreign nationals, and take bribes.

Adams had "not only accepted, but sought illegal campaign contributions" to his mayoral campaign, the indictment charged. But his corrupt relationships with foreigners, particularly officials from the Turkish government, dated back nearly a decade, according to the federal prosecutors in Lower Manhattan who filed the charges.

"As Adams' prominence and power grew, his foreign-national benefactors sought to cash in on their corrupt relationships with him," the indictment read, and Adams agreed to the scheme, "providing favorable treatment in exchange for the illicit benefits he received."

Besides using straw donors to take in illegal donations, Adams also was accused of accepting at least $123,000 worth of airline tickets, luxury hotel rooms, and flight upgrades as unreported gifts from a Turkish official or Turkish nationals. "Adams created and instructed others to create fake paper trails, falsely suggesting that he had paid, or planned to pay, for travel benefits that were actually free," the indictment said.

The most damning details of the case centered on events that took place in the summer and fall of 2021, shortly after Adams won the

Democratic primary for mayor, making him a virtual lock to win the general election. That September, a Turkish official told Adams that it was time to repay his government for their generosity. Specifically, the Turks wanted Adams to pressure the New York City Fire Department to help open a new Turkish consulate building in Manhattan without a fire inspection—a key part of the approval process for a thirty-five-story building. Adams, the feds charged, did as he was told, and a fire official responsible for the safety inspection was allegedly warned that he would lose his job if he failed to go along with the demand.

The feds were able to build the case in part because some of the people familiar with the alleged bribery and donation schemes had flipped and become witnesses. Despite New York's many bribery scandals over the years, including involving the political machine of Tammany Hall, a name still synonymous with corruption, the modern city of five boroughs had never seen a sitting mayor indicted.

After Adams became the first, he suggested that the charges against him were part of a political dispute with the Biden administration over immigration. "When the federal government did nothing as its broken immigration policies overloaded our shelter system with no relief, I put the people of New York before party and politics," he said. "I always knew that if I stood my ground for all of you, that I would be a target. And a target I became."

After the mayor entered a not guilty plea at his arraignment, his lawyer Alex Spiro stood outside the courthouse and accused the FBI and the Justice Department of trying to criminalize travel perks. "This case isn't even a real case. This is the airline upgrade corruption case," said Spiro, who had also represented Trump ally Elon Musk.

Both arguments were unconvincing to many New Yorkers, but they didn't seem to be the primary audience. The following month, Adams and Trump attended a Catholic charity event in Manhattan, where Trump, still battling criminal indictments while he ran for president, publicly aligned himself with the indicted mayor. "I know what it's like to be persecuted by the DOJ for speaking out against open borders," Trump said. "We were persecuted, Eric. I was persecuted and so are you, Eric." The comments were the first vivid example of how the second Trump term would be far different from the first.

For Trump, the battles over his indictments—four cases spread out over four different jurisdictions and three different prosecutors—were not simply to stay out of prison or to keep his political career alive. Trump's anger and desire for revenge served a political and even a legal purpose, but his rage against the Justice Department was also deeply personal, a visceral, instinctive reaction to his own experience.

"When a person has their home searched by the FBI, when a person experiences the full effect of a criminal investigation into their life, I don't know a single client who is not made bitter by that experience, however it turns out," said one lawyer involved in Trump's classified documents case. "Yes, he's a former president, and he may be the next president, but that anger never goes away. It stays with them for years, for as long as they live."

In 2016, Trump ran for president on a platform of "lock her up," arguing that his Democratic opponent, Hillary Clinton, should be prosecuted and in jail. By 2024, his message had changed somewhat. While his opponents should still go to jail, he argued, his allies or potential allies should not, even if they included a Democratic mayor.

Less than two months after Adams's indictment, Americans elected Donald Trump president.

In December, Adams requested and got a private conversation on FaceTime with Tom Homan, Trump's soon-to-be border czar. After the discussion, Homan, a deportation hard-liner who had publicly criticized Adams in the past, spoke glowingly of him. "I was wrong" about Adams. "I got a whole new outlook on the mayor today," he told *Dr. Phil*'s Phil McGraw, who had helped arrange the Adams-Homan meeting. "I got exactly and more what I was hoping for."

Days later, the president-elect told reporters he was considering pardoning Adams. "I think he was treated pretty unfairly. Now I haven't seen the gravity of it all but it seems, you know, like being upgraded in an airplane many years ago—I know probably everybody here has been upgraded," Trump said, referring to the reporters. "They see you're all stars and they say, 'I want to upgrade that person from NBC, and I'm going to upgrade him,' and that would mean you spend the rest of your life in prison."

Trump then praised Adams for his stance on immigration. "He made some pretty strong statements, like this was not sustainable, and I said you know what, he'll be indicted soon . . . and a few months later he was indicted."

Before even being sworn in as president, Trump made a public argument for pardoning Adams because the mayor was being persecuted for his alignment with Trump on an issue. It was an early indication of just how aggressively Trump would use the pardon power in his second term. What the president did not reveal was how, when it came to killing the Adams case, his administration would choose a far more destructive path than a simple pardon.

Days after Trump was sworn into office, Adams's lawyer Alex Spiro sent a letter to David Warrington, the White House counsel, seeking a pardon. Adopting the president's language, Spiro argued in his letter that Adams had been treated unfairly by a "weaponized" Justice Department: "President Trump has made clear his desire to reform the Department of Justice so that it is an agency that once again seeks justice and truth above all else. This case is a prime example," he argued.

Spiro's argument was greeted with enthusiasm, particularly from Emil Bove, who served in those early days as the acting number two of the Justice Department, personally executing many of the orders coming from Trump and Stephen Miller.

Bove reached out to Spiro directly, asking how the indictment was affecting Adams's ability to do his job. The question helped Adams's legal team (which included the well-connected Washington lawyer William Burck) fine-tune its arguments for killing the case.

The second week of the Trump administration, Bove called Danielle Sassoon, who was running the prestigious Manhattan federal prosecutor's office while it awaited a Senate-confirmed leader. Sassoon, thirty-eight, was no one's notion of a deep-state operative. A former clerk for conservative Supreme Court Justice Antonin Scalia, she was also a former colleague of Bove's, when they worked together years earlier in that office.

In the call, Bove said he didn't like the Adams case and indicated that he wanted it dropped. The mayor, Bove said, needed to be able to operate on the important issue of immigration.

Sassoon argued against dropping the case, adding that her prosecutors were about to add new allegations against Adams, for trying to destroy evidence. She also asked for time, suggesting they wait until Todd Blanche was confirmed as deputy attorney general.

Blanche, Bove told her, was "on the same page" on the Adams case, a cryptic answer that suggested, but did not say outright, that the yet-to-be confirmed government official had discussed the case with Bove. Blanche would later say under oath that he had had no such discussions about the Adams case before he was confirmed.

Bove told Sassoon to come to Washington on Friday for a meeting to discuss dismissing the case. Adams's lawyers Alex Spiro and William Burck were also at the meeting, where Sassoon once again tried to convince Bove that the case was righteous and the evidence showed the mayor was dirty.

As the meeting ended with Sassoon still refusing to cave on the issue, Bove got angry and demanded that one of Sassoon's prosecutors, who had been taking notes on the discussion, hand over everything he had written. There had been too many leaks about their discussions, Bove said.

It is not unusual for senior Justice Department officials to entertain arguments by defense lawyers in high-profile cases that the prosecutors who filed charges against this official or that company need to be reined in; such meetings have gone on at the department for decades, including meetings with lawyers for Trump before he was indicted.

What was unusual, and alarming to many Justice Department veterans, was the degree to which Bove, as a senior Justice Department leader, had adopted a rationale for dismissing the Adams case that deliberately and unapologetically ignored the facts and the law.

That same day, Bove took another step designed to rewrite recent history. In an internal memo, he directed the termination of more than a dozen federal prosecutors who had worked on cases stemming from the January 6, 2021, pro-Trump riot at the U.S. Capitol, justifying it on the basis that they were still within their probationary period as employees and, thus, easier to fire. President Trump, Bove said, had "appropriately characterized that work as having involved 'a grave national injustice that has been perpetrated upon the American people over the last four years.'"

Bove also claimed that the outgoing Biden administration had surreptitiously turned a bunch of temporary prosecutors into permanent hires, declaring that he "will not tolerate subversive personnel actions."

The following week, Pam Bondi was confirmed as attorney general on a mostly party-line vote. Soon after, Bove sent Sassoon a memorandum titled, "Dismissal Without Prejudice of Prosecution of Mayor Eric Adams." The two-page memo laid out many of the Bove arguments Sassoon had found so unconvincing in their earlier meeting.

Bove said the decision to not prosecute Adams had been reached "without assessing the strength of the evidence or the legal theories on which the case is based," a particularly maddening statement to the lawyers and agents who had spent years carefully building a case against the mayor.

Bove's memo then veered into a series of criticisms that could have come straight from a defense lawyer, or a politician. "It cannot be ignored that Mayor Adams criticized the prior Administration's immigration policies before the charges were filed," Bove wrote, before going on to specifically criticize the former U.S. attorney in Manhattan, Damian Williams. "These actions and the underlying case have also improperly interfered" with Adams's effort to campaign in the 2025 election. The pending prosecution "has unduly restricted Mayor Adams' ability to devote full attention and resources to the illegal immigration and violent crime that escalated under the policies of the prior Administration," Bove wrote.

Here, then, was the Trump administration's motives laid bare—they wanted Adams to help Trump on immigration issues, and an indictment, they reasoned, would make that harder. But they also wanted the case dropped "without prejudice," meaning that the administration could revive the charges at some future date.

To Sassoon and her prosecutors, this seemed like a particularly unethical way to dismiss the indictment, using the possibility of future charges as a kind of unspoken threat against Adams.

Bove had one more point to make in his memo—one that exemplified an entirely different vision of justice from that which the department had practiced for many decades. "Accomplishing the immigration objectives established by President Trump and the Attorney General is every bit as important—if not more so—as the objectives that the prior Administration pursued by releasing violent criminals such as Viktor Bout, the 'Merchant of Death,'" Bove wrote.

The reference to Bout had special meaning for federal prosecutors in New York. Viktor Bout, a former Soviet Army officer who became an infamous arms dealer, had been arrested in Thailand in 2008, part of an undercover DEA sting operation. Two years later, Thailand finally extradited him to the United States to face trial. In 2011, he was convicted at a trial in New York and sentenced to twenty-five years in prison. In the years since, his name had frequently surfaced as a possible chit in trading Russians in prison in America for Americans imprisoned in Russia.

A trade with Bout finally happened in 2022, when the Biden administration approved a deal to send Bout back to his country in exchange for Russia's release of Brittney Griner, a WNBA player who had been arrested in Russia for carrying a small amount of cannabis oil and sentenced to nine years in prison.

The Griner case was the subject of intense public interest, and of great frustration for U.S. officials who felt Vladimir Putin's Russia had plainly decided to detain and punish a high-profile American to use as bait for just such a swap.

When the Bout-Griner prisoner exchange happened on an Abu Dhabi airport tarmac, many Justice Department officials, particularly those who worked in Sassoon's office, were furious and frustrated. "If she were my relative, I would want to do the swap," said one. "But trading a notorious international arms dealer for a basketball player is madness."

There was a long history of such swaps, mostly related to espionage cases. KGB spy Rudolf Abel, who had been caught and convicted in New York, was swapped in 1962 for American spy pilot Francis Gary Powers, a trade memorialized in the film *Bridge of Spies*. There had been other spy swaps since, also involving Russians caught spying by federal prosecutors in New York.

What Bove argued, to the great frustration of Sassoon and her office, was that the logic of swapping spies between nations should now be applied to the Adams case: Drop the charges so Adams can help the administration on immigration issues.

But New York City was not a foreign country, it was . . . New York City, part of America, and in fact the nation's first capital.

The next day, Sassoon spoke again on the phone with Bove, this time joined by Bondi's chief of staff, Chad Mizelle. Mizelle's presence was another indication that whatever her conservative credentials and legal arguments, Sassoon had lost the fight to preserve the Adams case. Mizelle had a tendency to be dismissive and to talk about differing opinions as evidence of stunted intelligence.

Sassoon stood her ground. After the call with Bove and Mizelle, she crafted a long letter to Bondi, laying out all the reasons she thought Bove's demands not only were wrong, but violated basic principles of the Justice Department manual and rules of professional conduct for lawyers. Bove, she wrote, appears to concede "that Adams should receive leniency for federal crimes solely because he occupies an important public position and can use that position to assist in the Administration's policy priorities." Bove's comparison to the Bout case, she said, "was quite expressly a *quid pro quo*."

The Bout-Griner swap, she wrote "was a widely criticized sacrifice of a valid American interest (the punishment of an infamous arms dealer) which Russia was able to extract only through a patently selective prosecution of a famous American athlete. It is difficult to imagine that the Department wishes to emulate that episode by granting Adams leverage over it akin to Russia's influence in international affairs."

Sassoon also noted that her office was preparing to file a new obstruction charge against Adams based on evidence that he had "destroyed and instructed others to destroy evidence and provide false information to the FBI, and that would add further factual allegations regarding his participation in a fraudulent donor scheme."

Sassoon fired every conceivable rhetorical salvo against what Bove wanted, but seemed also to understand that the effort was probably futile. "In the event you are unwilling to meet, or reconsider the directive in light of the problems raised by Mr. Bove's memo, I am prepared to offer my resignation. It has been, and continues to be, my honor to serve as a prosecutor in the Southern District of New York," she wrote.

Bove replied the next day.

"First, your resignation is accepted," he said, in a letter filled with counter-accusations. He lectured Sassoon that she had "lost sight of the oath you took at the Department of Justice by suggesting that you retain discretion to interpret the Constitution in a manner inconsistent with the policies of a democratically elected President and a Senate-confirmed attorney general."

For all its bluster, Bove's letter made a key point about how the department was operating in the new administration. Justice Department lawyers swear an oath to "support and defend the Constitution against all enemies, foreign and domestic." They also vow to "well and faithfully discharge the duties of the office on which I am about to enter."

Generations of government lawyers have understood that oath to mean that they swear to follow the rules and principles of the Constitution. Bove's letter argued, against all evidence and past practice, that the oath was actually to follow any presidential command and to do whatever the president and the attorney general wanted.

Bove seemed determined to nip any disobedience in the bud. His letter also suspended the other New York prosecutors working on the Adams case, saying there would now be an investigation of their conduct in that case.

If he was trying to cow the notoriously independent Southern District of New York office where he had once worked, he did not succeed. Two days later, one of those prosecutors, Hagan Scotten, wrote Bove a message of unfiltered loathing for what he was doing to the Adams case and the department. "I am entirely in agreement" with Sassoon, Scotten declared. Bove's criticism of the case, and of the former U.S. Attorney Damian Williams, was absurd, the lawyer added. Scotten, a U.S. Army veteran, Bronze Star recipient, and former clerk for conservative Supreme Court Chief Justice John Roberts, was incensed. "No system of ordered liberty can allow the government to use the carrot of dismissing charges, or the stick of threatening to bring them again, to induce an elected official to support its policy objectives," he wrote. He also tried to make clear that he was not a Trump critic and could "even understand how a Chief Executive whose background is in business and politics might see the contemplated dismissal-with-leverage as a good, if distasteful deal." But any federal prosecutor, he said, "would know that our laws and traditions do not allow using the prosecutorial power to influence other citizens, much less elected officials, in this way. If no lawyer within earshot of the President is willing to give him that advice, then I expect you will eventually find someone who is enough of a fool, or enough of a coward, to file your motion. But it was never going to be me.

"Please consider this my resignation," he added. "It has been an honor to serve as a prosecutor in the Southern District of New York."

In the face of unyielding resolve from the Southern District of New York, Bove switched targets, but not tack. He took the Adams case away from New York and transferred it to the Public Integrity Section at Main Justice.

Bove seemed determined to make career Justice Department lawyers bend the knee.

If his former colleagues in New York wouldn't do it, the Public Integrity Section was a logical next step. Trump and his lawyers had a deep distrust of the lawyers running the section, which had been created to ensure uniform standards in corruption investigations around the country. Jack Smith, the former special counsel who had twice indicted Trump, had once run the section. And PIN had been intimately involved in many of the cases against Trump and his political allies in recent years.

Bove pressed the supervisors in the section to sign the court motion seeking dismissal of the Adams case. The section was still recovering from its sudden day-one decapitation, when their chief, Corey Amundson, was unceremoniously shipped off to the Sanctuary Cities Enforcement Working Group that was a dumping ground for department veterans the Trump administration wanted out of the way. Amundson's departure, however, meant that those immediately above and below him in the chain of command would be the next to face Bove's demands.

John Keller, the acting head of PIN after Amundson's removal, and Kevin Driscoll, a senior official overseeing the section, decided to resign rather than surrender, hoping their departures would convince Bove to back down. The two men first informed their deputies of what was happening and of their decision. Three deputies in the section, Marco Palmieri, Jennifer Clarke, and Rob Heberle, decided that they, too, would have to resign if they were asked to sign the motion.

The trio called in the rest of the section's lawyers who happened to be in the office, roughly half of the thirty-person staff, to explain the pressure coming from above. Bove's blitzkrieg of the section was just getting started. The corruption prosecutors had feared such a possibility, but they were still stunned.

That afternoon, the three remaining managers were summoned to a video conference meeting with Bove, who told them he wanted two line attorneys at PIN to sign the dismissal motion.

It was frustrating to PIN staff that Bove was so determined to have career lawyers sign the document. There was nothing preventing Bove, or any number of senior Justice Department officials in the administration, from filing the motion with their own signatures. But the lawyers suspected Bove wanted to make the dismissal look legitimate by having career lawyers do it. In the austere world of federal judges and lawyers, a document signed only by senior officials would serve as a kind of public distress signal from inside the ranks of career law enforcement officials, particularly given the swirling news coverage of the battle over the Adams case raging inside the department.

Talking to Bove via video, the three lawyers asked for more time. Bove refused.

So, the three resigned.

The next morning, which happened to be Valentine's Day, the section's remaining lawyers, roughly twenty of them, were summoned to a 9:45 a.m. video conference meeting.

Bove, a bald man with sunken eyes, struck a mournful tone. "Yesterday was a hard day I think for all of us," he said. "Danielle Sassoon was a"—he corrected himself—"*is* a personal friend of mine. It was hard for me, too."

He repeated the argument that their oath to uphold the Constitution meant "implementing the agenda that the President was elected to implement. It means following orders from the president and the attorney general, unless we view them as unlawful and unethical. Um . . . it means that there has to be a chain of command."

Bove emphasized the need for the lawyers to do what they were told. "These type of issues—chain of command, accountability to the one democratically elected official in the executive branch—they're really important, and there's no room for divergence from that if we're going to stay connected to what the rule of law really means in a democracy," he said.

Over the course of his nine-minute speech, Bove repeatedly emphasized how sad he was that so many people had resigned rather than do what he had demanded. "There are costs to this that hurt my heart," he said, convincing no one who listened to him.

After insisting that he understood why they were upset, Bove got down to business. "You guys, among yourselves, figure out who is going to file this motion. I need two people to put in a straightforward motion," he said. "Those two people, today, will emerge as leaders of PIN," he said, a remark that the others on the call immediately understood to be a dangle of promotions for anyone who did what he wanted. "Let's please just figure this out . . . so we can get past this."

But for Bove's voice, there was no other sound on the call. Many participants had muted themselves, and many had turned their cameras off. No one wanted to really engage conversationally with the man who seemed determined to become their sad-faced executioner.

He gave them an hour to decide.

The Public Integrity lawyers huddled to try to reach a decision. In the last forty-eight hours, at least a half dozen prosecutors had resigned over Bove's demands, and it now appeared that the whole section could be fired if no one volunteered to do his bidding.

Even before the video call, some had already written draft resignation letters. The fury of Ryan Crosswell, a marine turned PIN lawyer, represented a kind of generational split among the section. Older lawyers, who also tended to be supervisors, were more inclined to try to find a solution that spared people from losing their jobs. But for some of the younger lawyers in PIN, the principle was too important to worry about health insurance or mortgages.

But there was also a mountain of ongoing cases to worry about. At the moment Bove delivered his ultimatum, the Public Integrity Section was working on roughly two hundred cases, and if the section were decimated, many of those cases could wither and die.

With only thirty minutes remaining until Bove's deadline, one of the more senior lawyers in the section, Ed Sullivan, offered to put his name on Bove's motion. Sullivan's reasoning was somewhat unique. He had survived a previous scandal as a prosecutor in a corruption case that went sideways and felt his reputation would not suffer much by adding another to it.

Eighteen years earlier, Sullivan had worked on the case against Senator Ted Stevens, a Republican from Alaska. Stevens's conviction was rendered null when the judge found that the prosecutors had withheld crucial evidence that would have aided his defense. The fallout led to discipline and, sadly, the suicide of another prosecutor. Sullivan was ultimately exonerated by the internal investigation, but the stain lingered.

"This will be easier for me," he told his coworkers.

By volunteering, Sullivan offered them at least a plausible way out—preserving most of their jobs and their cases, at least for the time being. Some of his colleagues, particularly the younger ones, still didn't like the idea. But the ticking clock demanded an answer, so eventually Sullivan's offer became the decision.

Bove quickly accepted a single signer, as opposed to the two he had demanded. There was a further back-and-forth between Bove and Sullivan about what, exactly, the motion should say. Sullivan was not prepared to put his name on anything that criticized the New York prosecutors who had brought the case. Part of the reason was practical. The Southern District prosecutors were some of the best in the entire Justice Department, and they didn't really need Public Integrity's guidance or instruction the same way smaller offices around the country did.

Sullivan and the Public Integrity Section didn't actually know much of the granular details of the Adams case, and so were reluctant to take any position on the facts and the evidence behind it.

Eventually, Bove got fed up with the ongoing negotiation over wording, declared the conversation over, and insisted that the motion be filed. It was sent by the end of the day.

Sullivan signed it. Bove signed it, and so did Toni Bacon, the longtime Justice Department prosecutor who was temporarily serving as the head of the Criminal Division, overseeing the Public Integrity Section. To those who had worked with Bacon on past corruption cases, her role in the Adams case was deeply disturbing. "Toni is one of the foremost public corruption attorneys in the country, so she knows the Adams indictment is more than worthy of prosecution," said her former supervisor in Ohio, Ann Rowland, who could only surmise that Bacon's decision to sign the motion "was purely political."

The following Monday, Bacon summoned the entire Public Integrity Section into a conference room for a review of their cases. It was a nerve-wracking meeting, given everything they had just experienced on Friday. No one knew if Bacon would fire more people, order corruption cases to be dropped or closed, or present them with some new demand.

Bacon entered the conference room, sat down at the table, opened her computer, and began to read from her screen. The lawyers were baffled by her performance—an inept, lifeless version of a pep talk. "I need you to help make PIN great again," she said at one point, infuriating many of those in the room who took this as a declaration that they, rather than Bove, had done something wrong.

Some of the lawyers stared at Bacon in disbelief. Some stared at the ceiling.

Sensing the hostility in the room, Bacon seemed to realize her pitch had not been persuasive. "I can't want this more than you guys want this," she said.

When she finished speaking, the conference room was excruciatingly silent. She seemed to be expecting some response, maybe even a thank-you. Instead, the silence continued. And then the lawyers walked out.

CHAPTER 4

Find Out

When Alina Habba arrived as the new U.S. attorney for New Jersey, the top federal prosecutor for the entire state, she proudly told her new subordinates that her Secret Service name while working at the White House had been "Birkin," after the luxury Hermès handbags that cost anywhere from $11,000 to $225,000 each. Habba, it became clear to the prosecutors who worked for her, loved three things: Trump, Birkin bags, and guns.

When she met federal agents, she would often enthusiastically tell them about her love of firearms. To her, talking about guns was a way of trying to connect and build relationships in the new job. To many of the law enforcement officials who found themselves discussing weaponry with the new U.S. attorney, it felt like talking to a parent who was trying to be the "cool mom" from the movie *Mean Girls*.

Habba showed up to the job with no prosecutorial experience and little criminal law experience. Her ignorance showed in almost every conversation she had as a U.S. attorney. But she also arrived with a huge chip on her shoulder, frequently complaining about the "weaponization" of Biden-era prosecutors, New York state officials, and federal and state judges.

Often, she complained to her staff about the past Justice Department prosecutions of Trump. Habba had spent the prior year defending him in two civil trials, both of which she lost badly. Her conclusion from those cases was not that she had not performed well, or that the facts of the case were bad for her client, but that the judges, state officials, and huge swaths of the legal system were corrupt, politically motivated, and diabolically anti-Trump.

Habba, her subordinates soon realized, had a fierce desire to prosecute Democrats.

On her first day, she complained to federal law enforcement officials about a video that Newark's mayor, Ras Baraka, had posted about her. In taking the prosecutor job, Habba had vowed to go after MS-13 in the city. In his video, the mayor had invited Habba to "leave the beautiful country clubs of Bedminster," a reference to one of Trump's properties, "and come hang out with us here in the city of Newark." He suggested that she take a tour there with him and law enforcement officials. MS-13 was not an issue in his city, he said, where crime had been falling. "I do not want to jeopardize that with political grandstanding, trying to push Trump or MAGA agenda," he added.

"Did you see that video?" Habba asked. "He said there are no gangs in Newark."

But that wasn't what the mayor had said. He had said there was no MS-13 presence. Newark did have problems with gangs, including Bloods and Crips, but in 2025, MS-13 happened not to be one of them.

The distinction seemed lost on Habba.

Habba asked for a briefing on the office's public corruption investigations, which was a perfectly reasonable request for a new U.S. attorney. Over the years, the Newark U.S. Attorney's Office had investigated a number of people close to Baraka, including his brother. But the FBI and federal prosecutors did not have a viable case against the mayor.

After the briefing, Habba made it clear to her staff that she wanted the mayor charged with a crime, though she was unclear about which crime or what the evidence for any charge would be.

Senior FBI officials in the Newark field office began to get frequent calls from Habba demanding that they investigate the mayor. She told them, according to people familiar with the conversations, to put "every resource" into it.

After a few weeks went by and her office still had not charged Baraka with any crimes, Habba tried to force the issue with her staff. Sitting in a conference room named after Frederick B. Lacey, a legendary Republican prosecutor who sent New Jersey mobsters to prison, she asked a number of law enforcement officials to pursue criminal charges against Baraka and was met with significant resistance and concern from the career prosecutors in the room.

While her behavior behind closed doors increasingly left her staff with a sense of dread, her public statements rattled the Garden State's legal community. This was in large part because days after her appointment by Trump, Habba had declared her intention to use her job to help Republicans get elected—a huge transgression of proper prosecutorial conduct. "We could turn New Jersey red, I really do believe that," she told a conservative podcaster. "I think New Jersey is absolutely close to getting there. So hopefully while I'm there I can help that cause." She then added, incongruously, that she was "not a political person in that role, but the one thing I just want to do is make it safer."

Federal prosecutors are supposed to stay out of politics as much as possible, precisely because a necessary part of their job is investigating and prosecuting politicians. But before Habba had even started the job, she declared she would try to get Republicans elected. The obvious implication was that she might use the prosecutorial power to go after Democrats or decline to investigate any wrongdoing by Republicans.

Prosecutors have tremendous power not just to investigate, arrest, and imprison people, but also to ruin reputations along the way. For that reason, generations of Justice Department lawyers have been trained to scrupulously avoid using their jobs as political weapons. Habba had no such scruples. Egged on by Deputy Attorney General Todd Blanche and some of his senior advisors, Habba pushed for a raft of investigations of Democrats.

For her part, she insisted she hadn't even wanted the job, and over time many on the staff came to believe her on that point. She told others she'd agreed to become the U.S. attorney, a job that many lawyers revered, only because President Trump had explicitly pressed her to do it.

In her second week on the job, Habba announced on Fox News that she had opened an investigation into New Jersey's Democratic governor, Phil Murphy, in a dispute over how far state employees should go to help the Trump administration's immigration enforcement. "I want it to be a warning for everybody that I have instructed my office today to open an investigation into Governor Murphy" and the state's attorney general, she said.

Emil Bove pressed Habba and her staff to aggressively pursue the Murphy investigation. In Mayor Eric Adams, the Trump administration had seen a potential ally in cracking down on immigration, and they made a criminal case against him go away. In Governor Murphy, the administration saw a critic of the immigration crackdown and sought to build a criminal case against him.

Bove, in the spring of 2025, urged New Jersey prosecutors to issue a wide range of subpoenas related to the governor. Bove told prosecutors they could get subpoenas for anything and didn't need to justify issuing them. Habba took his instruction to heart, to the dismay of those who worked for her.

The standard for issuing grand jury subpoenas is low, but there is one. Prosecutors are not supposed to conduct fishing expeditions to see if they can find something derogatory. To issue a subpoena, prosecutors are supposed to be able to articulate how the information being sought would further their investigation. They are also supposed to limit the amount of material being sought, even if it's just to avoid creating unnecessary work for everyone involved.

At times, the prosecutors in her office debated whether Habba was a cunning master manipulator or so thick-headed that she really did not understand criminal law, ethics, or law enforcement operations. The longer she had the job, the more members of her staff came to believe she was acting not out of any grand scheme or strategy, but out of a frightening mix of stupidity and stubbornness.

In early May, Democratic politicians in the state, upset over the Trump administration's efforts to rapidly deport more than a million immigrants, went to Delaney Hall, an ICE-run detention facility near Newark Airport. Baraka, the mayor, was joined by three members of Congress, Bonnie Watson Coleman, Rob Menendez, and LaMonica McIver, for what they called an oversight visit and what administration officials called a cheap publicity stunt.

The members of Congress were allowed inside the facility, but the mayor was not. "Congressmen are different," an ICE agent told the mayor, an interaction captured on video. "This is the last warning. You will be placed under arrest." Baraka then walked out of the fenced-in parking lot and onto a public street with other protesters.

Habba and others saw their chance. In Washington, Deputy Attorney General Todd Blanche held a phone call with her and Ricky Patel, a senior ICE agent in Newark. Blanche ordered ICE to arrest the mayor on a misdemeanor charge of trespassing on federal property, according to people familiar with the order.

The notion that a deputy attorney general, the second-highest-ranking law enforcement official in the federal government, would make on-the-fly decisions to arrest a local official for a misdemeanor, and do so on the basis of a fairly minor interaction that was quickly defused, was unlike anything Justice Department officials or New Jersey's legal community had ever seen. The Trump administration's visceral loathing of anti-Trump demonstrations was starting to manifest itself in surprising ways.

In the spring of 2025, a senior FBI official was summoned to the office of Samuel Ramer, the FBI's general counsel. As the top lawyer for the FBI, Ramer held one of the most powerful, but obscure, positions in government. When the senior FBI official entered Ramer's office, he was told the FBI had to "do something" about a group of anti-Trump protesters at Trump Tower in Manhattan.

The senior FBI official assured Ramer that the NYPD had the situation in hand.

That wasn't good enough for Ramer, who angrily insisted the FBI had to make sure that protesters didn't get into "the boss's building."

It was a remarkable thing for the FBI's top lawyer to say. Ramer was seemingly ignoring the difference between federal and local law enforcement and demanding that the FBI somehow find a way to stifle protests that might anger the president or embarrass his company.

The senior FBI official was irate. His boss, he told Ramer, was the American people.

To veteran lawyers inside and outside the government, the Trump administration seemed increasingly determined to push past what generations of their predecessors considered good judgment, particularly when it came to the principle of prosecutorial discretion, a far-reaching term for the idea that not everything a prosecutor can do is worth doing.

Discretion means prosecutors should focus their limited resources on fighting the kinds of crime that matter most and the kinds of cases that do the most good. In practice, discretion means prosecutors don't charge every possible violation of the law they discover. Instead, they focus on the most serious conduct and the worst offenders in order to make communities safer. For example, in U.S. attorney offices around the country, prosecutors generally put minimum-dollar thresholds on the size of financial crimes they investigate, in order to avoid expending federal resources on small-scale crimes.

But the Trump administration set out to redefine prosecutorial discretion in favor of racking up arrests and deportations and making public examples of anyone who tried to get in their way.

When Newark's mayor was placed in handcuffs, Habba had finally gotten the arrest she wanted. A number of current and former law enforcement officials worried that the administration was rushing to charge the mayor without determining first whether Delaney Hall was federal property. (It wasn't.)

Within days, it became clear even to Trump administration officials that the charge against the mayor was so flimsy that they would have to dismiss it. So, they crafted a new plan, one that would camouflage their retreat on the Baraka case by creating new charges against one of the members of Congress who was there that day.

When agents had moved onto the sidewalk to arrest Baraka, there was a tense moment as members of Congress crowded around the mayor to prevent him from being taken away. Amid general pushing and shoving, McIver had raised her elbows, which made contact with the shoulders of an ICE agent. Habba and Blanche decided to charge her with assaulting a federal officer and impeding an arrest. To many law enforcement veterans, the charges seemed like overkill, the kind of thing that would not have been filed in any other context and, therefore, a particularly bad idea when filed against a politician.

At first, the administration thought it could convince McIver to publicly accept responsibility for what she had done, in exchange for a pre-trial intervention deal—the kind of resolution that is meant to resolve minor issues without a conviction. Habba planned to announce the deal with McIver at the same time she dropped the trespassing charge against the mayor, and to do it from a press conference podium at Justice Department headquarters in Washington.

But McIver decided not to take the deal and to fight the case instead. This left Habba's office with little choice but to face the indignity of dropping the case against Baraka, Habba's first and most desired target.

But Habba would not relent on charging McIver. She repeatedly claimed the administration had zero tolerance for assaults on law enforcement and never acknowledged the obvious contradiction of working for a president who, on his first day back in the White House, had pardoned hundreds of people who had done precisely that during the January 6 riot.

Habba didn't see any of these setbacks as a result of her own bad judgment. To her staff, she seemed utterly convinced that time would prove Trump and his team right—that the nearly million-dollar sanction against her by a Florida judge for unethical lawyering would be tossed out and that the courts and the country would eventually come around to the Trump administration's vision of justice.

When she talked like that, members of her staff worried that she was so thoroughly embedded inside a MAGA echo chamber that she could not absorb other kinds of information. That mindset proved particularly destructive to her chances of staying on as a U.S. attorney. Trump had made Habba's an interim appointment, a move that bypassed the normal Senate approval for such picks, but one that expired at 120 days. After that, the federal judges in New Jersey would get to select a temporary person to fill the U.S. attorney job. Sometimes, the judges picked the person the administration had already selected. Sometimes, they picked someone else.

As Habba neared her 120-day deadline, she campaigned hard for the judges' votes, launching a charm offensive to meet with the judges and assure them she was worthy of the job. "I am not political. I hate politics," she told them. They seemed skeptical, given her "turn New Jersey red" comment, the Baraka case, and her public announcement of an investigation of the governor.

In a private meeting, one of the judges inquired about Habba's media appearances and expressed concern about the impropriety of that conduct. In response, Habba promised that she would not do any more inappropriate television appearances. A few days later, she appeared on Fox News, in a tactical vest and baseball cap, talking about an ongoing fugitive-hunting operation.

In the world of federal law enforcement, such behavior was seen as unprofessional showboating, the kind of stunt that maybe a press-hungry local district attorney might attempt, but beneath the seriousness of a U.S. attorney position. Once again, Habba did not see the distinction.

In a private meeting, administration officials floated the possibility that if Habba were not confirmed, Trump might send Ed Martin, his attack dog and "weaponization" chief, to replace her. "Pick Habba or things will get much worse" was how many Newark lawyers interpreted that message.

Habba, in turn, thought her charm offensive toward the judges had gone well and that she would get the more permanent appointment to the job. Once again, she had badly misread the room. A former Justice Department official from the first Trump administration told Habba in July, as her 120 days were running out, that she didn't have the judges' votes.

Habba was floored.

The following week, the federal judges in New Jersey picked her deputy, Desiree Leigh Grace, as the next U.S. attorney. Blanche, the deputy attorney general, publicly attacked the judges on social media for acting out of "a left wing agenda." Habba, he said, was President Trump's choice, "and no partisan bench can override that."

Using an unorthodox personnel maneuver, the Trump administration fired Grace and installed Habba back in the job. She didn't last the year. An appeals court eventually ruled that her reappointment was unlawful and that she was not the legitimate U.S. attorney. Habba left New Jersey to go back to Washington and become an advisor to Pam Bondi, the attorney general. She departed with souvenirs, a set of challenge coins made specially for her.

Challenge coins are an old tradition in the federal government in which senior officials have a medallion made with a unique logo to commemorate the office they lead. Habba's challenge coin, which she designed, features a handgun being pulled from a Birkin bag. Above the gun were the letters "FAFO": Fuck Around, Find Out.

CHAPTER 5

Street Justice

When Ed Martin left the U.S. Attorney's Office in Washington, DC, in May, there was hope among many of the prosecutors in the office that the madness of the past four months would cease, or at least ease up. Among Martin's most infuriating moves had been his demotion of senior prosecutors to the low rungs of the ladder, assigning them rookie work like the daily stream of minor arrests.

At the DC prosecutor's office, moving down that ladder meant physically moving to a lower floor of the building. The U.S. attorney worked on the top floor, alongside that person's senior advisors. Public corruption and national security lawyers worked on the upper floors, just below the U.S. attorney. All the way at the bottom of the building, on the first two floors, toiled the prosecutors, many of them younger lawyers, who handled general crimes and misdemeanors.

Martin had sent a host of his most senior prosecutors down the elevator with boxes, under the guise of the office needing, he said, to focus more attention on street crime. To the staff, these moves were clearly meant as punishment for the political cases those prosecutors had worked or supervised before Martin's arrival.

But it wasn't the worst punishment Martin doled out. He and Emil Bove also simply fired people, including those who had worked on the January 6 cases or who had worked for Jack Smith, the special counsel tasked with investigating and prosecuting Trump.

So, when Martin's Senate confirmation ran aground, and he failed to officially enter Justice Department headquarters, some in the office felt a sense of relief: They were sure there was no way they'd end up with a boss as bad as Martin.

Then came Jeanine Pirro, who chose to forsake the performative public letters Martin had enjoyed issuing for swamping the courts with arrests so transparently bad that judges, juries, and many city residents openly questioned the integrity and honesty of her office.

A former district attorney in Westchester, New York, a wealthy suburb north of New York City, Pirro had once been a rising star in the Republican politics of the Empire State. But a tax evasion conviction for her husband and her own failed bids for both the U.S. Senate and the governor's mansion had snuffed out her political career. By 2025, she had spent more than a decade as a Fox News personality, often shouting her way through her show about her chosen targets, such as New York Governor Andrew Cuomo, U.S. Attorney General Merrick Garland, and in 2020, Dominion Voting Systems.

It was Pirro's claims about the last that cost her employer dearly. Fox News ultimately paid $787 million to settle a defamation suit brought by Dominion over on-air statements Pirro and other Fox personalities had made about the company's alleged participation in voter fraud in the 2020 election.

For that very reason, Pirro was a particularly galling pick to many DC prosecutors. In the run-up to January 6, she had been one of the loudest voices on Fox arguing that the 2020 election had been stolen. Her rabble-rousing was part of the general hysteria of false claims and angry refusal on the right to accept reality. That tsunami of denial had contributed mightily to the January 6 riot at the Capitol. Now she would run the very office whose staff had spent years prosecuting the criminal consequences of that rage.

Pirro faced her first major test as U.S. attorney just two weeks into the job. On the night of May 21, 2025, as a reception at the Capital Jewish Museum was ending, a man in a blue jacket stood outside the building on F Street trying to light a cigarette in the rain. Nearby, two Israeli embassy employees, Yaron Lischinsky and Sarah Milgrim, walked out of the building and were waiting to cross the street. Lischinsky and Milgrim were young, in love, and planning to get engaged. The man in the blue jacket, who seemed to be waiting for a larger group of people to emerge from the event, started following them, pulled out a handgun, and shot the couple in the back.

Both victims lay on the ground as the man in the blue jacket stopped to reload. Milgrim, a twenty-six-year-old from Kansas, screamed for help as she tried to crawl away. The man in the blue jacket fired at her again, until she collapsed back onto the street.

Then the gunman did something bizarre. He began mimicking Sarah Milgrim's panicked screams for help, trying to sound just like her. People still inside the Capital Jewish Museum, thinking he was a victim or a witness, brought him inside, offered him water, and comforted him.

A few minutes later, a police officer started talking to him, at which point the man's behavior again changed abruptly. "I did it for Palestine, I did it for Gaza," he declared. He was quickly arrested, and investigators found he had recorded the entire event on a camera strapped to his chest.

The killings shocked the country and ratcheted up concerns among already fearful Jewish Americans that anti-Semitism was becoming deadlier. "This is a horrific crime and these crimes are not going to be tolerated by me, and this office," Pirro declared at a news conference the next day. "We are not going to tolerate that anymore."

At the press conference, Pirro appeared poised and in command. If her suggestion that somehow the previous administration had tolerated hate crime murders struck those who worked in her office as a cheap shot, at least she seemed capable of talking like a serious prosecutor in a serious moment.

Toward the end of her prepared remarks, Pirro added a line whose significance was not immediately clear. "President Donald Trump appointed me to this position. This is the nation's capital. We should all be proud of this capital, and the president wants DC safe, and I and the partners behind me are going to do everything we can to make people proud of this city," she said.

In her first high-profile moment as the U.S. attorney, Pirro had performed well, embracing the American traditions of prosecutorial conduct in a way that was reassuring not just to the public but also to her staff. But she would soon embark on a very different course, one that would drive out more prosecutors, enrage judges, and alienate much of the city.

"This is Liberation Day in DC," Trump declared on August 11, standing before a White House Press Briefing Room packed with reporters and Cabinet officials. He invoked Section 740 of DC law, which gave him emergency powers to take control of the city's Metropolitan Police Department for thirty days. The law was meant to serve as a backstop in the event of a crisis so severe that the federal government needed to temporarily commandeer the local police force.

Such an emergency existed, Trump declared, and the emergency was street crime like carjackings, muggings, and murders.

The president's apocalyptic description of the nation's capital was unrecognizable to the majority of the people who lived there. Yes, Washington had crime, as did every other city. And yes, Washington had a particular problem with carjackings and car thefts—it was part of the city's criminal history stretching back decades. It also had a perennial problem with juvenile crime. But Trump's announcement was based on a fundamentally dishonest description of crime in the city. "Murders in 2023 reached the highest rate probably ever. They say twenty-five years, but they don't know what that means because it just goes back twenty-five years," he said. "Can't be worse."

That was simply false, as most of the city's older residents could have told him. There were 274 murders in Washington that year—a brutal 36 percent increase at a time when many other cities had seen violent crime begin to fall as the effects of the novel coronavirus pandemic eased. But that was a recent peak, not a historic high. The late 1980s and early 1990s were unquestionably the most crime-ridden years in the city's history. In 1991 alone, the city recorded 482 murders, marking the highest homicide rate in the entire country.

Standing beside the president as he spoke were his attorney general, Pam Bondi; FBI Director Kash Patel; and Jeanine Pirro. When it was Pirro's turn to speak, she embraced the president's view that Washington was too dangerous to visit. "We want a safe capital. We want to be able to bring our families here. We want to be able to come and enjoy the history that makes this place great. And unfortunately, we are not in that position right now," she said, angrily pointing her finger from behind the podium. "I see too much violent crime being committed by young punks who think that they can get together in gangs and crews and beat the hell out of you or anyone else." Pirro called for changing city laws to allow for tougher prosecution of juvenile offenders, declaring, "We need to go after the DC Council and its absurd laws."

Trump's executive order, however, was not about changing city laws, but law enforcement operations. His answer was to send hundreds of federal agents and more than two thousand National Guard troops into the streets to fight crime in a city where violence had already been falling for more than a year.

His orders had already gone out to law enforcement agencies. Small groups of U.S. marshals and FBI agents began conducting patrols the weekend before Trump's press conference. Given the nature of their training and regular duties, it was a haphazard assignment.

Trump's FBI director, Kash Patel, liked to say his goal was to "let good cops be cops," but the phrase grated on many of the agents under his command, who were not, in fact, cops. The FBI is not a federal police force, but rather, a nationwide agency of investigators. They don't patrol streets, and unless they were police officers before they joined the FBI, most of them have never walked a foot patrol. The same is true for agents with the Drug Enforcement Administration and the Bureau of Alcohol, Tobacco, Firearms, and Explosives. Deputy U.S. marshals, who were also assigned to street patrols in Washington, perhaps come closest to having some relevant job experience, as many are involved in guarding federal courthouses.

Trump and Patel's vision of the FBI was that tough guys with badges were essentially interchangeable, and therefore, if the president wanted something done on the streets of a particular city, it didn't matter what counterintelligence, child sex crimes, or white-collar fraud case the agents were already working; they should follow orders and go out—just as thousands of agents around the country had done when enlisted to help with Trump's immigration crackdown.

In Washington, many of the federal agents were put on DC streets two nights a week and handled their regular work duties the other three days of the week. But their colleagues and prosecutors found that the new split responsibilities cost them more than just two days a week. The night shifts left some agents bleary-eyed and worn out when it came to performing their day jobs.

Complaints that this was overtaxing the FBI workforce were met with little sympathy from administration officials. Erik Siebert, the U.S. attorney in Northern Virginia who had once worked as a DC cop, said the agents should "drink more coffee."

In the first days after Trump's announcement, little seemed to actually change on Washington's streets. The president couldn't simply snap his fingers and put thousands of men and women in uniform onto city streets within hours. It took several days for troops and agents to start appearing in significant numbers. One of their first landing spots was Union Station—long a source of complaints about the homeless and mentally disturbed people who hung around its entrance.

As August wore on, the number of troops and agents on the street grew. Often, they were used for what officials called "visible crime deterrence"—their mere presence, the administration reasoned, would scare away the bad guys.

The administration also deployed significant numbers of agents from Immigration and Customs Enforcement and Border Patrol, many of them from out of state. Those agents used the assignment to arrest undocumented immigrants, causing the first real friction between city officials and the administration. As food deliverymen became a frequent, easy target of ICE agents, some city officials worried that the crime crackdown might have been just an excuse to flout the city's sanctuary policies and hunt for immigrants. There was ample evidence to justify such suspicions. Attorney General Pam Bondi ordered the city's mayor, Muriel Bowser, to assist in "the enforcement of federal immigration law" to find and detain "aliens unlawfully present in the United States."

Stephen Miller, Trump's senior aide who oversaw law enforcement and immigration issues, was determined to raise the number of immigration arrests nationwide to three thousand a day or more. To many immigration enforcement veterans, the number seemed impossible.

But in Washington, where Miller and others could even more closely observe the results, the agency fanned out to rack up numbers, and they got them. In the first six months of the Trump administration, ICE agents made only about eighty-five arrests in the nation's capital. But in the first month after Trump's declaration, they arrested about a thousand people, according to officials.

At the beginning, that happened largely at new traffic checkpoints, where local cops pulled over vehicles for minor infractions, and immigration agents then questioned the people in the vehicles. That type of tag-team work to question people's immigration status had long been barred by city law. Now the administration decided it was fair play.

It wasn't just more agents and more effort. Department of Homeland Security officials made a key change in the legal standard for arresting people. Federal case law had long established that to arrest an immigrant without a warrant, ICE agents needed to meet a "probable cause" standard—that is, there was a reason to believe the person was both in the country illegally and likely to escape if not arrested.

Trump's Homeland Security officials, however, decided that the standard should be the lower bar of "reasonable suspicion." The courts have defined reasonable suspicion as when a law enforcement official has some information that justifies questioning or detaining someone, but not arresting them. A reasonable suspicion can't be a hunch or a guess, but it is often not much more than that.

Suddenly, by lowering the standard for who could be arrested, ICE was about to round up people who would typically have been questioned and released by immigration agents, either because they were legal residents or because they were already following a legitimate process to stay in the country. Instead, as part of Trump's crime crackdown in Washington, those people were handcuffed and sent to a detention facility, driving up the number of ICE arrests.

One of those numbers was José Escobar Molina, a forty-seven-year-old father of two who set up scaffolding at construction sites around the nation's capital. Around six o'clock on the morning of August 21, 2025, Escobar Molina was walking to his work truck in the Mount Pleasant neighborhood of Washington when two unmarked vehicles pulled up. Two plainclothes agents jumped out and grabbed him.

"I have papers!" Escobar Molina yelled.

"No, you don't, you are illegal," one of the agents answered, according to a sworn statement he gave later about the arrest.

Placed handcuffed into the back of a black Suburban SUV, Escobar Molina tried to convince the driver that he did have Temporary Protected Status (TPS), and though it had expired, he had applied for an extension in time, as the law required.

"Shut up, bitch! You're illegal," the agent told him, Escobar Molina later recounted.

He was taken first to a city police station, then to a parking lot near the Pentagon in Virginia, where he was placed inside a van that took him to an immigration detention facility in suburban Chantilly.

There, he was put into a packed holding cell.

When he got a chance to speak to an agent inside the holding facility, he again tried to explain his immigration status and that he should be released. The agent claimed, wrongly, that TPS status didn't matter anymore.

Escobar Molina was then transported to another detention facility, a two-hour drive to Richmond. There, an officer finally admitted the obvious. "Sorry you had to live through this," the ICE officer told him. "These are new officers, they do not know what they are doing." The officer apologized three times.

Nearly twenty-four hours after his arrest, Escobar Molina was finally let go. His son, a U.S. citizen, had to drive two hours to pick him up.

After Escobar Molina was released, he became part of a lawsuit against the government. Federal Judge Beryl Howell ruled largely for the immigrants who had sued, many of whom were, like Escobar Molina, simply released after DHS officials admitted the reality of their specific cases.

Howell noted in her ruling that immigration enforcement is usually a civil, not a criminal, legal process. The Trump administration appeared to have taken the position that all immigrants who were potentially subject to deportation were therefore criminals, the judge wrote in an exhaustive eighty-eight-page ruling. That, the judge said, was "plain wrong."

She also upbraided administration officials for changing the standard for arrest from probable cause to the lower "reasonable suspicion" and for acting as if the two were somehow the same thing. They were not, and the agencies knew it, she said in her ruling.

By the time Judge Howell issued that ruling, in late 2025, it was clear that Washington had served as the Trump administration's guinea pig for doing similar things in other cities: Chicago; Charlotte, North Carolina; and Minneapolis all faced versions of Trump's immigration blitz.

On the second week of the Washington crackdown, Trump's deputy chief of staff, Stephen Miller, Secretary of Defense Pete Hegseth, and Vice President JD Vance took what was meant to be a triumphant tour of the city's train station, where he and his entourage were met by anti-Trump protesters whose angry chants echoed off the cavernous plaster-and-gold-leaf ceiling.

Walking across the station's marble floors past white granite arches, Miller said the city had been a morass of crime, filth, and fear, and that this would now change, thanks to the president. Generations of city residents, he claimed, had suffered through awful conditions until Trump got involved.

But Miller's description was about forty years out of date. Union

Station had seen terrible times, but that was back in the 1980s, when the ceiling started to fall down in chunks and the building was closed to the public. By the early 2000s, the city's train station was in far better shape than it had been in decades. Trump's decree, however, meant that Union Station would end the year ringed by military Humvees and National Guard troops with little to do all day but smile for pictures with tourists.

A day after Miller's tour of Union Station, Trump decided to give a victory speech to federal law enforcement agents at a U.S. Park Police facility in Southeast Washington. Rather than cover the speech, I decided to go to the place where Trump's crime rhetoric would have to come into contact with reality: the courts.

The E. Barrett Prettyman Courthouse sits on the north side of Pennsylvania Avenue, between the Canadian embassy and the Department of Labor. Built after World War II, the older section of the Prettyman Courthouse is ugly but carries the dignity of history, including the courtrooms where the Watergate scandal defendants met justice.

I went to the courthouse because sources had told me of an ongoing fight between Jeanine Pirro, the U.S. attorney, and her prosecutors over one of the cases arising from Trump's DC crime crackdown. Police had arrested a man for being a felon in possession of a weapon, but there was a problem with the case. The search that found the two guns had been clearly unconstitutional, according to the prosecutors who looked at the facts. Pirro had demanded that the man be charged anyway. The back-and-forth inside her office went on for days, and in the meantime, the guy sat in jail, waiting to see a judge.

"They don't care much about the facts of these cases, or the law, they just want to rack up arrest numbers that they can talk about at the White House," complained one frustrated law enforcement official who very much liked to prosecute criminals, but who believed there was a right way and a wrong way to do it.

Besides yelling at her subordinates about the gun case, Pirro had given a much broader and more consequential order. She told prosecutors to charge the most serious possible crime in every case, according to people who received the instruction. "Prosecutorial discretion appears to be dead," another frustrated employee marveled on the day they received Pirro's instruction. "It's been replaced with 'charge them all, and charge the stiffest possible count in every case, and let the judges and juries sort it out.'"

A *New York Times* colleague, Nicholas Bogel-Burroughs, dug through court records to find a likely name of the person in the gun case I had been tipped about: Torez Riley, a thirty-seven-year-old with a criminal record who had been arrested shortly after walking into a Trader Joe's grocery store. So, I went to see Riley's first court appearance, thinking an afternoon in court would tell me something more about the turmoil inside the Justice Department. What I found was that the Trump administration had caused a new kind of crisis, this time in the court system, as judges had to wrestle with a deluge of shoddy cases based on improper arrests or overcharging.

The American court system has long relied on what lawyers call the "presumption of regularity," a phrase that means judges trust what prosecutors say in court. The presumption of regularity generally means that judges view federal prosecutors as careful, honest people unless someone can show evidence otherwise.

But the sudden rush of cases that prosecutors were bringing in August 2025, in an apparent desire to jack up arrest figures, made some judges question whether they should still trust what prosecutors said.

Waiting for the clerk to call the Riley case, I got a chance to see others. I watched as deputy U.S. marshals opened a door in the back of the courtroom, revealing a steel holding cell with other people arrested in the president's crackdown. Deputy U.S. marshals retrieved one of the men from the holding cell—Mark Bigelow, a part-time deliveryman for Amazon—and brought him into the courtroom.

In the early-morning hours of August 19, Bigelow had been sitting in the middle row of a van parked in Northeast Washington, across the street from his grandmother's house. As the clock struck midnight, Bigelow turned twenty-eight years old. Two of his friends sat in the front seats, and there were drinks in the vehicle, according to court papers.

More than a dozen cops and federal agents—city cops, FBI agents, DEA agents, and even State Department Diplomatic Security Service agents—stopped to question the men. "We were chilling, not smoking or anything, just chilling and laughing, and they rolled up, like twenty of them, and started harassing us," Bigelow told me.

First, the agents spoke to the men sitting in the front of the van. As the police questioned those men, Bigelow left the vehicle and tried to walk back inside his grandmother's house, but other agents stopped him. Peering into the van, an officer spotted "a second cup containing an alcoholic beverage in the middle row seat," at which point one of the agents decided to arrest Bigelow, according to court papers.

"The dude picked up a cup from out of the back of the car, and he held the cup toward me," Bigelow recalled. "This is your cup," the officer said, according to Bigelow. The officer said Bigelow was being arrested on a POCA charge—DC cop talk for "Possession of an Open Container of Alcohol."

"That cup is empty," Bigelow answered. "There's nothing in that cup, so how is that a charge? You didn't see me hold that cup anyway, so how is that possession?"

Some of the other agents involved in Bigelow's arrest didn't even know what he was being arrested for.

As Bigelow was being put into a police vehicle, the handcuffed man became angry, according to court documents. "Get off me! Y'all too little, bro!" he yelled at an ICE agent. Bigelow told me he was trying to be loud enough to wake his grandmother, hoping she might come outside and talk the officers into releasing him.

"They were just trying to wrestle me down into the car, but I was like, 'What am I being arrested for?'" he recalled. Bigelow, the agents said, made "contact" with them by kicking one agent in the hand and another in the leg. Under Pirro's new directive, this earned Bigelow a charge of assaulting, resisting, or impeding a federal officer, a felony with a potential sentence of eight years in prison.

When public defender Elizabeth Mullin was assigned to represent Bigelow roughly two days after his arrest, he was just one of a torrent of new cases that, weeks earlier, would have been handled as misdemeanors in a lower court, if there had been any charges at all. Mullin, a former federal prosecutor, told Magistrate Judge Moxila Upadhyaya she was certain Bigelow would never have been arrested but for Trump's order to flood the streets with as many federal agents as possible.

"He was caught up in this federal occupation," Mullin said in court, arguing that her client had done nothing to deserve being arrested in the first place and that the agents had grossly overstated the struggle after his arrest to justify a felony charge. "This was a case created by federal law enforcement."

After Bigelow came the gun case I had been tipped about, the case against Torez Riley.

The internal dispute among prosecutors over the Riley case was not about their being soft or tough on crime, it was about making smart choices about which cases to put in front of the judges who sat in Washington courtrooms. There are basic principles that guide prosecutors' charging decisions, but chief among them is a simple goal: Try not to lose. In seeking to carry out Trump's orders for a crime crackdown, Pirro charted a course for her office that was likely to cause them to lose again and again and again.

Riley was arrested after a city police officer spotted him near a grocery store and thought his bag looked suspicious. So, the cop stopped him, opened the bag, found two handguns, and arrested Riley. The Fourth Amendment of the Constitution says police must have a good reason to stop and search someone on the street. A cop's guesses aren't good enough, even if guesses sometimes turn out to be right. The Bill of Rights requires that police must have objective information to justify searching someone.

The cop who stopped Torez didn't have that, and losing the case potentially meant much more than just one guy walking free. In a jurisdiction like Washington, DC, where judges can be quick to criticize the actions of a police officer or a prosecutor, prosecutors have to worry about weak cases that might lead to an appeals court putting greater limits on how all officers conduct stops and searches in the future. It is difficult for prosecutors to predict which particular case might tick off a judge, but they typically try to avoid reckless choices. To many prosecutors with decades of experience in the district, the Riley case that Pirro had insisted on pursuing was a disaster waiting to happen.

None of this was mentioned at Torez's initial court hearing. Mullin, the public defender who had represented Bigelow, also had Torez as her client, and she argued that the long delay in bringing him to court meant he should be released. The judge was unconvinced, and neither seemed to understand that part of the reason Torez hadn't appeared in court until then was that his case had been the subject of a dayslong fight between Pirro and her staff about whether the arrest itself was improper.

The next case to be called was that of Edward Dana, a thirty-year-old who was first arrested by police over complaints that he had vandalized a light outside a restaurant. Sitting at the defense table, Dana rocked back and forth as the prosecutor detailed a long history of arrests and mental illness. Bystanders had noticed him being arrested and had called out to him, asking what was happening. Such interactions became frequent in the city, as residents were deeply skeptical of and sometimes hostile toward the law enforcement agents moving in packs down the streets.

Once placed in a police car, Dana began angrily denouncing the Trump administration. "I'm not going to tolerate fascism," he declared, adding that he would "protect the Constitution by any means necessary. And that means killing you, Officer, killing the president, killing anyone who stands in the way of our Constitution."

The officer driving Dana to jail immediately got on his radio and asked his dispatcher to notify Secret Service. "He just made threats to kill the president."

Once again, Pirro's instruction would come into play, as an angry outburst while handcuffed in the back of a police car was turned into a federal felony charge. Many veteran cops would say the ramblings of a clearly disturbed individual already in cuffs in the back of a police car are rarely turned into a fresh charge. But Trump's order meant that a new definition of justice was being deployed on the streets of Washington.

As the ride to jail continued, Dana began to sing. Once he got to the jail, he continued to yell and quarrel and aggravate the police.

Dana's case was meaningful in one way that the others weren't. Chief among the complaints about crime by Trump and his supporters had been that Democratic city leaders in Washington and elsewhere had coddled criminals and refused to address the problems that homelessness and untreated mental illness created for the rest of society. Many city residents who were not Trump supporters also thought it was well past time for the city to do more about those problems.

To some city residents, Dana was the type of person who made people afraid for their safety. But to Dana's lawyer Mullin, this was the kind of case that would normally have been handled by a mental health court, and the crackdown had once again done more harm than good. "He is not a danger," Mullin told the judge. "The danger here is having federal agents roaming the streets."

The prosecutor on the case, Conor Mulroe, argued that mental health problems were not an excuse to harass passersby and businesses. By that point, Judge Upadhyaya, who had grown tired of Pirro's brand of post-arrest argument, had tried to politely nudge the prosecutor into at least discussing with the defense lawyer some sort of reasonable compromise over whether Dana could be safely released from jail until his case was resolved, but the prosecutor was noncommittal and evasive.

"I know what you're doing, and I just have no tolerance for it," the judge snapped at Mulroe. "There has to be a commonsense application of the law."

It was a plea more than a command.

I had come to court curious about a single case and had happened upon a vivid display of the consequences of Trump's decree: Aggressively stupid and stupidly aggressive police work. Prosecutorial intransigence. People sitting in jail on bad cases that judges didn't have enough time to scrutinize.

As a young reporter, I spent more than six years covering courts and crime scenes in New York, and I have spent countless hours since in other courtrooms. Courtrooms have a rhythm that is instantly familiar to people who spend a lot of time there, but none of the cases I saw that day made sense to me. I was shocked by the kind of charges the Trump crackdown was producing.

In the weeks that followed, the three cases I observed that afternoon were all abandoned by Pirro's office, a silent admission of the glaringly obvious flaws in the work by the agents, cops, and prosecutors who had brought them.

While sitting in holding cells together, Bigelow and Riley had bonded, praying that they would be released soon. Both men were confident the charges would not stick, because the body cameras of the arresting officers and agents would show that they were racially profiled, in Riley's case, and simply harassed in Bigelow's.

"We prayed together, because we knew it was bogus. Twenty guys rolled up on me, driving in a line like something out of *America's Most Wanted*," Bigelow said. Riley's arrest, Bigelow said, "was racial profiling for real. They only arrested him because he's Black and has a bookbag."

While Bigelow's charges were eventually dismissed, the arrest had serious consequences. He lost his delivery job, and a company that was considering him for a full-time position said it was no longer interested. "I hope nobody else goes through that," said Bigelow. "They forget that we're still citizens and humans out here."

When the case against Dana was dismissed, another magistrate judge who had been wrestling with the flood of crackdown cases criticized Pirro's office for how they handled it. Judge Zia M. Faruqui, who had previously worked as a prosecutor in the same office, decried what he saw as a dangerous degradation of standards there. "These catch-and-release arrests have caused presumed-innocent people to spend days detained at the D.C. jail," he said in anger. "This goes against our constitutional norms."

As he dug into the data, he got even angrier.

In August and September, prosecutors had filed ninety-five cases by criminal complaint, a legal mechanism more hurried than charging someone by grand jury indictment. Of those ninety-five cases, prosecutors eventually requested that twenty be dismissed. This meant that in just two months, Pirro's office had dismissed the same number *of her own cases* that the office had dismissed in a ten-year span, from 2014 to 2024, covering more than four thousand cases.

To Judge Faruqui, this approach had turned justice into a "roller coaster." And it wasn't just judges who were pushing back. Grand juries—made up of everyday citizens asked to hear evidence in private and decide if there was probable cause to believe a specific person had committed a crime—began rejecting some of the charges Pirro's prosecutors put in front of them. Many federal prosecutors go their entire careers without ever encountering a grand jury rejection of a case. In Pirro's office after Trump's crackdown, these "no true bills" became a regular event.

It's a stale joke in the criminal justice system that prosecutors wield so much control over grand juries that they could indict a ham sandwich. Trump's crackdown would show that in Washington, DC, in 2025, jurors found a sandwich more credible than the prosecutors. Here is that story.

Gregory Lairmore had worked for the Customs and Border Protection agency for twenty-three years when, in August 2025, he got an unusual assignment. He was to go out on patrol in Washington, DC, as part of the president's crackdown. Lairmore was an information systems specialist, and he was not accustomed to night patrols. Nevertheless, he was one of the hundreds of federal law enforcement agents sent out into the streets by order of the president.

So, on a warm night that month, he stood on the corner of U Street and Fourteenth in Northwest Washington, a popular part of the city, full of restaurants and bars. Lairmore wasn't doing much besides standing around, or as he would later call it, conducting "high visibility crime prevention."

Standing at a busy intersection with about ten other law enforcement officials, Lairmore was focused on testing a cell phone program meant to show law enforcement officials where other nearby agents are.

Sean Dunn, a paralegal at the Justice Department, happened to be on the same corner that night and was incensed by the presence of Lairmore and his colleagues. Red-faced, and holding a Subway sandwich, Dunn walked up to Lairmore and began screaming at him. In a pink polo shirt and light-colored shorts, Dunn hopped up and down with rage as he berated Lairmore, calling him a fascist. Amused bystanders began filming the interaction with their phones.

Dunn's diatribe ended in dramatic fashion: He hurled his footlong sandwich at Lairmore's chest. Before the salami hit the sidewalk, Dunn was already running away as fast as he could. In the first seconds, it looked like he might outrun the agents, but eventually they caught up with him.

With that, "Sandwich Guy" became an internet sensation—a hero to those city residents and others who hated Trump's police state play-acting and a villain to Trump supporters who wanted to see government force stamp out public disorder.

The video was undeniably entertaining, but there were serious consequences for Dunn. He was fired from his job at the Justice Department, and the administration recorded its own video of a pack of heavily armed agents going to Dunn's apartment to re-arrest him in the case.

Pirro released her own video, talking tough about Sandwich Guy. "He thought it was funny. Well, he doesn't think it's funny today, because we charged him with a felony," she says in the video shot in her office. "So there, stick your Subway sandwich somewhere else!" Folding her arms like a local television anchor, she smiled triumphantly.

Grand jurors, however, rejected the Dunn case, refusing to indict him for a felony, one that carried a possible eight-year prison sentence.

So, Pirro settled for a misdemeanor case, which didn't need a grand jury's approval.

At trial, the star witness was Lairmore. The sandwich "kind of exploded all over," he testified. "I could feel it all through my ballistic vest," and "smelled the onions and the mustard."

The defense countered with video showing that the sandwich had stayed intact inside its wrapper.

After seven hours of deliberations over two days, the jury found Dunn not guilty.

One juror felt the whole exercise was absurd. "We're supposed to be looking at the evidence, but a clear majority felt it was nonsensical, like, 'Don't waste our time or money,'" the juror told *The Atlantic*. "If he was trying to lure law enforcement away from innocent people, I think he's a hero. He was trying to do the right thing, and he was getting very, very angry and frustrated, and I think a lot of people can relate to that."

Pirro's full-tilt embrace of Trump's crackdown brought a new wave of resignations from the office that had hoped their worst days had ended when Ed Martin left. Veteran prosecutors realized that in some ways, Martin was a better bad boss than Pirro, because he struggled to get even a single terrible case off the ground. Pirro, by contrast, launched dozens of cases that many of her own staff thought should never have been brought, at least not as felonies.

To agents in Washington who had been trained to high standards, it was a deeply demoralizing time, as the administration seemed hell-bent on misusing law enforcement personnel—sometimes for show, sometimes to punish political enemies, and sometimes to stroke the egos of the people running the government.

Weeks into the crackdown, FBI Director Patel posted a triumphant message on social media about some of the recent arrests his agents had accomplished, including a drunk driving case.

"God, what are we even doing anymore as an agency?" bemoaned one veteran after seeing Patel brag about a DUI. "We're the nation's preeminent law enforcement agency and we're doing a DUI, and we have federal agents out inspecting food trucks to see if they had the right permits. How in the world is this the best use of our resources?"

In December 2025, Patel claimed the FBI had doubled the number of arrests from 2024. In January, he claimed the number had tripled. There was little confidence among rank-and-file agents that either figure was accurate. And the price of Trump's avowed crackdown on crime, according to many of the people carrying out his orders, was fewer arrests of substance. While agents stood on street corners like beat cops, federal drug prosecutions plummeted 10 percent in 2025, a Reuters review of case records showed. That was the lowest level the Justice Department had seen since the late 1990s. And the number of people charged with money laundering fell a staggering 24 percent.

Within the FBI, agents worried that the changes wrought by Trump and Patel might be irreversible. The political leaders of the country seemed to be learning to misuse the FBI as dial-a-cops, with agents being sent on a whim to this or that city to make low-level arrests. Trump and Patel had made it far easier for their successors to use FBI agents as errand boys and goons.

CHAPTER 6

Bodies in Motion

This is so, so fucked up," the lawyer thought, her eyes darting across the information on the computer screen. A career veteran of the Justice Department's Office of Immigration Litigation, she had been struck by the same feeling many times in the first months of 2025, but on a random day in late March, the feeling hit home while she was perusing a shared drive on a work computer.

By that point, the lawyer was already deeply disillusioned with not just the people in charge of the department, but also the mid-level managers who seemed increasingly willing to discard reality, reason, and their own sense of justice in the name of survival in the second Trump administration.

"I was frustrated with leadership in the office, and I just started poking around on the shared drive, and I found this folder," the lawyer said. It was marked "AEA," after the Alien Enemies Act, a rarely used wartime law that authorized the detention of citizens of foreign countries in times of war, invasion, or "predatory incursion." The law hadn't been used since World War II, when it was invoked against Japanese, Germans, and Italians in America.

What she found in the folder was a series of internal government emails describing the pressure her colleagues had been under to keep the courts from stopping the Trump administration's unprecedented use of the Alien Enemies Act. The emails showed the back-and-forth among Justice Department and Department of Homeland Security officials while they fought against lawsuits over the deportations and removals of immigrants earlier that month to a maximum security prison in El Salvador known as CECOT.

"As far as I could tell from reading the emails, it seemed like DOJ leadership told DHS to violate a court order," said the lawyer, whose account is reported here for the first time. Ultimately, she decided to become a whistleblower for the Justice Department's internal watchdog, the inspector general.

"I personally don't think there could be any dispute that Emil Bove told DHS to violate this court order, but I wanted someone to review it, and maybe follow up with the people who were on those email chains. I thought there should be some type of investigation. I also thought, these documents were on a shared drive, and you wouldn't necessarily put emails about your cases in a shared file."

Someone, the lawyer thought, had put the emails there for a reason—so that there would be a paper trail of the administration's efforts to ignore and lie to the courts.

Days earlier, on Friday, March 14, another lawyer in the immigration litigation office, Erez Reuveni, was formally notified that he was being promoted. Reuveni's ascension came at a challenging time for the new Trump administration, when many in the office worried about how far they might be pushed to defend new Trump initiatives. The administration aimed to end birthright citizenship, and there was talk of sending migrants to the military detention facility in Guantánamo Bay—two propositions that many of the lawyers in Reuveni's office considered not just illegal but abhorrent.

Reuveni had worked at the Justice Department for nearly fifteen years, as a career government lawyer in both Republican and Democratic administrations. Up to that point, he had exemplified a key principle of a government lawyer, in that he had little to no input on policy choices, and his responsibility was to advocate in court for policies set by the White House or federal agencies.

During the first Trump administration, Reuveni was one of the government lawyers defending the president's travel ban that first targeted seven majority-Muslim countries. He also defended the administration's efforts to speed up deportations and bar migrants' access to asylum at the southern border, and he sued the state of California during the first Trump term over its sanctuary city policies.

March 14 was a Friday, and Justice Department headquarters was mostly empty, for security reasons, as the president was due to give a speech in the building's Great Hall at the end of the day. But Reuveni and his colleagues were working in their federal office building nearby, and around lunchtime they were summoned to a meeting on the fourth floor of Main Justice, where the deputy attorney general works. The lawyers gathered in the DAG's conference room to hear from Blanche's deputy, Emil Bove. Reuveni's boss, Drew Ensign, was there, along with James McHenry, who had briefly served as acting attorney general in the early days of the administration and who now worked for Blanche, and Paul Perkins, another Blanche aide.

Blanche, the deputy attorney general, was not at the meeting at first, but he did drop by at one point to speak privately with Bove. After Blanche left, according to Reuveni, Bove told the lawyers that the president would soon sign a proclamation invoking the Alien Enemies Act against citizens of Venezuela. Invoking the wartime law would allow the administration to bypass the regular immigration court processes and deport undocumented immigrants with little to no due process.

This wasn't entirely shocking to the assembled lawyers, because news reports had surfaced in recent days indicating that the administration was heading in that direction. The Trump administration was fed up with the refusal of Venezuelan President Nicolás Maduro to take back his country's own citizens on the U.S. deportation list. So, instead, the United States would start sending them to a third country.

Soon after Trump had signed off on the Alien Enemies Act, Bove explained, at least one plane, and probably more, would take off from Texas carrying Venezuelan migrants. The administration expected immigration lawyers to sue to try to stop them, but Bove stressed that the planes needed to take off "no matter what," Reuveni later recounted.

It was possible, Bove conceded, that a court order would block the migrant removals before they could be carried out. But according to a whistleblower account Reuveni would later file, Bove said the Justice Department would have to consider telling the courts "fuck you" and ignoring any such order. Others in the room were stunned, and several people exchanged nervous glances. After an awkward silence, the meeting attendees were ushered out of the conference room.

Reuveni was dumbstruck. He had never heard any Justice Department official, in any administration, argue that the department could simply ignore a court order. Some of the other lawyers in the room tried to reassure each other that, however the case went, the Justice Department would make clear to Department of Homeland Security officials that all court orders should be followed.

President Trump, the former reality television star, liked to make a production of signing proclamations and executive orders from a desk at the White House. He would frequently summon reporters in to watch him do so. In the ceremonies, an aide would read out loud what the new declaration would do and then hand to Trump a dark leather folder holding the declaration. The president would sign the declaration, offer some color commentary on the subject, and then hold the document up for the cameras—a routine that became a popular internet meme.

When it came to invoking the Alien Enemies Act, the process was far more secretive. Trump signed the document on the afternoon of March 14, but he did it behind closed doors at the Justice Department, just minutes before he gave an angry speech that encapsulated his desire to punish the people in the department he viewed as disloyal and unleash prosecutorial power against his perceived enemies.

Presidential visits to Main Justice are rare. Biden never spoke at the

Justice Department while he was president. President Obama went twice, once to deliver a speech to mark new limits on some of the post-9/11 surveillance programs that had been exposed in greater detail during his presidency, and once to attend a farewell to his first attorney general, Eric Holder.

President Trump didn't come that day to talk to the building's employees, most of whom had been told to stay home for reasons of security. The audience was dominated by his aides and advisors and the new political leadership of the department. Seated in the front row of the audience, Attorney General Blanche chatted with his deputy, Bove, and with Miller about their action plan for the document the president had just signed.

I was in the hall that day for the president's speech, but I was distracted. While the public uncertainty surrounding the Alien Enemies Act was important, I spent most of that day scrambling with my colleague William Rashbaum to try to confirm information we'd developed from sources that the department was close to finalizing a prisoner deal that sounded bizarre. The United States planned to send El Salvadoran gang leaders awaiting trial back to their home country. It was a scenario that alarmed some veteran law enforcement officials, who feared that such a move would not only demolish important cases carefully built over years, but would do so in a way that could get valuable informants killed.

What we did not know, as the president waited behind a giant blue curtain to be introduced, was that all these stories were about to merge into one, and untangling it would reveal a great deal about how the president and Stephen Miller intended to use the Department of Justice.

Wearing a bright white suit, Attorney General Bondi spoke before the president. Next to her onstage was a giant pile of what appeared to be bricks of drugs wrapped in plastic. On top of the pile was a large cardboard box labeled DEA EVIDENCE.

It was not DEA evidence. It was a prop.

The pile of fake drugs, Bondi said, "represents" 180 kilograms of fentanyl, which would be enough, in theory, to kill ninety million people. "That should terrify everyone," she said.

Fentanyl was unquestionably a major problem in society and had been for years, and it was admirable for the Trump administration to try to combat it. In 2022, roughly 110,000 Americans died of drug overdoses, and almost 70 percent of those deaths were due to opioids like fentanyl. The number of opioid deaths had been on a dizzying climb for more than a decade. Fentanyl deaths made the "crack epidemic" of the 1980s seem insignificant: Back then, drug overdoses killed about five thousand people a year. By the 2020s, overdoses killed that many Americans every three weeks.

And fentanyl killed Americans in a uniquely perverse way for U.S. drug culture. The highly potent drug was laced into all manner of pills and powders without the users' knowledge, making fentanyl a poisoning epidemic as much as a drug epidemic. The number of overdose deaths peaked in 2022, began falling in 2023, and in 2024 dropped by a record margin, to more than eighty thousand. When Trump was sworn into office in 2025, he inherited a drug problem that, like crime, was already getting better.

When it came time to introduce Trump, Bondi declared, "We are so proud to work at the directive of Donald Trump," emphasizing that her Justice Department's job was to obey whatever orders the president issued.

President Trump took the stage that afternoon with a grin, smiling at his former defense lawyers, who now sat in the front row as the leadership of the Justice Department.

A year earlier on the campaign trail, Trump had declared to supporters, "I am your justice. And for those who have been wronged and betrayed, I am your retribution." Now that he was president again, he made clear in his speech that the person he thought had been most wronged by the Justice Department was him. "They spied on my campaign, launched one hoax and disinformation operation after another, broke the law on a colossal scale, persecuted my family, staff, supporters, raided my home Mar-a-Lago, and did everything in their power to prevent me from becoming president of the United States," he said.

Jack Smith, the former special counsel who had charged Trump for his alleged mishandling of classified documents and with trying to obstruct the certification of the 2020 election results, was "scum," Trump declared. So was Andrew Weissmann, a senior prosecutor from the days of Special Counsel Robert Mueller's investigation of possible ties between Russia and the 2016 Trump campaign.

Trump said he was disappointed that Tom Homan, his border czar, wasn't there for the speech. Homan, he said, was "a fantastic guy, a great guy." To public corruption prosecutors who knew the truth about the investigation the administration had frozen in place, Trump's praise of Homan was a particularly galling moment. Some wondered if the president was taunting them.

Trump's speech wasn't just bombast. He hinted at news to come that weekend, mentioning Tren de Aragua. "We've caught hundreds of them, the Venezuelan gang, which is as bad as it gets. And you'll be reading a lot of stories tomorrow about what we've done with them," he said. "You'll be very impressed, and you'll feel a lot safer, too, because they're a vicious group."

The president was being coy, in part, because the original plan for the Alien Enemies Act was a kind of legal blitz—to sign the document and put bodies on planes that same night, Friday, sending hundreds of migrants to a high-security prison in the dark. Under the secret terms of the deal, no one would be the wiser until the morning, when El Salvador's president, Nayib Bukele, planned to post videos of the prisoner transfer on social media.

But the administration found that just as they could not throw open all the prison bars for January 6 defendants within hours of Trump's being sworn into office, they also could not throw people into a foreign jail that quickly. After all, it had taken ICE more than a week to round up more than one hundred Venezuelans from as far away as New York and Florida and bring them to a detention facility in Texas.

The international transfers were put off until Saturday, setting the stage for a conflict that symbolized the Trump administration's antagonistic, dismissive posture toward the courts.

Just after midnight Saturday, the American Civil Liberties Union filed an emergency court request to stop what they suspected would be the removal of five Venezuelan migrants from the United States. The matter landed in the lap of James E. Boasberg, the chief judge of the federal courthouse in Washington, DC.

That morning, Boasberg issued a temporary restraining order barring the government from removing the five Venezuelans. He also scheduled a 5 p.m. hearing to dig into the larger question of whether the administration could legally remove people under the Alien Enemies Act without giving them due process, that is, fair treatment through the judicial system.

The lawyer representing the government at the hearing was Drew Ensign, who had been at the meeting a day earlier with Reuveni where Bove suggested they might need to say "fuck you" to any judge who tried to stop the deportation flights.

Boasberg's first question for Ensign was a simple one: When did the president sign the proclamation invoking the Alien Enemies Act?

Ensign said he didn't know.

"But fair to say this afternoon?" Boasberg prodded.

"Your Honor, I don't know the answer to that question," Ensign replied.

At that point, Lee Gelernt, a lawyer for the ACLU, interjected that that proclamation had been signed the day before, Friday.

The judge then asked Ensign if deportations and removals were imminent. "When I say imminent, I mean in the next twenty-four or forty-eight hours?"

"Your Honor, I don't know the answer to that question," Ensign replied. "We can certainly investigate that and report back to you. But I don't know the answer to that."

Reuveni and another colleague listening on the public line for the hearing had a horrible, sinking feeling when they heard Ensign's answer.

"Oh shit," the colleague texted Reuveni. "That was just not true."

The same colleague added: "He knows there are plans for AEA removals within the next 24 hours."

"Yes he does," Reuveni texted back.

Adhering to the court's traditional deference to government lawyers as straight shooters, Boasberg decided to take a break so that Ensign could ask his superiors if there were such flights planned soon.

"I will try to get people as quickly as possible and find out that information," Ensign assured the judge.

After a thirty-eight-minute break, Ensign's answers were no better, though he claimed there were "national security issues" that prevented him from answering the judge's question in a public court. "I do not have additional details I can provide at this time," he said.

The virtual hearing had a public dial-in line so reporters and others could listen to the discussion. Ensign dangled the possibility that maybe tomorrow he could brief the judge privately, without the public listening in. The judge immediately turned off the public line to allow such a briefing then and there.

Once they were in private, however, Ensign dodged again, saying he might be able to provide the details in the days ahead, but couldn't do so now. The Trump administration, through Ensign, seemed determined not to tell the judge what it was doing.

Gelernt then told the judge it was the ACLU's understanding that two of the flights had just taken off from Texas, and another was due to take off in about fifteen minutes.

Each evasion by Ensign only made the hearing stranger. The government was unwilling to tell him what it was doing, while the civil liberties group suing the government seemed to have a minute-to-minute breakdown of details that Ensign claimed were national security secrets.

Gelernt, the ACLU lawyer, implored the judge to do something before it was too late. "They may be sent to Guantánamo. They may be sent to El Salvador. It seems like many of them already have been sent to El Salvador. They are in real danger, I can't express that strongly enough, if they end up in a Salvadoran prison," the lawyer said.

Boasberg decided there was too much at stake to let the flights happen before the legal issues had been sorted out. He ordered Ensign to "inform your clients of this immediately, and that any plane containing these folks that is going to take off or is in the air needs to be returned to the United States." The people on those planes "need to be returned to the United States. However that's accomplished, whether turning around a plane or not embarking anyone on the plane or those people covered by this on the plane, I leave to you. But this is something that you need to make sure is complied with immediately."

Listening remotely, Reuveni relayed the judge's command in real time to try to make sure the Department of Homeland Security complied. Once the hearing ended, the lawyer was certain that when additional hearings were held the following week, the Trump administration was going to lose, badly. He expected Boasberg would issue a court order barring any similar flights from anywhere in the country.

"This doesn't end with anything but a nationwide injunction," Reuveni texted his supervisor, August Flentje. "And a decision point on fuck you," he added, another reference to Bove's remark from the day earlier.

Flentje wondered if Ensign would be sanctioned by the court.

"Jesus," Reuveni replied.

By 8:10 p.m., two flights of migrants, carrying about 230 people, had landed in Honduras.

"Guess we are going to say fuck you to the courts," Reuveni texted a colleague. "Super."

"Well Pamela Jo Bondi is," the colleague replied. "Not you."

For the next several hours, Reuveni tried to get DHS officials to respond to emails about what they were doing. Had the planes turned around? Were they bringing the migrants back? To someone with Reuveni's experience, this was a simple enough question. In the past when the U.S. government wrongly deported someone, it simply brought them back. But now the Justice Department lawyers couldn't get a straight answer on whether DHS officials had even told their employees about the judge's order.

Later that night, Department of Homeland Security officials, who were responsible for any deportations or removals, told Reuveni that they were not going to give their employees any instructions on the issue until they had heard from Bondi, the attorney general.

In ignoring or only half-answering Reuveni's questions, the administration seemed to want to keep some of its own lawyers in the dark about what it was doing and planned to do.

Reuveni thought that handing the passengers over to El Salvadoran authorities late on Saturday night would be a clear violation of the judge's order.

Around midnight, he was told by Ensign that the Justice Department would soon send an explanation to the court that the administration believed it had not violated Boasberg's order because the two planes had left U.S. airspace before 7:46 p.m., when the judge's written order—as opposed to the oral order, which was issued more than an hour earlier—was entered into the court docket.

None of the career lawyers involved in the case believed the Justice Department could argue with a straight face that a judge's order issued at a hearing didn't take effect until it appeared in written form in the docket. Reuveni was told that Bove would file that written explanation himself, which at least took the pressure off the career attorneys to go into court to face the wrath of a federal judge whose order had been ignored.

But Bove eventually backed out of such a filing, leaving Reuveni's office on the hook to explain, in legal terms, what had just happened. Just as he had done with the motion to dismiss criminal charges against New York City's mayor, Bove seemed to want the veneer of legitimacy that would come from putting career lawyers' signatures on court filings.

At 7:46 a.m. Sunday, Nayib Bukele, the president of El Salvador, posted a screen shot on social media of a news story about Boasberg's order blocking the transfer of Venezuelans under the Alien Enemies Act. "Oopsie . . . Too late," Bukele wrote, adding a laughing emoji. Elon Musk, the billionaire Trump ally, quickly replied with his own laughing emoji.

Twenty minutes later, Reuveni sent an email to DHS and DOJ officials trying yet again to confirm that they had complied with Boasberg's orders and asking for the status of the people on the three Saturday flights. Reuveni pointed out that for the administration to comply with the order, no one who had been removed from the United States as a result of the Alien Enemies Act proclamation should be taken off the planes in El Salvador. They should be returned to the United States while the court cases played out. He also asked if there were discussions at higher levels of Justice, Homeland Security, and the State Department that he should know about.

He got no response.

Bukele, however, filled in the gaps, posting a video on X of heavily armed El Salvadoran guards marching chained prisoners off planes. The men, forced to walk bent over, some of them with their heads almost to their knees, were herded onto white school buses. The buses were driven to the Terrorist Confinement Center, or CECOT, where the men were videotaped on their knees, having their heads forcibly shaved. The faces of some of the prisoners were recognizable to their horrified families. The lawmen all wore masks.

The United States had agreed to pay Bukele's government millions of dollars a year to house the prisoners, which Bukele called "a very low fee for them, but a high one for us."

As upset as Reuveni and some of his colleagues were about the events of March 15, things were about to get a lot worse in court for his office. In the days that followed, the career lawyers struggled mightily to make the administration's statements in court align with what the government was actually doing, or not doing, when it came to removing or deporting immigrants.

As a government lawyer, Reuveni viewed his job as giving honest answers to the court about what officials had done, in a way that followed the law so that judges did not punish the administration with onerous, far-reaching restrictions. That was how he had done his job for years, even when the first Trump administration tested the limits of what the law would allow. As heated as those legal battles were, the administration did change course as it went, adhering to whatever new lines were drawn by federal judges. When it came to the 2017 travel ban, for instance, the final version was vastly different from the first one imposed by Trump.

In late March 2025, it dawned on Reuveni that the task before them was different, and far more difficult because whatever legal advice he was giving Homeland Security officials, they were getting other instructions in backchannel discussions with Justice Department leaders like Bove and Blanche.

The court hearings on the issue were a disaster, as judges grew suspicious of the answers and nonanswers they were getting. The government lawyers giving those answers increasingly worried their own careers would be tarnished by accusations of lying to the court. "At this point, why don't we just submit an emoji of a middle finger" in the next court filing, Reuveni texted a colleague in frustration.

It didn't help that the president himself publicly disavowed having had anything to do with the presidential signature that launched the planes in the first place. "I don't know when it was signed, because I didn't sign it," he declared on March 22, eight days after the White House said he'd signed it.

"Other people handled it, but Marco Rubio has done a great job and he wanted them out and we go along with that. We want to get criminals out of our country," the president told reporters. A week after the flights, it was increasingly clear that many if not most of the individuals frog-marched off planes in the middle of the night did not have significant criminal records, and some had been locked up and shipped to a high-security prison based primarily on supposedly suspicious tattoos or items of clothing.

In the rush of news, Trump's denial was quickly forgotten, but it's striking that the president disavowed having signed a document he publicly bragged about just a week earlier. And it was particularly bizarre given how often Trump claimed that his predecessor Joe Biden was so mentally incompetent that aides used an autopen to authorize many of his key decisions.

As immigration lawyers and reporters dug into exactly who had been shipped to an El Salvador prison and why, it became increasingly clear that the Trump administration often couldn't or wouldn't distinguish between immigrants and criminals.

The Trump administration's "Alien Enemy Validation Guide" used a point system for deciding whether migrants were part of Tren de Aragua. Eight points, according to the guide, were enough for the individual to be identified as a gang member. Tattoos "denoting membership/loyalty" to the gang were worth four points, the guide said. But tattoos were not the only marker. If an agent decided the person "displays insignia, logos, notations, drawings, or dress known to indicate allegiance" to the gang, that was also worth four points. What kind of clothes fit that description? Homeland Security officials said that members "dressed in high-end urban street wear," and in particular Chicago Bulls jerseys or Michael Jordan gear.

So, under the administration's math, having suspicious tattoos and wearing suspicious clothing, like that of a Michael Jordan fan, was all it took for a person to be declared a member of the Venezuelan gang and shipped to prison.

One of the men shipped to CECOT under those rules was Andry José Hernández Romero, a gay makeup artist. The thirty-one-year-old's tattoos included a crown above the word *Mom* and another crown above the word *Dad*, according to his lawyers. Hernández Romero, a federal agent wrote, had "tattoo 'crowns' that are consistent with those of a Tren de Aragua member."

Inside Reuveni's office, some lawyers were growing more upset by the day as new revelations came in about the people now locked in CECOT. "There are times I think what's happening is the result of incredible malevolence and incompetence," one staffer told me. "And there are times I think I am witnessing a criminal conspiracy within the government to violate people's civil rights, and nobody in a position of responsibility seems to care. Where the fuck is Congress? Is the inspector general dead?"

Those two questions would haunt many Justice Department employees in 2025, including Reuveni. In late March and early April, he often worked past midnight, stuck between the unbending demands of administration officials and the ceaseless questions from courts about what they were doing.

Friday, March 28, was such a night. Facing a court deadline, Reuveni tried to craft a legal strategy for the Trump administration that would not blow up in their faces as soon as a judge looked at it. To that end, he sent emails to Homeland Security and Justice officials, trying to get clarification that the administration wasn't trying to ship more migrants out of the country, which would likely violate one of the court orders now in place.

Annoyed by the questions Reuveni was asking, James Percival, a lawyer at the Department of Homeland Security, fired back at him after midnight. "My take on these emails is that DOJ leadership and DOJ litigators don't agree on the strategy," he wrote. "Please keep DHS out of it." He then added, "Figure out what DOJ's position is and get back to us. DHS has one position from the top of the agency to the bottom. DOJ needs to do the same."

"What is that position?" Reuveni emailed back at Percival and the group.

"Ask your leadership. Holy crap guys," Percival wrote back.

The exchange marked what had become a growing problem for lawyers at the Justice Department. Their colleagues at the Department of Homeland Security, who were also their clients, seemed to be trying to get away with lying to the court. And as the cases went on, the Justice Department lawyers came to suspect that their own bosses were encouraging that behavior.

As ugly as the internal discussions with DHS were becoming, Reuveni was determined to keep doing his job ethically. In an email sent at 12:42 in the morning to Percival and more than forty other government lawyers and officials, the fifteen-year Justice Department veteran put his foot down. "We can't file the briefs then," he wrote. "If planes are taking off or will take off with people covered by the injunction as these briefs say[,] we cannot file the briefs as written."

That sparked a series of frantic phone calls from higher-ups at the department.

Reuveni had pressed them for two acknowledgments: that a judge's order amounted to a nationwide injunction, and that some instructions would be issued to DHS personnel explaining the judge's order. Over the 1 a.m. phone calls, Reuveni convinced agency leaders to concede the first point, but they refused to bend on the second, and they did not issue any instructions to DHS staff.

The person who did receive new instructions that Sunday was Reuveni. Ensign, who had spent his court hearings with Boasberg playing dumb, told Reuveni to stop sending emails with a lot of DHS recipients, particularly Percival, the DHS official who had snapped at him in a post-midnight message.

The paper trail was becoming worrisome to Trump administration officials, and they wanted it to stop.

Reuveni emailed them anyway, asking if any instructions on the court order had been sent to DHS personnel. An answer came in the form of phone calls with Ensign, who told him that leaders at DHS had concluded that no instructions would be issued to agency staff.

For the Trump administration, the silence served a purpose. On Saturday, a flight from Texas carrying seventeen migrants, described by the Trump administration as criminals, left Texas for the military detention camp in Guantánamo Bay, Cuba. The following day, a military plane transported the same seventeen people to the maximum-security prison in El Salvador.

The next morning, Secretary of State Marco Rubio announced that the men, who he said were members of Tren de Aragua and another violent gang, MS-13, were now also in CECOT.

To an increasing number of lawyers in the Office of Immigration Litigation, the new administration seemed willing to flout court orders to keep sending migrants to that prison.

Reuveni felt he had to figure out who these men were and what legal authority the administration had used to ship them away. Once again, he asked DHS officials.

"These are not questions for DHS," wrote back Joseph Mazzara, the agency's top lawyer. "DHS has nothing to do with this operation as far as I'm aware." Talk to the Defense Department, the DHS lawyer added.

A minute later, Mazzara replied again, to make a second point. "And for the record, do not make any representations to the court regarding DHS on the matter of this reported flight."

The problem with Mazzara's answers was glaringly obvious to Reuveni. If ICE, which was part of DHS, had taken the detainees to Guantánamo from Texas in the first place, and was responsible for them while at Guantánamo, how could the agency have had no role in their removal from the United States?

"These folks were in DHS custody at GTMO, were they not? And they were moved from ICE custody in TEXAS to GTMO, were they not?" Reuveni answered.

Mazzara did not reply.

Reuveni then called Charles Young, the top lawyer at the Defense Department, to try to figure out what had happened. Young told Reuveni he had not known about any court injunction, and he sounded upset that he had been kept in the dark, the Justice Department lawyer later recounted. To Reuveni, there was just no way that flight to El Salvador had not violated the court order. Lawyers at the State Department shared his concerns.

By the following day, Tuesday, Reuveni was running out of options. Yaakov Roth, a senior Justice Department official, called him to say that Bove was "very unhappy" with the way Reuveni had been contacting lawyers at other agencies to determine if the Justice Department had violated court orders. Roth told Reuveni to stop emailing lawyers at other agencies. As much as possible, Roth said, Reuveni should communicate by phone.

By this point, it was clear to Reuveni that he was fighting more than just his client, the Department of Homeland Security, whose silence seemed designed to ignore court orders. He was now lined up against the leaders of his own agency.

Reuveni could reach only one conclusion: the leadership of the Departments of Justice and Homeland Security had deliberately schemed to violate a court order.

Thanks to the administration's secrecy and obstinance, its legal problems were metastasizing. One of the men shipped out to CECOT on Saturday, March 15, was a twenty-nine-year-old man named Kilmar Ábrego García. Born in El Salvador, Ábrego García had come to the United States when he was sixteen. For years he had been living in Maryland with his wife, son, and stepchildren. Ábrego García had been arrested on March 12 and, three days later, put onto a plane to El Salvador. Within days it became clear that ICE had mistakenly removed him in violation of an immigration judge's 2019 order.

When the facts of the Ábrego García case first came to light, the solution seemed obvious to Reuveni and his colleagues at the Office of Immigration Litigation. It's not like the federal government never made mistakes. When it did, everyone—from the courts to senior Justice Department officials—agreed that the answer was simple: just return the person to the United States. That had for many years been the rule. The Trump administration, however, did not want to.

Reuveni was assigned to represent the federal government in a lawsuit brought by Ábrego García's lawyers, and he took the case in part because he didn't want the more junior lawyers to be buffeted by the demands of a case that had quickly become a high-profile legal test of the Trump administration's immigration agenda.

That week, he conferred with DHS officials who wanted to say not only that Ábrego García was a member of MS-13, but that he was a top leader of the notorious gang. Reuveni told them that this kind of claim had to be backed up with facts in a sworn statement by an immigration official.

DHS officials provided a sworn statement acknowledging that through "administrative error, Abrego Garcia was removed from the United States to El Salvador," which the agency official called "an oversight." The statement didn't go so far as to declare Ábrego García an MS-13 leader, stating only that he was "purported" to be a member of the gang.

Behind the scenes, as the two sides in the Ábrego García case prepared to go to court, Reuveni tried to get the State Department and Homeland Security officials to start efforts to bring him back. He was told that they would engage on that only if Justice Department leaders—Reuveni's own bosses—approved it.

Instead of getting approval, Reuveni got criticism. One of Blanche's deputies, James McHenry, sent instructions that Reuveni should stop making requests of other agencies when it came to the Ábrego García case, stop asking for facts to buttress the case, and tell the judge she didn't have jurisdiction to second-guess what the administration had done here, given that the man was no longer on U.S. soil.

Once again, Reuveni felt like his bosses were ignoring their ethical obligations in order to advance the administration's immigration agenda at all costs. Those senior leaders of the department would not have to go to court to explain all this; Reuveni would.

On Friday, April 4, Reuveni walked into the Maryland courtroom of Judge Paula Xinis for a hearing on the Ábrego García case. Lawyers for the man said their client had been shipped away based on the shaky claim of a years-old informant and on the detainee's wearing a Chicago Bulls hat and hoodie.

"This was an illegal act," the judge declared. "From the moment he was seized, it was unconstitutional." She then lectured the government on the most basic parts of due process and the Bill of Rights. "If there isn't a document, a warrant, a statement of probable cause, then there is no basis to have seized him in the first place," she said. Xinis ordered the U.S. government to bring him back in three days.

Reuveni tried a Hail Mary request. Repeating what was in the DHS official's sworn statement about the mistake that had led to Ábrego García's removal, Reuveni admitted the error and asked for the court's patience. "Give us, the defendants, one more chance to do this" without a court order compelling his return, Reuveni said. "That's my recommendation to my client, but so far that hasn't happened." Walking out of court, Reuveni looked at his phone and saw a torrent of messages, most of them responding to the minute-by-minute press coverage of the hearing.

Ensign called him almost immediately and asked why he hadn't claimed in court that Ábrego García was a terrorist. The question, Ensign said, was being asked by the White House.

To Reuveni, the question was bizarre, particularly coming from a fellow government lawyer. It was one thing for the Trump administration to constantly seek to blur the distinction among immigrants, criminals, and terrorists. It was a very different thing for government lawyers to engage in similar distortions of reality.

For one thing, Reuveni saw no evidence to support the claim that Ábrego García was a terrorist. For another, even if that were true, *terrorist* was not some magic word that invalidated legal procedure and due process. And finally, as any lawyer would know, because the department had not made such an argument in court filings, Reuveni couldn't just spring it on the judge in the subsequent hearing, a point he'd already made to Ensign.

By that evening, the Trump administration was in full damage-control mode as it tried to counter a raft of stories about the hearing in which Reuveni admitted Ábrego García had been removed from U.S. soil by mistake. The admission merely echoed what DHS had said in an earlier court filing, but the hearing had put greater public attention on the screwup.

Now senior administration officials began circulating a new proposed court filing, to make the argument that Ábrego García was a terrorist.

Reuveni increasingly felt like the administration's demands of Justice Department lawyers were dangerous and unrelenting. Once again, the internal discussions about what to say in court stretched past midnight. Reuveni spoke to his boss, August Flentje, around 1:20 in the morning, repeating the same objections he had raised to Ensign after the hearing.

Flentje told Reuveni he should submit the brief as the higher-ups demanded, and that he had signed up for the responsibility to do so when he accepted the new job of acting deputy of the office.

Sitting in his living room, his wife asleep upstairs, Reuveni thought for a moment about what it meant to be a lawyer for the Department of Justice, and what it didn't mean. "I didn't sign up to lie," he told Flentje.

Before nine o'clock that Saturday morning, Reuveni was suspended, placed on administrative leave, by Todd Blanche and Pam Bondi. A week later, he was fired.

The firing of Erez Reuveni horrified his coworkers, many of whom considered him one of the hardest-working attorneys the Trump administration had. "Erez did nothing wrong, nothing," said one Justice Department lawyer, repeating a sentence I would hear over and over in the months that followed. "And if he can be fired, then any of us can be fired, for anything or for nothing."

Joe Darrow, a longtime immigration lawyer at the Justice Department who had decided to quit, used his farewell email to coworkers to put down in writing what everyone around him was thinking and talking about. "I can't with a clean conscience defend actions by our clients that I cannot square with even the most tortured reading of the U.S. Code and Constitution, or basic principles of fairness and humanity," he wrote.

"What was done to Erez is *wrong*. He was presented with an impossible situation, and merely told the truth, acted reasonably, and did his best to avoid an adverse order against the government. That is our job description, full stop," Darrow wrote. Firing Reuveni, he wrote "was a warning, and an act of intimidation against us all. It signaled that we will no longer be able to do our jobs professionally and ethically if doing so is perceived to conflict with full-throated support of a partisan agenda."

Reuveni became both a hero and a cautionary tale to lawyers throughout the department. His experience suggested that when trapped between judges who demanded clear answers and superiors at Trump's Justice Department who refused to provide them, an honest lawyer could not survive.

Shortly after his firing, Reuveni dropped by a Maryland brewery for a colleague's retirement party. The lawyers there gave him a standing ovation.

Reuveni's ouster solved none of the Trump administration's problems when it came to the Ábrego García case. In fact, they got much worse. The Supreme Court ruled in April that the government had to "facilitate" Ábrego García's return. While his advocates hailed it as an important legal victory, senior Trump administration officials interpreted the ruling's use of the word *facilitate*, rather than *effectuate*, to mean they didn't have to bring him back; they only had to try.

And they didn't try particularly hard, at least not at first. When they finally did bring him back to the United States, in June, it was to face new charges of human smuggling, over a 2022 traffic stop in Tennessee. State troopers had pulled Ábrego García over, found eight passengers in the vehicle, and suspected that he was transporting migrants illegally for money, but he was not charged or ticketed at the time.

Once Ábrego García was back in the United States, the administration continued to suffer setbacks in court as they tried to either convict or deport him to some other country.

Rob McGuire, the acting U.S. attorney in Nashville, claimed in court that his office had reached the decision on its own to bring the new charges of human smuggling. Internal Justice Department emails from April, however, showed that Aakash Singh, a top deputy of Todd Blanche, had urged the case forward.

A judge who looked at the emails found that they "may contradict" McGuire's prior claims "that the decision to prosecute was made locally and that there were no outside influences."

Singh wrote in an April 30 email to McGuire that charging Ábrego García was "a top priority" for Blanche's office. McGuire replied, "We want the high command looped in." Weeks later, McGuire emailed his own staff to say that he had not received "specific direction" from

Blanche's staff, but he added that he had heard "anecdotally" that they "would like Garcia charged sooner rather than later."

Once again, Justice Department officials, who have a sworn duty as officers of the court to be honest, appeared to have been caught playing fast and loose with critical facts about their own conduct.

Another branch of government was about to confront the same problem, and expose its own impotence.

CHAPTER 7

The Corpse of Congress

O ver my dead body," one Justice Department lawyer immediately thought upon hearing that President Trump planned to nominate Emil Bove to become an appeals court judge in Philadelphia. The lifetime job on the Third Circuit was one rung below the Supreme Court, and it was possible that this appointment, while prestigious, was intended as a stepping stone.

Bove had served as the tip of the spear for many of the administration's most punitive and aggressive moves in the Justice Department. Inside the DOJ, few were more despised than Bove.

Nominating Bove was both a reward for past service to the president and a rebuke to the career lawyers of the Justice Department who had come to view Bove as a raging villain in the building. Behind closed doors, he could lose his temper and scream at subordinates who frustrated him. In more public settings, he was cautiously cool and measured, even when pushing lawyers beyond their ethical limits.

Bove's confirmation hearing in June 2025 served as a test of Senate Republicans' loyalty to Trump, and of the Democratic minority's ability to delay or stop the administration. Outside Congress, current and former Justice Department officials who had watched Bove punish and fire good people solely for the positions they held or the cases they worked, hoped to torpedo his nomination.

The Republican chairman of the Senate Judiciary Committee, Charles Grassley of Iowa, began the June 25 hearing by praising Bove's résumé and reputation and decrying the reporting and criticism around him. Bove, he said, "has been the subject of an intense opposition campaign by my Democratic colleagues and by their media allies," Grassley complained.

A day before the hearing, Reuveni's lawyers at the Government Accountability Project had filed a lengthy and detailed whistleblower complaint to the committee. When I broke the story of Reuveni's account for *The New York Times*, the administration denied the thrust of the claims and attacked the reporting. "This is disgusting journalism," Blanche said in a written statement, calling Reuveni's accusations "utterly false."

Blanche, who was Bove's boss, claimed that he was also present at the key meeting where Reuveni claimed Bove had suggested the department say "fuck you" to a judge, and he had never heard such a comment. However, according to Reuveni, Blanche had entered the meeting room briefly, spoken to Bove privately, and then left before Bove made the comment.

While Trump nominees tend to go on the attack in congressional hearings, Bove understood he had to play defense, given the allegations against him. He told the senators that there was a "wildly inaccurate caricature of me in the mainstream media. I am not anybody's henchman. I'm not an enforcer. I'm a lawyer from a small town who never expected to be in an arena like this, not until Todd called me and gave me an opportunity to participate in some of the most historic and significant legal battles of our lifetime."

He added: "I'm proud of what Todd and I accomplished as part of President Trump's defense team."

The top Democrat on the committee, Richard Durbin of Illinois, raised Bove's standoff with Public Integrity prosecutors over dismissing the Mayor Adams case. "Did you state, suggest, or imply that any individual who agreed to sign the brief would be rewarded?" Durbin asked.

"I'm sorry, I don't follow the question," Bove replied.

"Well, you needed someone to sign that brief," Durbin explained. "Was there any suggestion they be treated any differently because of it?"

"No," Bove replied.

Though no one said it at the hearing, an audio recording had been made of Bove's conversation with the Public Integrity lawyers. On the tape, he clearly suggested promotions for whoever signed the Adams motion. And Ed Sullivan, who signed it, did become the acting head of the Public Integrity Section.

Senator Corey Booker, a New Jersey Democrat, also pressed Bove on the issue. "You . . . told them that whoever signed the motion would emerge as the new leaders of the Public Integrity Section?" he asked Bove.

"I don't recall saying that," Bove answered.

"You don't know if you said that or not?"

"I don't recall saying that," Bove repeated.

Bove's claim that he could not remember was important. It is certainly true that many witnesses don't remember the specifics of past conversations when asked about them under oath. But in congressional testimony, outright lies carry the risk of being charged with a crime. So, claiming not to remember is a legally safe answer for a witness to fall back on when the truth is politically or personally painful.

Booker noted that Ed Sullivan had been promoted to acting head of the Public Integrity Section. Bove, however, denied there was a "causal relationship" between Sullivan's signing the document and his subsequent promotion.

"He's fucking lying," someone with direct knowledge of that conversation texted a colleague while watching the hearing.

In the committee room, the senator from New Jersey thought the same thing. "I'm hoping," Booker said, "that more evidence is going to come out that showed that you lied before this committee."

But Booker's questions, and Durbin's, highlighted a frequent flaw in congressional hearings. Both lawmakers knew more than they let on when they grilled Bove, but both also rushed through the key questions, trying to cover as many areas as possible without pinning Bove down. Booker in particular asked a number of compound questions that allowed Bove to deny the assertion without necessarily saying which part of the question he disagreed with.

Television and movies have left much of the public with an expectation that confirmation hearings involve dramatic confrontations. The reality is that such hearings rarely kill nominees. Typically, if a nominee is to flame out, it will happen prior to a hearing. If anything, a confirmation hearing will often lock members of the president's party into public support of the nominee.

In early May, well before the first stories suggesting Emil Bove could be nominated for a judgeship, the Justice Department lawyer who had stumbled upon a shared folder full of alarming internal emails about sending Venezuelan migrants to El Salvador filed a detailed whistleblower complaint with the Justice Department's inspector general.

The complaint, filed both electronically and via FedEx delivery, described allegations and evidence that Bove had committed brazenly unethical activity in directing lawyers to deal with lawsuits related to the Alien Enemies Act, according to people familiar with the material.

The Inspector General's Office had gone eerily quiet once Trump became president. The new administration fired more than a dozen inspector generals at various agencies, but at the Justice Department, the long-serving inspector general Michael Horowitz was left untouched. Inspectors general, or "IGs," as government employees usually call them, are often unpopular with administration officials who resent IG reports critical of how the agencies are run.

Horowitz was different. Trump liked Horowitz and often cited his past findings against former FBI Director James Comey, Comey's deputies, and Justice Department officials. Horowitz had sharply criticized how surveillance warrants were obtained related to the investigation into Russian interference in the 2016 election and how the investigation of Hillary Clinton's use of a private email server had been handled.

But when it came to possible wrongdoing by the second Trump administration, Horowitz was far more circumspect—nearly silent. And his office, when it received the whistleblower complaint about Bove's role in shipping Venezuelan migrants to an El Salvadoran prison, did nothing for weeks. Horowitz's staff did not contact the whistleblower and made no moves to investigate the claims.

Grassley, the committee chairman, claimed Reuveni's allegations against Bove had been raised by partisan schemers trying to derail a Trump nominee. But the reality was that the first whistleblower who reported Bove's conduct had come forward well before there was any suggestion that Bove would be nominated for anything. And that complaint had nothing to do with the confirmation process, and for weeks the whistleblower had been waiting silently for someone, anyone, to care.

And Bove's testimony did have a problem. His answers to the committee were contradicted by what he said on the audio recording of his meeting with Public Integrity prosecutors.

A person with the recording reached out to an old colleague to ask for advice about what to do. "Get a fucking lawyer," the colleague said. The person began to think of themselves as a soon-to-be whistleblower.

To the person with the recording, the weeks after the Bove hearing, while everyone waited for the committee's vote on his nomination, seemed to crawl. It was a painful lesson in how Congress worked, or didn't. "Nothing was happening," the person with the recording recounted. "The staff said they were working on getting meetings to discuss the recording. I could not believe how difficult it was for these people to sit down in a room and talk."

Some Democratic staffers wanted the person to simply come forward publicly with the recording, whatever the consequences for their career. The person, in turn, wanted some assurance from a Republican, possibly Thom Tillis of North Carolina, that if they did make the recording public, Tillis or other Republican lawmakers would take it seriously and act on the evidence.

But Tillis, not having heard the recording, seemed noncommittal.

Failing to reach some kind of understanding with any Republican on the committee, Democrats began to prepare to fight the Bove nomination on the floor. But peeling off multiple GOPers, as they would need to do to stop a full Senate vote, was a tougher task than peeling off a single committee Republican.

Shortly before the committee vote, a new wrinkle emerged. *The Washington Post* reported that another whistleblower had emerged with evidence that contradicted Bove's sworn testimony about the Adams case. Though it wasn't specified in the story, the evidence was a recording of the conversation.

Complicating matters, however, was a simultaneous announcement within hours about the first whistleblower, the one who had accessed the shared folder. Between Reuveni, the folder whistleblower, and the recording whistleblower, it was becoming difficult for lawmakers to keep track of everyone who was coming forward with derogatory information about Bove.

The Justice Department inspector general only made the matter more confusing. When congressional staffers asked for an explanation of this new purported whistleblower account about Bove, the Inspector General's Office first claimed not to have any such document. The IG only found the complaint after the whistleblower's lawyer showed them copies of the delivery receipt.

To people who had risked their careers and reputations to make whistleblower disclosures, the Bove confirmation process left them deeply disillusioned.

The person with the recording of Bove talking to Public Integrity lawyers concluded that the Republicans simply were not interested in evidence that Bove had lied to the committee or misled them.

For the first whistleblower, the one who had stumbled across the shared folder of emails, the Justice Department job had become depressing and demoralizing long before her complaint got lost. "It's very frustrating to first get no response, and then be told, 'Oh wait, we do have it, but we're still not going to do anything with it.' It just didn't matter at all," the person said, crying again while recounting the experience.

The lawyers who sought to stop Bove's nomination failed. They failed in part because they had too much faith in the movie script version of the confirmation process, where righteous lawmakers expose the truth about shady behavior. They failed, too, because they were naive about the degree to which lawmakers would conduct a good-faith, lawyerly examination of Bove's record. And they failed because the political math of his nomination was more important than any fact or feeling about his character.

But there was a time, and not very long ago, when the Senate took its responsibilities more seriously. Congress has never been a role model of maturity, but over its history it has had moments of deliberation, focus, and action. Article I of the Constitution created Congress as the most powerful branch in government. Article II created the presidency as a secondary branch, to execute the laws passed by Congress. But for decades, and especially since 2010, the first branch of government, Congress, has been conceding more and more power to the presidency.

The recent and rapid decay of Congress is largely the result of a shift, mostly in GOP politics, that began in the first term of President Barack Obama. The Tea Party movement sent a faction of combative right-wingers to the House of Representatives, and the presence of that faction meant that even when Republicans had a majority, they often did not have a functional majority, because a key bloc of lawmakers refused to go along with the kind of compromises needed to get laws passed. What had been a two-party system of government became a two-and-a-quarter-party system, and the two-and-a-quarter-party system became unmanageable. Bit by bit, the parts of Congress that wielded real power—the appropriators who not only spent the money, but also took a protective posture toward the federal agencies they oversaw—became less relevant and influential.

The Founding Fathers designed Congress to control the government purse, while the president would wield the sword of foreign policy and the military. But in the past two decades, as Congress failed again and again to make real spending decisions and pass anything other than emergency, stopgap budgets, the power of the purse slowly dissipated.

In 2025, the withering of Congress rapidly accelerated. Trump demanded and got far greater control over federal agencies, tariffs, and spending. The courts sometimes curtailed his most aggressive power grabs, but the Republicans who controlled both chambers of Congress either cheered or were silent. When the year ended, Congress could claim credit for only three things of any significance—Trump's "Big Beautiful Bill," which seemed destined to blow a massive hole in the federal debt; the longest shutdown in the history of the U.S. government; and a law forcing the release of FBI files about sex trafficking millionaire Jeffrey Epstein.

House Speaker Mike Johnson, seeking to keep a razor-thin and fractious majority from damaging itself further, kept his members out of session for long stretches of 2025. Congressional Republicans were so absent from the government that in the fall, Trump liked to joke to associates that he was both the president of the country and the Speaker of the House.

Steve Bannon, the populist podcaster and former presidential advisor in Trump's first term, dubbed Congress the "state Duma," a sarcastic comparison to the Russian legislature that serves a rubber-stamp role for President Vladimir Putin.

By the summer of 2025 at the Justice Department, many career lawyers agreed. It wasn't simply that Congress's power dynamic with the presidency had changed. For decades, Congress had acted as a check and a critic on the Justice Department. Legislative pressure on the Justice Department had long come from a basic assumption that Congress had a responsibility to monitor, regulate, and improve how the department functioned. In 2025, the Republican-led Congress seemed more inclined to abandon the department.

CHAPTER 8

The Library of Secrets

In early 2026, FBI Director Kash Patel flew to Italy, where his schedule showed he spent about as much time watching Olympic hockey as he did in work meetings. When the US men's team won gold, he chugged a beer inside the locker room, hopping up and down in glee with the much-larger athletes. By then, he had established a pattern within the bureau of taking trips that combined significant personal leisure activities with work events. He also regularly took time to fire career agents who had worked on past cases he didn't like. Many senior FBI agents came to think of Patel as a kind of live action role-playing FBI director, while the bulk of the agency's day-to-day decisions were made above him, by Stephen Miller.

"It is chaos, every day in here," said one FBI veteran.

Since being sworn in as the director of the Federal Bureau of Investigation on February 21, just before his forty-fifth birthday, Patel had been determined to bring sweeping changes to the Bureau. Many rank-and-file agents felt change of some kind was desperately needed for an agency whose headquarters building was a crumbling, leaky mess and whose middle name, some often joked, was "Bureaucracy."

But the transformation wrought on the FBI by Patel, Trump, and Stephen Miller had gone far beyond the elusive goals of efficiency or transparency. To those who worked for Patel, his decisions seemed fueled by a perpetual sense of grievance and suspicion toward his own employees, and he appeared to define his primary mission as punishing anyone deemed disloyal to the president.

Patel had never been shy or coy about what he thought of the FBI. In his 2023 book, *Government Gangsters*, he called the Bureau "a threat to the people" and argued for the top ranks of the agency to be removed. He also wrote a children's book, *The Plot Against the King*, a fable about the dangers of what Trump and his supporters called the deep state.

Patel's path to the top of the FBI was far different from that of his eight predecessors, dating back to J. Edgar Hoover. Some, like William Webster and Louis Freeh, had been judges. Others, like Christopher Wray and James Comey, had served in senior positions at the Justice Department. Patel, by contrast, had been a mid-level federal prosecutor for less than five years and, before that, a public defender. His ascendancy to the top of the nation's premier law enforcement agency showed that in the Trump administration, the credential that counted most was fealty to the president, which Patel had in abundance.

Patel grew up on Long Island, the child of Indian immigrants. After graduating from law school in 2005, he struggled to find a job with a big corporate law firm and instead became a public defender in Florida.

In 2013, he got a new job, working in the National Security Division at Justice Department headquarters. Former coworkers recalled him as someone who seemed to nurse resentments against those in high positions, whether it was judges, prosecutors, or agency bosses. In a lot of the stories he told about himself from that period, Patel seemed to play the role of David facing off against Goliath, and Goliath was often his boss's boss.

In 2017, he went to work for Republican Congressman Devin Nunes, who chaired the House intelligence committee. Patel came into the job at a pivotal moment, as the FBI investigation into Russian election interference and the possibility that Russian operatives had conspired in some way with Trump associates was kicking into high gear.

Patel distinguished himself by being one of the first voices to declare the Russia investigation a frame job and a hoax. The Justice Department, he later wrote, was in the grips of "endemic corruption" by prosecutors who "lie, leak[,] cover up or twist the truth." That, he said, is how the deep state worked to try to "take down" President Trump in his first term.

Patel's criticism did not arise entirely out of whole cloth. An inspector general investigation would later conclude that a series of FBI applications for surveillance of a little-known Trump campaign advisor, Carter Page, had been predicated on faulty information, and one FBI lawyer later pleaded guilty to doctoring an email to make Page's behavior seem more suspicious than it was.

The inspector general, while sharply critical of the FBI's work on the surveillance applications, eventually concluded that the Bureau's work across the board on such applications had been riddled with all manner of mistakes and flaws, suggesting it was less an issue of political bias and more one of a system that had operated in such intense secrecy that the quality of its work had not received proper scrutiny.

Patel didn't see human error, incompetence, or institutional sloppiness in the faulty work. He saw proof of a liberal conspiracy by government employees.

After his time in Congress working for Nunes, Patel joined the first Trump administration, taking a series of jobs where he often clashed with those around him and struck experienced government hands, ranging from Attorney General Bill Barr to National Security Advisor John Bolton, as hopelessly out of his depth.

Throughout Trump's first term, Patel showed a great knack for getting the president's ear and convincing him that others were not doing enough for him—particularly Christopher Wray, the FBI director chosen by Trump in 2017. By 2019, Trump had soured on Wray, and Patel, it seemed to FBI executives, was constantly egging the president on with new, false accusations against the Bureau.

When the Trump administration ended, Patel moved full time into the world of MAGA-friendly videos and podcasts and had his own podcast at *The Epoch Times*, a newspaper that promoted right-wing disinformation. "There are no coincidences," Patel liked to say on his Epoch TV program.

He also courted the conspiratorial QAnon movement, which built a devoted online following around the idea that President Trump was in a secret battle with a powerful cabal of child molesters. "The Q thing is a movement a lot of people attach themselves to," he said in a 2022 interview. "I disagree with a lot of what that movement says, but I agree with a lot of what that movement says."

In late November 2024, Trump announced on social media that he would nominate Kash Patel to serve as the next FBI director. Patel had "played a pivotal role in uncovering the Russia, Russia, Russia Hoax, standing as an advocate for truth, accountability, and the Constitution," the president-elect wrote. Under Patel, he said, the FBI will end the "crime epidemic," dismantle gangs, and stop human and drug trafficking at the border.

The announcement showed just how much the FBI would be changed by Trump. The tradition of letting FBI directors carry over between administrations hadn't even lasted until Inauguration Day. In choosing Patel over Christopher Wray, Trump couldn't even argue that he didn't want someone else's pick in the job, given that it was he who had picked Wray in 2017 to become the director. By law, FBI directors were appointed to ten-year terms, a period meant to insulate both the institution and its leader from the political pressure of elections. Within the FBI, many agents considered Trump's announcement to be an unofficial obituary for the ten-year terms of FBI directors and whatever independence such terms provided.

Patel did not arrive quietly. Just days after his confirmation, he launched into a profane tirade at agents and staff who had been assigned to sift through reams of documents about Jeffrey Epstein, the millionaire sex offender who died in a Manhattan jail cell in 2019. Since that suicide, the horror of Epstein's crimes, and the suspicion that others had escaped justice of any kind, had gradually taken up more and more of the public's attention, at least in part because of Trump's allies. Patel had promised to deliver on those expectations, even if his motivational skills were extremely off-putting.

"You gotta get this fucking done!" he hollered at the FBI employees, according to people on the receiving end of his outburst.

Patel, his deputy director, Dan Bongino, and Pam Bondi, now the attorney general, had all fed the flames of speculation surrounding Epstein and his powerful friends, but now they were in charge of agencies that at least in theory held all the answers. The pressure was on them to deliver what they'd promised to voters, politicians, podcasters, and social media influencers.

For years there had been online chatter of a secret Epstein "client list," which would supposedly show not simply that Epstein had paid young girls, many of them from the same high school, to engage in sex acts with him, but that he had served as a kind of pimp to the rich and famous. But there was a problem: There was no such client list, according to investigators I had spoken with over the years.

That didn't mean Epstein's friends and associates were all blameless or unaware of what he had done, or would have cared even if they had known. But the public expectation of Epstein's having funneled dozens of victims to a powerful pedophile network was not supported by the evidence in the case files, according to many current and former federal investigators.

Patel, Bongino, and Bondi had promised to deliver the Epstein files to the public. In the Trump administration, senior officials often performed for an audience of one: President Trump. But that one-man audience got much of his information from a variety of social media influencers, podcasters, and other extremely non-official sources, so when it came to doing their jobs, the leaders of the Justice Department and the FBI often had to worry about not simply what the White House thought, but also what influencers like Laura Loomer, Charlie Kirk, and Joe Rogan thought.

As they started their jobs running the FBI, Patel and Bongino wanted badly to deliver on the promises of releasing the Epstein files, so much so that hundreds and hundreds of agents and other Bureau staffers were put on a crisis footing to review documents for release.

Managed by Patel and Bongino, the FBI's review of the Epstein files was a rushed, rage-inducing mess. Instead of being given the full training on how to review and redact documents, agents received only crash-course instructions before being handed files to sort through. At its core, the job was to black out any references that could identify victims or reveal "personally identifiable information."

Each time the FBI agents thought they had finished the job, they were told there had been serious errors and that they needed to do it over again. This went on for weeks, leading to more tongue-lashings from Patel, who at one point "reminded" them that the administration wanted him to fire them all anyway, so they had better work harder, according to people who received Patel's version of a pep talk.

Some of that work was done in an FBI documents facility in the small Virginia city of Winchester. Some was done in New York, where the second federal case against Epstein had been investigated and where Epstein later hanged himself with a bedsheet in a jail cell.

But wherever the agents worked on the Epstein files, it always seemed to lead to the same unavoidable conclusion: Their new top leader was prone to angry outbursts. Bongino, for all his wide-eyed, vein-popping anger as a podcaster, was often more receptive to basic discussions of facts, according to agents who interacted with both men.

The Bureau, a large organization with roughly 12,000 special agents around the country, is a massive machine capable of deploying a small army of sharp-thinking investigators to run down every findable fact and witness. Hoover originally thought of the FBI as an agency that would operate much like the vaunted Pinkerton detective agency, in which an East Coast investigator could get a tip and then, based on that tip, get a West Coast counterpart to rapidly interview someone with critical information to solve the case.

But Hoover's vision for the FBI became grander, and more cerebral, than that. To pay for his law studies at George Washington University, he started working at the Library of Congress, earning thirty dollars a month. Studying how the nation's premier library catalogued information, he learned that it was not good enough simply to file away information—that information had to be easily searchable and findable, because often the key to unlocking a crime was knowing where to look for information the FBI already had.

Hoover believed in hiring, training, and deploying the best possible men to investigate crimes. He also believed in creating a library of the information produced by those investigators that could be easily and effectively searched, in order to solve not just one particular case in the moment but potentially solve future cases.

The FBI was born and conceived as a weapon—against criminals, spies, and anyone perceived to be trying to weaken the United States. In his era, Hoover aimed that weapon at bank robbers, Communists, and spies. He also used the weapon in some disturbing ways, targeting dissidents and activists like Martin Luther King Jr.

The FBI has always been a weapon, but it has also always been a library of secrets.

As his Bureau grew, its files became a key source of Hoover's power, and the power of every director who followed him. The FBI carefully guarded the information it gathered. Countless informants, tipsters, and everyday citizens brought information to the Bureau. Some of it was deeply personal, and much of it was nonsense. But in that sea of nonsense were eddies of information vital to solving a case or changing the minds of presidents or lawmakers on a particular subject.

By 2025, the data files of the FBI, now digitized, had grown beyond anything Hoover could have imagined. As FBI director, Patel had access to vast quantities of information, government secrets, and expertise, but it did not seem to change how he thought about the FBI or its workforce. In many ways, he was still the voice in Epoch TV videos declaring there was no such thing as a coincidence.

Patel's deputy, Dan Bongino, was cut from similar cloth. A highly successful right-wing podcaster before taking the number two position at the Bureau, Bongino was the first deputy FBI director not to have come from the ranks of agents. Deputy director of the FBI is generally considered one of the hardest jobs in Washington, serving as a kind of 24/7 chief operating officer of the Bureau.

Just as the FBI had never seen a director like Patel, it had also never seen a deputy director like Bongino. Shortly before he took the job, Bongino declared on his podcast that the FBI knew who was responsible for leaving pipe bombs outside the Republican and Democratic Party headquarters buildings in Washington the night before the January 6, 2021, riot at the Capitol. "The FBI knows who this person is," Bongino declared, calling it "an inside job."

Once in charge of the FBI, Patel and Bongino seemed to veer from one self-declared crisis to another. The Bureau had spent years developing expertise in different areas: Chinese espionage, terrorist groups, cybersecurity. Some of its staff held PhDs in their fields. But Patel and Bongino had a habit of throwing any kind of personnel at any problem, careening wildly from one target to the next in a way that drove many FBI managers to distraction.

Those managers also struggled when it came to Patel's impulse to rush to offer public details of ongoing sensitive investigations. On September 10, 2025, a gunman on a roof at Utah Valley University shot and killed the right-wing activist Charlie Kirk—a killing that deeply rattled the Trump administration, where many senior officials knew Kirk personally.

In the moments following the fatal shot, fear swept through the crowd at Utah Valley University. Unsure where the gunman was, people screamed and ran in every direction to get away. Hours after the shooting, a young man in a car was detained for questioning—a fairly common event in a fast-moving manhunt, and one that in and of itself usually doesn't mean much as detectives and agents scramble for evidence.

But Kash Patel quickly posted on social media, "The subject for the horrific shooting today that took the life of Charlie Kirk is now in custody." His announcement was met with huge relief, which quickly gave way to greater confusion. At a press conference in Utah, law enforcement officials said they were looking for a suspect, which didn't make sense when Patel had already declared that they had caught the guy.

Patel's announcement was the most egregious example of one of his habits that rank-and-file agents found deeply frustrating. Time and again, the agents noticed, in planning meetings and quick conference-call discussions about some new investigation, the FBI director and the deputy director would focus on social media posts capable of getting the attention of the president, his aides, and the broader MAGA community. In doing so, they often raced ahead of their knowledge and understanding of facts on the ground. The agents were hunting a killer while their bosses were hunting retweets. Kirk was the most high-profile example, but not the only one.

Less than two hours after Patel had declared that the suspect in the Kirk killing had been captured, he took it back. "The subject in custody has been released after an interrogation by law enforcement," the FBI director posted. "Our investigation continues and we will continue to release information in the interest of transparency."

Even some conservatives and Trump administration officials found Patel's "post first, ask questions later" style maddening, particularly when it came to a case they cared about as much as the Kirk killing. In December, after a gunman shot up a Brown University classroom, Patel prematurely announced that a "person of interest" had been captured in a nearby hotel room. Just as in the Kirk case, that person turned out to be neither interesting nor the gunman.

It wasn't just a public relations problem.

Just before Halloween 2025, Patel revealed on social media that a fast-moving FBI investigation had thwarted a potential terrorist attack in Michigan. His announcement caught federal prosecutors by surprise, given that they were still reviewing the evidence and had not made charging decisions. Investigators feared any one of the suspects around the country could suddenly flee or strike out because of the director's rush to speak. One of those individuals, a nineteen-year-old man in New Jersey, was later arrested at Newark Liberty International Airport, where he had hurried to try to get out of the country after he saw the news about the investigation.

As the leader of the FBI, when Patel wrongly announced that a gunman had been caught, something he did more than once, he defended those mistakes as the unfortunate but irrelevant consequence of making the FBI more transparent. In his formulation, the intentions of others could never be trusted, while his intentions could never be doubted.

By the morning after Kirk's killing, Utah investigators and FBI agents had done a great deal of investigative work but had not yet identified the suspect. They had scoured security camera footage from the school and found images of the gunman, but his dark hat, sunglasses, and American flag shirt didn't give them a name. In the video, his right leg seemed unnaturally stiff, suggesting he had hidden the rifle in his pant leg while walking through the campus.

Patel had been in New York when the shooting happened, and that morning he convened an online meeting about the investigation before he flew out to Utah to personally oversee the work.

The FBI director started the call with a profanity-laced tirade at his agents for not having told him earlier that they had found an image of the suspect, a criticism that ignored the written material he had already been sent with the image. The newest tongue-lashing was a fresh reminder to FBI agents—not that they needed one—that the FBI director was not much of a reader. Furious, Patel kept going with his tongue-lashing, declaring that he would not tolerate any more "Mickey Mouse operations" from his own agency.

Despite the public questions and private criticism from their boss, investigators were optimistic they would catch the gunman. On the first night of the manhunt, they had found the murder weapon in nearby woods.

"We are confident in our abilities to track that individual," Beau Mason, Utah's Department of Public Safety commissioner, said at a press conference. "If identification takes longer than expected, we will seek the public's help by releasing those images." Investigators at both the federal and state level had growing confidence in the power of facial recognition technology and digital license plate readers, tools that allowed analysts to sift through huge haystacks of seemingly useless data to find the proverbial needle.

Patel ordered the public release of images of the suspect to generate leads and tips from the public. It worked. The mother of a twenty-two-year-old Utah man named Tyler Robinson thought the images looked like her son. She asked her husband, and he agreed, setting off a series of conversations that ultimately led the family to bring Robinson into a sheriff's office to surrender.

At the press conference announcing that the real killer had been captured, Patel ended his remarks with a message for Kirk: "Rest now, brother. We have the watch, and I'll see you in Valhalla."

From beginning to end, Patel's response to the crisis in Utah had been an emotional roller coaster. But the mercurial director of the FBI was not just responding to crises, he was creating them.

CHAPTER 9

Burn Bag

Room 9582 in FBI headquarters is a high-security space for handling classified information, known in government jargon as a SCIF, for Sensitive Compartmented Information Facility. The manual for the technical specifications of a SCIF runs more than two hundred pages, with a solution—soundproofing, deadbolts, and specially coated windows—to counter every conceivable kind of penetration or compromise.

In June 2025, FBI Director Kash Patel sat for a long conversation on Joe Rogan's podcast, the most popular in the nation. At press conferences, Patel often seemed jumpy and overcaffeinated, in such a rush to get his words out that he sometimes garbled them. On Rogan's podcast, though, he was relaxed, wearing a black hoodie and smoking a cigar that he fired with a torch lighter. Rogan began the conversation by blowing a large cloud of smoke from his own cigar, which wafted past both their microphones. Rogan's studio was part of his multimillion-dollar home in Austin, and while it had soundproofing, it was no SCIF.

Rogan began the interview by asking Patel what his new job was like.

"It's effing wild," the forty-five-year-old director of the FBI replied.

Patel had a revelation to share with Rogan, who loved to talk about conspiracy theories. The FBI director told Rogan that he had recently found a secret vault of documents at the FBI. Those papers, he insisted, would help him prove the argument he had been making for years, that a series of FBI leaders dating back to 2016, most especially the former director James Comey, had deliberately set up Donald Trump with investigations based on falsified information about links to Russia.

"Just think about this," Patel told Rogan. "Me, as director of the FBI, the former 'Russiagate guy,' when I first got to the Bureau, found a room that Comey and others hid from the world in the Hoover Building, full of documents and computer hard drives that no one had ever seen or heard of. Locked the key and hid access and just said, 'No one's ever gonna find this place.'"

Patel was talking about Room 9582 in FBI headquarters.

"Whaaaat?" Rogan replied. "What's in there?"

"A lot of stuff," said Patel, eager to talk at length about the issue. "You know how I caught these guys? Because these guys were so arrogant, they would write everything down, and I found the documents."

Amazed, Rogan asked why they would have done that.

"They're so arrogant, they think, 'No one's going to catch us, I'm going to write everything down. We're going to put it in a lockbox, we're going to put it in a vault, and no one's going to find it,'" Patel said. "Well, you know what? I found the vault, and now I'm going to work."

Rogan ate it up.

"This is unprecedented behavior that's tolerated and coordinated with the media," the comedian turned podcaster said. "Like, that's dangerous for the country, but people are so ideologically captured, they're so locked in to their party . . . that they're willing to do a very un-American thing."

Patel's fantastical account, born out of corkscrew logic and threadbare legal theories, would eventually lead to cascading crises within U.S. attorney offices of the Justice Department. It would also lead to criminal charges against a former FBI director and a critical test of the federal court system.

On July 14, a little more than a month after Patel told millions of Rogan listeners about the supposed vault of dirty secrets, Todd Gilbert was sworn into office as the new U.S. attorney in Roanoke, overseeing all federal prosecutions in the Western District of Virginia.

The fifty-four-year-old Gilbert was a lifelong Republican. As a college student, he had interned for George Allen, the Republican congressman who would eventually become Virginia's governor. Gilbert had also gone into politics, serving twenty years in the state legislature, representing the Shenandoah Valley, and rising to become the Speaker of the Virginia House of Delegates. Before launching his political career, he had worked as a local prosecutor in the area. To become U.S. attorney, he had given up his elected position, his legislative leadership post, and his law firm work.

"In my heart, I have always been a prosecutor," Gilbert said after taking an oath to uphold the Constitution.

On his very first day, he got a phone call that would wreck his new job. The call was from Kash Patel, the FBI director.

Gilbert was told his office had to take on a hugely complex investigation into possible mishandling or destruction of classified documents—documents that had been found in burn bags in Room 9582 of FBI headquarters. But that wasn't all. Patel wanted the investigation of Room 9582 expanded so that prosecutors would examine the conduct not just of their immediate predecessors, like former FBI director Christopher A. Wray and his deputy, Paul Abbate, but also those stretching back nearly a decade, to James Comey and events in 2016 and 2017.

Patel also wanted Gilbert's investigators, whose mostly rural district in Western Virginia rarely handled national security cases, to investigate whether any former Obama-era intelligence officials, particularly former CIA Director John Brennan, had lied to Congress about a 2017 intelligence assessment that concluded Russia had attempted to interfere with the 2016 presidential election.

To Justice Department veterans, everything about the call was strange. For one thing, FBI directors didn't typically assign U.S. attorneys to open up cases—particularly not cases against former FBI and CIA directors. Those kind of instructions should come from Justice Department headquarters. And they were not the kind of cases that were assigned to Roanoke, Virginia. And Gilbert was in no position to push back, because he had not yet been confirmed by the U.S. Senate.

The task given to Gilbert that July, by Patel rather than Gilbert's own bosses, was to investigate what some law enforcement officials came to derisively refer to as "the Grand Conspiracy." The theory, pushed often by Patel, Trump, and a host of others, was that Comey and his allies had concocted and manipulated the FBI's Russia investigation to harm Trump's chances of winning the election. When it didn't work, Comey and his cabal of senior officials in multiple agencies had knowingly perpetuated a lie about Trump ties to Russia in order to cripple his presidency.

In fact, Comey's actions in the run-up to the 2016 election unquestionably harmed Clinton, while his FBI largely kept quiet about the Russia investigation, which was still in its infancy.

The FBI's Russia investigation, dubbed Crossfire Hurricane, was marred by significant problems and misjudgments, and Patel can genuinely claim to have been among the very first people to point them out. But most of that case, which could have caused great harm to Trump's candidacy if it had been revealed during the campaign, was kept under wraps during the 2016 election, while Comey badly damaged Clinton's chances of winning by revealing just eleven days before the election that he had reopened an investigation into her use of a private email server when she was secretary of state.

When Trump won that election and became president, he inherited Comey as his FBI director. The president fired him after less than four months, fed up with the FBI investigation of his current and former aides. Trump was also furious at Comey because the FBI director wouldn't publicly declare that Trump himself was not under investigation. The Trump administration's rationale offered for Comey's firing was that he had treated Clinton unfairly.

Comey's sudden dismissal led in turn to a special counsel investigation by his predecessor as FBI director, Robert Mueller, that dogged Trump for another two years before it petered out without proof being found of a Trump-Russia conspiracy. Politically, the end of Mueller's work resolved little—a host of Democrats believed Mueller had suffered a lack of will to deliver a decisive criminal case, and more than a few Republicans criticized the entire investigation as unfair.

Trump blamed Comey more than anyone, and by 2025, the former FBI director seemed to have cemented his place in Trump's brain as the number one target of his revenge campaign. Patel, Trump's FBI director, was the president's eager hunter. After years spent pushing the Great Conspiracy claims against Comey and others, the FBI director planned to use the contents of Room 9582 to prove his theory.

Gilbert, the prosecutor in Western Virginia, was told that "burn bags" of secret documents had been found in a room at FBI headquarters, and inside those bags were documents that cast the entire Russia investigation in a new, more sinister light. There is nothing inherently suspicious about burn bags containing secret documents. Generations of spy hunters have used the large, heavy-duty brown paper bags with red-and-white stripes as a trusted method of preventing secret government documents from being thrown out in the trash where someone could discover them. When officials no longer needed a physical piece of paper, it could be safely put into a burn bag. Once a bag was full, it was stapled shut and taken to an incinerator. Burn bags were far less necessary in the computer age, but still occasionally useful, even if only as last-minute wrapping paper for a goodbye gift to a departing agent.

A week after the call to Gilbert, the FBI formally opened the investigation, with a written report called an "electronic communication." The FBI report said that five burn bags had been found in Room 9582 that contained "a variety of classified and unclassified records." The classified material "related to the FBI's Mar-a-Lago search, the January 06 Capitol breach, the Crossfire Hurricane investigation" and included a classified appendix to a report issued in 2023 by Trump-era Special Counsel John Durham, who had investigated the way the FBI had handled the Russia investigation. One of the authors of the FBI report launching Patel's investigation was Jack Eckenrode, a seventy-eight-year-old former agent who had previously worked the Durham investigation. Now Eckenrode was investigating how a document from his investigation had been handled.

Patel had vowed to change how the FBI operated, and the burn bag investigation was wildly different from a typical Bureau investigation. The people tasked to review what had happened with the burn bags were his "director's advisory team," a group consisting mostly of retired agents, many of them Trump-supporting critics of the previous two FBI directors, to see if anything untoward or criminal had happened. Billed as an advisory committee, they often seemed to take a leadership role in investigations outside the regular chain of command.

Because SCIFs are secure rooms, Patel's team was able to quickly determine who had checked in and out of Room 9582, and they came to believe the burn bags had been placed inside the room in the days before and after Trump's January 20 inauguration. Attention quickly turned to Paul Abbate, the deputy director who had been unceremoniously jettisoned on day one of the new administration.

As FBI veterans learned what Patel and his team were investigating, they were alarmed but also baffled. How could FBI officials have mishandled classified documents by placing them in a SCIF, the very place designed to keep them secure? What did it matter which documents were put into burn bags when the bags were in a SCIF and when the FBI's classified system is built to retain the information on computers anyway? And wasn't the far more obvious, and innocent, explanation that a senior official forced out by the Trump administration had simply cleaned out his or her office after many years in the job?

And even if there were suspicious answers to some of those questions, it was hard to grasp why the investigation had been assigned to the hills of Western Virginia rather than to Washington, DC, where FBI headquarters sits.

Patel and Bongino were adamant that the case not be handled in the nation's capital. Like many in the Trump administration, they were deeply skeptical that judges and juries in Washington would take seriously any cases against the president's enemies. The administration was also deeply worried about leaks to the press—an odd thing to suddenly care about after the director had announced the investigation on the most popular podcast in the country more than a full month before the FBI officially opened the case.

To get the case out of Washington, they used an elastic notion of jurisdiction.

In the same way that Justice Department headquarters is a collection of government buildings around the Washington area, the geographical footprint of what agents call FBI headquarters is similarly spread out across an assortment of office buildings. The FBI stores necessary documents at its Central Records Complex, where billions of pages of records are sorted by robots and people. This massive FBI library is located in Winchester, Virginia, a small city about seventy-five miles west of Washington, perhaps best known to historians for having changed hands seventy-two times in the course of the Civil War. The FBI records warehouse in Winchester was Patel's hook for placing the burn bags investigation in the Western District of Virginia.

One document was of particular interest to Patel and his team—a September 7, 2016, letter from the CIA to the FBI. The letter said the CIA had received intelligence that Clinton planned to try to tie Trump to Russia. By the time that letter was sent, Clinton campaign officials had repeatedly argued on television that there were suspicious links between the Republican candidate and Russia. Nevertheless, Republicans in Congress characterized the CIA memo to the FBI as proof that Comey and his deputies at the FBI had been explicitly warned that the Russian allegations were hogwash and a political dirty trick by the Clinton campaign. In that chapter of Patel's Grand Conspiracy, Comey had decided to ignore the CIA's warning and investigate anyway because his real aim was to hurt Trump's political fortunes.

When Comey was questioned about the 2016 letter in testimony before Congress on September 30, 2020, he said he didn't remember seeing it and didn't recall that issue being brought up with him.

So, when Patel and his advisory team were told that a copy of the document had been left in a storage closet by the FBI director's office, and then later taken to Room 9582, they immediately smelled a rat.

Among the discovered documents were notes apparently written by Comey from the same period. One of the notations said, "HRC plan to tie Trump." The next bullet was "HRC Health."

Patel and his team viewed this as further proof of their theory, which was dumped into Gilbert's lap hours into his new job.

Many U.S. attorneys come into the job with significant prior experience as federal prosecutors. Those who do not, like Gilbert, tend to lean heavily on the career staff, especially in the first few months as they learn how the office works. Gilbert relied on a senior career prosecutor, Zachary Lee, to advise him. Lee had worked in the office for twenty years and was widely respected both by the prosecutors who worked for him and by the defense lawyers he opposed in court.

Gilbert and Lee thought the way to handle the strange case was to take it seriously and do a thorough and careful job. Gilbert emphasized to his subordinates that however unusual or risky the assignment was, the prosecutors in his office should conduct it by the book—even if he needed them to explain to him what the book said.

But all around them, there were warning signs.

The FBI director got daily or near-daily briefings on the progress in the case, a frequency of briefings typically reserved for manhunts or national security crises. Gilbert, still uncertain why he was receiving so much direction from Patel and so little from the deputy attorney general, Todd Blanche, repeatedly tried to get guidance from Blanche. One time, he even drove to Washington unannounced to ask Blanche for some guidance on how to handle the case. Blanche was often busy and couldn't find time to talk to Gilbert about it. Instead, one of his deputies, Aakash Singh, would urge Gilbert to keep aggressively pursuing it. But Singh wouldn't or couldn't address the legal and factual questions Gilbert had about the case. Instead of pointers, Gilbert got platitudes.

The law, it seemed clear to him and Lee, gave legal jurisdiction (what lawyers call "venue") to the Western District of Virginia on only one of the issues Patel wanted investigated—the question of how the secret papers had gotten into the burn bags and whether there had been any criminal scheme to hide or destroy them. But the two other issues—whether Comey had lied in his congressional testimony in 2020 and whether Brennan, the former CIA director, or others had lied to Congress about the 2017 intelligence assessment of Russian election interference—had no legitimate venue in Western Virginia, they concluded.

Within a matter of weeks, Gilbert's office was able to convince leaders at the FBI that those two other branches of the case should be investigated elsewhere. The Comey testimony case was assigned to federal prosecutors in Eastern Virginia, because the hearing in question had taken place during the pandemic, and Comey had appeared remotely from his home in the northern part of the state. The intelligence assessment case was assigned to federal prosecutors in Philadelphia.

In conducting a diligent review of the facts, Gilbert ran afoul not just of the FBI leaders but of White House officials, too. About two weeks after he got the case, the administration ordered him to demote Zachary Lee and take another lawyer, Robert Tracci, into the office as his deputy, apparently to ensure that Gilbert pursued the case aggressively.

Tracci had worked briefly in the office before, but was not remembered fondly. More than one person warned Gilbert to be careful—Tracci was the kind of person who tried to look good by making his colleagues look bad.

With those warnings in mind, Gilbert assigned Tracci to a pending drug trial, and demoted Lee as he was told to, but he still relied on the office veteran for advice. He also gave Lee a new title: executive assistant U.S. attorney.

Gilbert was under pressure on two related fronts. First, he and his prosecutors did not think the evidence the investigators had gathered from FBI witnesses about the burn bags justified impaneling a grand jury, which would be a necessary step to securing an indictment. Gilbert was also pressured, according to people familiar with the events, to further demote or punish Lee and to give Tracci a bigger role in the decision-making.

Gilbert refused to do that to Lee, and in mid-August the administration decided to get rid of him. Sergio Gor, a powerful White House official, called Virginia Governor Glenn Youngkin. Gilbert was going to be fired, Gor said, and the governor should not try to stop it. The decision had already been made.

Gilbert had lasted just thirty-seven days.

Shortly after being forced out, he posted a GIF on social media from the Will Ferrell comedy *Anchorman*. In the scene, Ferrell has just survived a nonsensical street fight with rival news stations and is back at his office, relaxing with a beer. "Boy, that escalated quickly!" the Will Ferrell character exclaims with surprise.

With Gilbert gone and Lee preparing to resign, Tracci was put in charge of the U.S. Attorney's Office. The investigation pressed forward, egged on mostly by Patel and some members of his advisory team.

Prosecutors on the burn bag investigation wrote a lengthy analysis, called a declination memo, describing why the facts and law had led them to the conclusion that no criminal charges were warranted over the documents in Room 9582. The senior FBI agent on the case endorsed the declination memo's findings.

For his part, Gilbert declined to talk about what had happened. He soon took a new job at a county prosecutor's office.

The damage from the burn bag case had been substantial, but it did not stop in Western Virginia. The political pressure to deliver revenge for the president did not abate; it just changed direction, to the other federal prosecutor's office in Virginia.

The head of that office, Erik Siebert, had the connections and experience to be a great U.S. attorney. As a young man, he'd worked as a police officer in Washington, DC, before going to law school. In 2010, he became a federal prosecutor in the Eastern District of Virginia. EDVA, as it was called by the people who worked there, was one of the most respected federal districts in the country. In addition to the regular criminal workload, the office also ran a steady stream of national security cases, given that the district contained the Pentagon, CIA headquarters, and the large military presence in Norfolk.

On the first day of the new Trump administration, the forty-six-year-old Siebert was made the U.S. attorney in the Eastern District of Virginia, one of the trusted Republican lawyers who took immediate control of key prosecutors' offices around the country, including in Washington and New York.

Siebert was an enthusiastic advocate for the new administration, promoting the federal crackdown on immigration and the president's declaration of a crime emergency in Washington, DC. It was Siebert who, when some on his staff worried about the drain on resources, particularly for FBI agents forced to suddenly work night shifts every week, said the agents should "drink more coffee."

Siebert was temporarily appointed under a section of federal law that allowed him to serve as an interim U.S. attorney for 120 days. As that period came to an end in May, the state's two Democratic senators recommended that Trump nominate Siebert to keep him in the position. As the nomination proceeded through the Senate, the judges in the district, following another part of the federal vacancies law, unanimously appointed him to continue in the job.

In a time when Trump and Democrats could rarely agree on anything, Siebert's appointment was the rare exception.

It would not last long.

After the Western District federal prosecutors' office went through a tumultuous August wrestling with the burn bag case, the White House revenge campaign turned its focus to Siebert's office.

Ed Martin, the former temporary U.S. attorney in Washington who had become the Justice Department pardon attorney, held weekly meetings to try to push forward mortgage fraud investigations against a handful of Trump enemies: New York's attorney general, Letitia James;

California Senator Adam Schiff; and a far more recent target, Lisa Cook, a member of the Federal Reserve Board whom Trump had decided he wanted to replace so he could have a greater say over interest rates.

James was a target for one obvious reason: She had sued Trump and his businesses in civil court in New York, and won, at least at first. In 2024, the judge in that case ordered Trump and his companies to pay more than $450 million, though an appeals court later threw out the dollar amount as excessive. The James case was a central part of Trump's argument that Democrats had harnessed "lawfare" against him, bringing the kinds of charges and lawsuits that would never have been filed against anyone else. As evidence, his legal team pointed to James's campaign rhetoric vowing to investigate Trump as soon as she was elected.

Trump's enmity for Schiff dated back to his first term, when the California congressman had served as the top Democrat on the House of Representatives' intelligence committee and had been an outspoken critic of the president. Trump accused Schiff of leaking and hyping the Russia investigation. Schiff had also been one of the congressional leaders on the impeachment case against Trump.

The mortgage investigations probably never would have gone as far as they did but for Ed Martin, who led the Justice Department's "weaponization working group." On paper, Martin reported to Todd Blanche, but in reality, he mostly did as he pleased, confident in his direct line of communication with the president and others in the administration. At times, Martin seemed to be running his own fiefdom within the Justice Department, one dedicated to delivering scalps for the president.

Even more than Martin, the mortgage cases were pushed fervently by Bill Pulte, the head of the Federal Housing Finance Agency and chairman of mortgage giants Fannie Mae and Freddie Mac. Pulte, thirty-six, was no prosecutor, but in April 2025 he made a criminal referral to the Justice Department against Letitia James, claiming she had falsified information in mortgage paperwork to get a more favorable interest rate. In July, Pulte leveled a similar allegation against Schiff, suggesting the senator had claimed two different places as his primary residence in order to get a lower rate. The next month, he leveled similar accusations against Cook.

Pulte's aggressive finger-pointing irritated even Justice Department leaders pursuing their own questionable criminal cases against Trump critics. In an administration where law enforcement officials were already willing to pursue weak facts and novel theories to bring criminal charges against Trump's enemies, Pulte seemed to go the furthest. He didn't just make criminal referrals, he publicly campaigned for criminal charges to be filed, and he egged Trump on to help him browbeat the department into filing cases, according to people familiar with the internal discussions.

On the Letitia James case, career prosecutors in Norfolk looked at the evidence and found little to support the notion that James had intentionally lied on the mortgage forms to save money. Proof of intent is a critical component in mortgage fraud cases, as the paperwork is complex, often handled by brokers or other middlemen, and few homebuyers bother to read or understand the stacks of fine print.

Investigators scrutinized two mortgages in Norfolk that James had taken out. One was for a single-story home bought in 2020 for $137,000. The accusation pushed by Martin and Pulte was that while James had indicated to her mortgage broker that she planned to use the house as a second home, she had instead rented it to her grandniece and her family. One of the key flaws in the case, however, was that the grandniece did not appear to pay rent.

The administration calculated that, even if its accusations were correct, James would have stood to save a total of $18,933 by the time the mortgage was paid out in 2050—which averaged out to something like $50 a month.

In July, Blanche summoned FBI agents, Virginia prosecutors, and Pulte to a meeting at the Justice Department to talk about the James investigation. The meeting began with a presentation by the FBI agents, who emphasized the lack of evidence of criminality surrounding the mortgages on the two Norfolk properties.

After the FBI agents finished, Blanche weighed in, declaring in no uncertain terms that there was no criminal case to bring against James for either property. When Pulte's aides at the meeting tried to argue or interject, Blanche shot them down.

For the agents and prosecutors on the case, it was encouraging to see the deputy attorney general back them up and put Pulte and his team in their place. But that optimism was short-lived. Within days of the meeting with Pulte, law enforcement officials heard that the White House still wanted to see James charged.

And it would not give up on going after Comey, either. Siebert was handed the Comey testimony investigation in mid-August, after the Western District prosecutors successfully argued against taking it. It was the second time in three months that the office had been pressed by Blanche's office to investigate Comey.

In May, the former FBI director had posted a photo on social media of seashells arranged to read "86 47," the slang reference "86" meaning "get rid of"—in this case, the forty-seventh president. Trump and his supporters, however, called the message a threat of violence. Comey denied that this was the intent, noting that the term is often used for throwing a rowdy patron out of a bar or restaurant.

The next morning, prosecutors in the Eastern District of Virginia were told to investigate the seashells. Secret Service agents tracked Comey and his wife as they traveled from the North Carolina seashore to their home in Virginia.

Comey agreed to sit down with Secret Service agents for an interview, and he asserted again that he had had no intention at all to post a threat or encourage violence. Given those statements, Secret Service believed there was no point in opening a criminal investigation. Blanche's office disagreed, and pressed both the FBI and Secret Service to pursue a case. But the Secret Service did not report to Blanche—the agency was part of the Department of Homeland Security—and senior officials at the Secret Service refused to open a full investigation, which made it easier for the FBI and the federal prosecutors in Virginia to also say no.

The seashells incident was significant for what it said not about Comey, but about Blanche and the Trump administration's desire to pursue Comey. The hunters, as Trump put it, had caught the scent of prey and wanted more. When Siebert was handed a new Comey investigation in mid-August, he was put in an even tougher position than his colleagues in the western part of the state had been, because he faced a difficult deadline. Comey had testified on September 30, 2020, which meant the five-year statute of limitations was about to expire, and if he was to be charged, it had to happen before then. That gave his prosecutors about a month and a half to gather evidence, analyze it, and decide whether to charge a former FBI director with a crime.

Between the Comey and James cases, Siebert was stuck in a vise, under increasing pressure to produce the outcomes Trump and his advisors wanted. FBI agents assigned to the Comey testimony case scrambled to review documents at FBI headquarters, trying to check them against Comey's answers to Republican lawmakers who had grilled him nearly five years earlier about the Russia investigation and the Clinton email investigation.

Entering 2025, Comey wasn't exactly a sympathetic figure. Trump and Republicans loathed him. For their part, many Democrats blamed him, with justification, for inadvertently helping make Trump the winner of the 2016 presidential election when he broke long-standing Justice Department protocol by publicly reopening the investigation into Hillary Clinton's emails in the final days of the race. The limp ending of the Russia investigation only added to some liberals' sense of disappointment in him.

But there is a big difference between being unpopular and being a criminal. By the fall of 2025, there was also good reason to doubt whether federal prosecutors in Washington, who had a wealth of experience assessing cases about false testimony to Congress, would see any merit in the facts of the Comey case. Many veteran Public Integrity prosecutors thought it was a glaringly weak case and not worth pursuing.

At the Senate hearing, Comey had been called to explain and defend his decisions.

One of his inquisitors, Texas Republican senator Ted Cruz, mentioned prior testimony Comey had given in 2017, when he was asked if he had ever authorized someone else at the FBI "to be an anonymous source in news reports about the Trump investigation or the Clinton administration."

Right away, there was a problem with Cruz's question. He'd meant to say "Clinton investigation," but what he actually said was "Clinton administration." In everyday conversation, that kind of flub is inconsequential. But when you're trying to build a criminal case that someone lied to Congress, it's a problem. At a trial, prosecutors would have to show that the person intended to lie. Confusion about the question's meaning could undercut any claim that Comey had deliberately misled Congress.

There was another basic structural problem with the conversation as evidence of a crime. Cruz had asked Comey about an episode involving Comey's former deputy director, Andrew McCabe.

Here I should note that Cruz's question was about reporting that I did years ago when I worked at *The Wall Street Journal*. In October and November 2016, I wrote a series of stories about internal conflicts at the FBI and Justice Department around McCabe's role in an investigation of the Clinton Foundation. Those stories led McCabe to try to determine who had leaked material to me. But instead of uncovering whoever was mad at him inside the FBI workforce, the person McCabe came closest to getting charged with a crime was himself.

"As you know, Mr. McCabe, who works for you, has publicly and repeatedly stated that he leaked information to *The Wall Street Journal*," Cruz said at the September 2020 hearing, which was a significant mischaracterization of what McCabe had said to investigators. At the hearing, Cruz accused Comey of being "directly aware of" and having "directly authorized" McCabe's actions.

Cruz then asked, "Now what Mr. McCabe is saying and what you testified to this committee cannot both be true. One or the other is false. Who's telling the truth?"

Comey responded calmly, "I can only speak to my testimony. I stand by the testimony you summarize that I gave in May 2017."

"So your testimony is that you never authorized anyone to leak and

Mr. McCabe, if he says contrary, is not telling the truth, correct?" Cruz asked.

"I'm not going to characterize Andy's testimony, but mine is the same today," Comey answered.

The Cruz-Comey exchange was a textbook example of the limits of hearings in a broken Congress. A lawmaker garbled key facts, raced through his questions, and mostly failed to land a "gotcha" moment.

Senators are notorious for hurrying their questions at hearings, racing to fit as much as possible into the five minutes they typically have with a witness. Politicians who love to talk tend to pile multiple factual elements into a single query and tend to cut witnesses off before they give their full answer. Elected officials also rarely ask the kind of follow-up questions that would clarify exactly what a witness's answer meant.

As political theater, the Cruz-Comey exchange was unremarkable. As the legal basis for charging someone with intentionally lying to Congress about material facts, it was a hot mess. Nevertheless, the Trump administration barreled forward with a plan to charge Comey. The president's desire for revenge would not be denied, even if it meant wrecking another U.S. attorney's office.

CHAPTER 10

Weapons Drawn

By September 2025, the heat from the top of the Trump administration to do something with the James Comey and Letitia James investigations had reached a boiling point. Time was running out on Comey's case—the statute of limitations meant it needed to be indicted soon if it was going to be done at all.

Patel and others in the administration wanted Comey charged for two sets of statements: the first, in response to questions from Senator Lindsey Graham, about an intelligence document sent from the CIA to the FBI in September 2016 about a supposed Clinton campaign plan to tie Trump to Russia. This was the document that had been found in a storage closet and taken to Room 9582. When asked about the document, Comey repeatedly said he didn't remember getting it.

"That doesn't ring a bell with me," he said.

Patel and others wanted his claim that he could not remember to be charged as a criminal lie.

The case against Comey was contorted and chaotic. One problem was that although Comey was asked about authorizing McCabe to leak, Patel and others wanted to charge that answer as a lie about other alleged leaks. Specifically, they wanted to charge that Comey had lied because, they said, he had authorized Daniel Richman, a law professor friend of his, to share information with a *New York Times* reporter about private conversations Comey had had with Trump. The public disclosures of the details of those conversations had led to the appointment of Robert Mueller as special counsel to investigate Trump over possible Russia ties. Comey readily admitted that he had hoped the coverage would spur the appointment of a special counsel, and an inspector general later faulted him for leaking the details, but federal prosecutors who had examined those events over the years found no crimes in them. Now the administration wanted to see Comey charged with lying about his interactions with Richman when he was asked specifically about McCabe—the kind of legal bank shot that seemed absurd to the career prosecutors who were asked to look at it.

The other problem with the plan to prosecute Comey was that his denial in 2020 was really just a reiteration of what he'd said in his 2017 testimony. So, the prosecution theory of the Comey case wasn't just a bank shot; it was a double bank shot.

Blanche, through his deputies, pressured both the FBI and the federal prosecutors to charge the case. As a result of that pressure, a kind of split started to emerge between the agents, some of whom believed a chargeable case existed against the former director, and the prosecutors, who were more skeptical.

Three of Blanche's deputies—Aakash Singh, Christopher-James DeLorenz, and Diego Pestana—spoke regularly with the prosecutors, urging them to be tough, be aggressive, and see the case through. But Blanche also kept a certain distance from the conversations, leaving his aides to relay his wishes.

The pushiest of the three was Pestana. When prosecutors outlined the ways in which the evidence was weak, Pestana suggested the prosecutors were weak—a particularly galling critique given that he had never worked as a prosecutor and was beating the drum to indict a former FBI director. Blanche, for his part, was said to be furious that prosecutors had written a memo describing the weaknesses of the case—the clumsy congressional questioning, the grasping desire to turn an answer about one person into a lie about another, and more basic uncertainty of Comey's intent. The FBI had been told to draft a criminal complaint to charge Comey, while prosecutors had been told to draft an indictment.

On the weekend of September 13, Patel began telling people that Comey would be charged in three days. But then no charges were produced in the FBI director's three-day window, nor even a draft of a criminal complaint. Patel's big talk seemed to have done little other than ratchet up the administration's pressure on Siebert's office.

Siebert started warning his superiors at the Justice Department in September that the facts simply could not produce viable criminal charges. "Erik Siebert would happily charge Comey if he thought there was any kind, *any kind* of case, to make against him," one Justice Department official told me in the middle of the month. "But there's not, and it's not a close call."

It was hard to even see who a prosecution witness against Comey would be. Investigators questioned Richman, whose answers closely tracked those he had given years earlier in one of the previous investigations. Back then, federal prosecutors had closed the case without charges.

So, if Siebert couldn't call Richman to testify, what would a Comey trial even look like? Some lawyers familiar with the facts of the case began to derisively refer to it as a "no witness case."

On Thursday, September 18, Aakash Singh called Siebert to warn him that the president planned to fire him. The next day, ABC News reported the planned firing, though, curiously, the reason given for Siebert's dismissal was the James case. That made little sense inside the Justice Department, where everyone understood that the time pressure was all centered on the Comey case. When reporters at the White House asked Trump about the ABC News report, Trump confirmed it. "I want him out," he said. Letitia James, he added, was "very guilty of something."

Trump then went on to make it sound like he didn't want Siebert as a U.S. attorney anymore because Virginia's two Democratic lawmakers

Tim Kaine and Mark Warner liked him. "When I saw that he got approved by those two men, I said pull it, because he can't be any good," the president said.

The process for nominating U.S. attorneys—the top federal prosecutors in each state, each with enormous sway to investigate or prosecute the most important cases—requires bipartisan compromise by design. In states where both senators are in one party and the president is in the other party, a system called "blue slips" is used to ensure that the U.S. attorney pick is acceptable to everyone. If a senator cannot abide a particular person as a U.S. attorney in their state, they won't issue a blue slip letting their nomination go to the committee for a vote. The blue slip system forces the two sides to find a person they can each live with.

Compromises like that were designed to ensure credibility and confidence in the people running the Justice Department, regardless of which party was in power, but Trump had no interest in those kinds of compromises. If anything, he blamed Senate Republicans for defending the blue slip tradition.

For Siebert, the larger debate around blue slips didn't matter much. Publicly reprimanded by the president, he submitted his resignation late that Friday. His top deputy, Maya Song, was fired.

The very next day, the president posted a message on social media that seemed to strip away any veneer or pretense about his desire for the Justice Department to exact his revenge. "Pam:" the message to the attorney general began, as if he meant it to be a private discussion. "I have reviewed over 30 statements and posts saying that, essentially, 'same old story as last time, all talk, no action. Nothing is being done. What about Comey, Adam 'Shifty' Schiff, Leticia??? [*sic*] They're all guilty as hell, but nothing is going to be done.' Then we almost put in a Democrat supported U.S. Attorney, in Virginia, with a really bad Republican past. A Woke RINO, who was never going to do his job. That's why two of the worst Dem Senators PUSHED him so hard. He even lied to the media and said he quit, and that we had no case. No, I fired him, and there is a GREAT CASE, and many lawyers, and legal pundits, say so. Lindsey is a really good lawyer, and likes you, a lot. We can't delay any longer, it's killing our reputation and credibility. They impeached me twice, and indicted me (5 times!), OVER NOTHING! JUSTICE MUST BE SERVED, NOW!!!"

The brazenness of a president publicly demanding that his attorney general produce criminal charges against specific political foes was breathtaking. The command seemed to strip away any fig leaf of fairness at the Justice Department—so much so that Hillary Clinton spoke out, rising to the defense of James Comey, the person whose 2016 decisions had done so much damage to her campaign. "Imagine if Richard Nixon had just tweeted out the Watergate scandal rather than putting it on secret tapes. That's what this is," she wrote.

The "Lindsey" whom Trump referred to in his message to Bondi wasn't immediately clear, so aides clarified that he meant Lindsey Halligan, his choice to be the new U.S. attorney in Virginia. Halligan, a White House aide, had never worked as a prosecutor before. She was practicing insurance law when she met Trump at one of his golf clubs in 2021. They hit it off, and she joined his legal team the following year.

A former Miss Colorado USA beauty pageant contestant, Halligan viewed her boss as a victim of the Justice Department and was part of the small team of lawyers who went to the department headquarters in 2023 in an unsuccessful effort to convince senior officials not to indict him. Before suddenly becoming U.S. attorney, her biggest government appointment had come in March 2025, when Trump instructed her, via executive order, to "remove improper ideology" from the Smithsonian Museums. Halligan told *The Washington Post* after she got the museum assignment that she defined improper ideology as "weaponizing history," adding, "We don't need to overemphasize the negative to teach people that certain aspects of our nation's history may have been bad."

Halligan was sworn in as the interim U.S. attorney for the Eastern District of Virginia on Monday, September 22. Three days later, she walked into an Alexandria grand jury room and secured an indictment of James Comey, making him only the second FBI director to be indicted, after L. Patrick Gray, an acting director during the Watergate era who was charged with conspiring to violate civil rights by authorizing illegal break-ins against Weather Underground suspects. The charges against Gray were eventually dropped.

The moment the Comey indictment was filed, it seemed obvious that it had been something of a nail-biter inside the grand jury room. An indictment requires a minimum of 12 "yes" votes to indict on a particular charge, and the Comey indictment had mustered only 14 out of 23 grand jurors to accuse him of two crimes: lying to Congress (in answer to Cruz's questions about authorizing someone at the FBI to give information to the press) and obstruction of a congressional proceeding. Halligan had also tried and failed to indict Comey on a third charge: that he had lied to lawmakers when he said he didn't remember getting any intelligence document from the CIA about a Hillary Clinton plan to tie Trump to Russia.

Halligan's first indictment did not go smoothly. When she got to the courtroom, she sat down first at the defense table. That was a minor faux pas compared with what came next.

Handed the paperwork, the magistrate judge, Lindsey Vaala, was flummoxed. "So this has never happened before. I've been handed two documents that are in the Mr. Comey case that are inconsistent with one another," Judge Vaala said. "There seems to be a discrepancy. They're both signed by the foreperson."

One of the documents said the panel had failed to concur on an indictment, but it did not specify that the rejection was for the criminal charge about Comey's having supposedly lied to Senator Graham.

Halligan struggled to clear things up. "So I only reviewed the one with the two counts that our office redrafted when we found out about the two—two counts that were true billed, and I signed that one," she told the judge. "I did not see the other one, I don't know where that came from."

"You didn't see it?" Vaala pressed. "So your office didn't prepare the indictment that they—"

"No, no, no," Halligan tried to explain. "I prepared three counts. I only signed the one, the two-count indictment. I don't know which one with three counts you have in your hands."

"Okay," the judge said, unimpressed. "It has your signature on it."

"Okay. Well," Halligan said, seemingly at a loss for what to say. With no clear answers from the only prosecutor who had signed the indictment, the court published both versions of it, another rarity for a judicial system that prides itself on carefully curating its docket.

Even though the president had been publicly demanding an indictment of James Comey, when it actually happened, the reality of it still shocked many federal law enforcement officials who had deep faith in the basic fairness of the justice system.

The Comey indictment was particularly galling to prosecutors in the Eastern District of Virginia, where the case was filed. Comey had once been a senior prosecutor in that office, overseeing the federal prosecutors in Richmond, the state capital. He was remembered by the older lawyers, prosecutors, and judges as a popular, charismatic young man on the rise. For him to be charged as a criminal on facts that did not on the surface make much sense was offensive not just to their sense of right and wrong, but also to their belief in the diligence and care of the American legal system.

Hours after his indictment, Comey declared he still had faith. "My heart is broken for the Department of Justice, but I have great confidence in the federal judicial system and I'm innocent," he said in a video posted online.

His son-in-law Troy Edwards Jr. worked in the Eastern District as a national security prosecutor. Within hours of his father-in-law's indictment, Edwards resigned in a one-sentence letter addressed to his new boss, Halligan. "To uphold my oath to the Constitution and country, I hereby resign as an Assistant U.S. Attorney for the Eastern District of Virginia in the Department of Justice effective immediately."

Halligan wasn't done. Weeks later, she secured an indictment against Letitia James, charging the New York attorney general with lying to financial institutions to get a mortgage for the home a relative lived in.

Nine months into the second Trump administration, the president's Department of Revenge had finally produced big results. The career prosecutors who had thought Ed Martin wasn't smart enough to deliver an indictment were proved wrong.

But as soon as the Comey and James cases faced scrutiny in a public courtroom, they began to crumble. Lawyers for Comey and James wasted little time attacking the indictments. The first defense argument was also the simplest: Halligan's appointment as the U.S. attorney, immediately after the firing of Siebert, had violated federal law, and because she was the sole prosecutor in both cases, the indictments needed to be tossed out.

The second main argument struck at the motives of the two cases—that the Trump administration had engaged in vindictive prosecutions driven not by pursuit of justice or the law, but by the desire to exact revenge on people the president hated.

Such arguments are long shots in most cases. But in the Comey and James cases, the defense lawyers had Trump's angry demands for their prosecution in a social media post the day after he fired Siebert. The defense lawyers could also point to years' worth of other social media posts by the president to show how badly he wanted them both charged with crimes.

There was a third plan of attack against the Comey and James cases, and to some Justice Department veterans, it was the most important: The evidence was laughably weak, did not support the charges, and therefore the cases had to be dismissed.

This last point mattered a great deal to the prosecutors who had been fired, demoted, or threatened as a result of finding no basis to charge the cases. A victory on the facts would in many ways be vindication for the dedicated, mostly faceless workforce of the Justice Department, against their own leaders. The defense lawyers' court filings focused primarily on the first two arguments, but each filing contained elements of all three lines of attack.

Because the James and Comey arguments challenging the legality of Halligan's appointment were nearly identical, they were heard together in mid-November. A judge from outside the district, Cameron McGowan Currie, was brought in from South Carolina to hear the case. A courtroom full of reporters and lawyers attended the hearing, with a second overflow courtroom for a few dozen others to watch the proceedings on a closed-circuit feed.

Just a few weeks shy of her seventy-seventh birthday, Judge Currie was skeptical of the arguments made by Justice Department lawyer Henry Whitaker that there had been nothing amiss with Halligan's appointment, and even if there had been, it was a harmless error that should not hamper the cases themselves. Whitaker had the difficult task of arguing that the administration could put whomever it wanted into U.S. attorney positions for as long as it wanted.

Comey's lawyer, Ephraim McDowell, began with a series of legal points about the federal law of appointments.

Judge Currie moved quickly to a question that bothered her. "Are you aware of any evidence of whether a declination memo was prepared in the Comey matter?" she asked McDowell. In the Justice Department, prosecutors often write either a prosecution (or "pross") memo when they think charges are warranted, or a declination memo when they are not. Such memos are carefully guarded secrets inside the department, but news reports before Comey's indictment indicated that career prosecutors had memorialized their objections to any charges being filed.

By asking the question, Judge Currie signaled that she was very interested in the most basic question raised about the indictments: Was there good evidence to support them? McDowell said he didn't know, but the judge's question set the tone for the hearing, and it was not going to be an easy one for Halligan and her team.

James's lawyer, Abbe Lowell, argued that when Halligan walked into the grand jury room to seek an indictment against his client, she may have called herself the U.S. attorney, but under the law, she was just a private citizen pretending to be a prosecutor.

After Lowell, the judge heard from Whitaker, who had joined the Trump administration from the Florida attorney general's office.

Once again, Currie quickly interrupted the questions of legal interpretation with a basic fact problem. She had received the grand jury transcripts and tapes in the Comey case, "and there is a missing section of what occurred," she declared.

Whitaker had few answers.

The judge's last question for Whitaker was a carefully laid trap. "Do you believe," she asked, "that *U.S. v Trump*, decided by Judge Cannon . . . was wrongly decided?"

The question was dangerous for Whitaker because Trump administration lawyers were not about to suggest that Judge Aileen Cannon had wrongly dismissed charges against the president. But Cannon's rationale for dismissing the classified documents charges had been that the special counsel who filed them, Jack Smith, had been improperly appointed. It was a version of the legal argument now being made by Comey and James against Halligan, only with the political roles reversed.

Whitaker argued that questions about a special counsel appointment were too different from those about a U.S. attorney appointment and that any issues with Halligan's appointment amounted to no more than a "paperwork error."

As the hearing went on, it seemed clear that Currie would eventually rule that Halligan's appointment had violated federal law. Less certain was what she would do about that—dismiss the Comey and James indictments or let them stand?

The next day, Halligan wrote to the judge to address her concerns about the missing time period in the grand jury transcript, which amounted to roughly two hours. There was no transcript for that period, Halligan wrote, because the grand jurors spent that time deliberating among themselves. "I had no interaction whatsoever with any members of the grand jury" in that time frame, she wrote.

Days later, a magistrate judge in the same courthouse, William E. Fitzpatrick, dealt another blow to the prosecution, ruling that Halligan had made a "fundamental and highly prejudicial" misstatement of the law to the grand jury that indicted Comey. "The court is finding that the government's actions in this case—whether purposeful, reckless or negligent—raise genuine issues of misconduct," Judge Fitzpatrick concluded.

Fitzpatrick, who had a wealth of experience as a former prosecutor in the office before becoming a magistrate, said, after reviewing a transcript of the grand jury proceedings in the Comey case, that Halligan had apparently mischaracterized the law to grand jurors when she suggested Comey could not avoid testifying at his future trial. In fact, the Fifth Amendment of the Constitution guarantees that defendants do not have to testify in criminal cases. The judge said Halligan also seemed to have suggested to the grand jury that there was additional evidence that she had not presented to them.

Judge Fitzpatrick also voiced concern over the apparent gap in the grand jury transcript. He cast doubt on Halligan's explanation, saying it seemed all but impossible for her to have followed proper procedure to formulate a modified two-count indictment of the former FBI director. If he was right about that, Fitzpatrick wrote, "then the court is in uncharted legal territory."

Judges rarely scrutinize the inner workings of a prosecution so closely, but Halligan, Trump, and Bondi had all but dared the courts to ask such questions, given the soap opera drama that preceded the Comey indictment.

Investigations are complex, and most judges prefer not to go looking for problems inside prosecutors' work. But in the Comey case, every rock they turned over seemed to reveal a new screwup or deliberate misuse of prosecutorial power.

Just two days after Fitzpatrick's criticism, another federal judge in Virginia, Michael Nachmanoff, held a hearing with Comey, his lawyers, and prosecutors over the question of whether the case was a vindictive prosecution by the Trump administration.

The Comey indictment had rattled the nation's legal community more than almost any other step Trump took in his second term. Some of the best lawyers in the nation had offered to represent him, wanting to defend basic principles of American justice. That was the principled reason to want to help Comey. But many lawyers also have the hunting instincts of sharks, and to them, the prosecutors lined up against Comey looked like fat, dumb fish.

The lawyer who stood up for Comey at Judge Nachmanoff's hearing looked more like a law professor than a predator. Bald and bespectacled, Michael Dreeben had spent more than thirty years in the Solicitor General's Office of the Justice Department, the office that handled Supreme Court arguments. Widely considered one of the foremost experts on appellate criminal law, Dreeben had served in both the Robert Mueller and Jack Smith special counsel offices. That had earned him significant respect from many attorneys, but it also meant that some conservative lawyers, including some Supreme Court Justices, had come to disagree sharply with Dreeben when it came to corruption cases.

Dreeben rose that day in court to speak on behalf of a client, but he was also arguing for a legal standard that many attorneys feared was being demolished by the Trump administration's endless appetite for retribution.

"This is an extraordinary case, and it merits an extraordinary remedy," the lawyer began. "The president's use of the Department of Justice to bring a criminal prosecution against a vocal and prominent critic in order to punish and deter those who would speak out against him violates the Constitution."

Dreeben walked the judge back through Trump's September 20 social media post, the one in which he demanded that James Comey, Letitia James, and Adam Schiff be prosecuted, writing, "We can't delay any longer, it's killing our reputation and credibility."

Dreeben noted that the president hadn't declared "We can't allow a wrongdoer to escape justice," but instead, had framed the need for indictments as critical to his reputation and credibility. Trump had mentioned in the post how many times he had been indicted by others and added that "justice must be served, now" in all capital letters, and ending with exclamation points.

"If this is not a direction to prosecute," Dreeben told the judge, "I really would be at a loss to say what is."

Judge Nachmanoff pointed out that Trump had gone even farther in remarks to reporters. "You know, they were ruthless and vicious. I was impeached twice. I was indicted five times. It turned out to be a fake deal. And we have to act fast," Trump had said in September shortly after ousting Siebert. "One way or the other. One way or the other. They're guilty, they're not guilty, we have to act fast. If they're not guilty, that's fine. If they are guilty, or if they should be charged, they should be charged. And we have to do it now."

The judge asked Dreeben if he thought Halligan was a "stalking horse or a puppet" of Trump's—was she following orders or making charging decisions on her own?

"She did what she was told to do," Dreeben replied.

Dreeben said it wasn't only the Comey and James cases in which the Justice Department had shown they would do whatever Trump ordered them to do. Days earlier, after emails to and from the dead sex offender Jeffrey Epstein had surfaced mentioning Trump, the president publicly ordered his attorney general to launch an investigation into Democrats and Epstein. Bondi immediately complied.

Back to the Comey case, Dreeben reminded the judge that two sets of prosecutors had looked at the same evidence and concluded that no charges should be brought, and then Trump fired one of his own prosecutors to get an indictment before the statute of limitations ran out.

It was time, Dreeben argued, for the courts to rein in a president so eager to abuse and misuse his own Justice Department. "This has to stop," the lawyer said. "This court is the first to confront the issue of whether a message needs to be sent to the executive branch, that you can prosecute for legitimate prosecutorial reasons, and you can strike hard blows so long as they are fair, but what you cannot do is allow the president to take advantage of his authority over the executive branch, to use it as a cudgel to damage and intimidate his political opponents."

Lindsey Halligan sat at the prosecution table listening but not reacting. Arguing on her behalf was Tyler Lemons, who until September had been a federal prosecutor in North Carolina. Lemons's presence was another tacit admission of the stench coming off the Comey case. None of the career prosecutors in Virginia would take part in it, and Halligan apparently could not be expected to make legal arguments in court over the case she had brought.

Lemons tried to counter Dreeben's presentation by arguing that the judge should examine only whether Halligan, not Trump, had a personal animus toward Comey.

Judge Nachmanoff quickly put Lemons on the defensive by asking if career prosecutors had written a memo declining to charge Comey before his indictment.

Lemons stammered, already a deer in the headlights facing a question he had to have known he would be asked. "In the course of— In the course of a prosecution there are— As Your Honor is well aware, there's multiple discussions of the propriety of charges, the overall investigation, and what specific charges are appropriate," he said, filling the courtroom with words without information. "At this point, my position would be that the, whether a declination memo existed or not, is something that would be a privileged matter that I have not gotten permission from my client, the Department of Justice, to disclose one way or another."

From the outset, Lemons found himself in the same dangerous posture that Drew Ensign had been in when he claimed months earlier in a different courtroom that he didn't know if planes full of migrants were flying out of Texas. These were the kinds of questions their Justice Department bosses simply did not want them to answer.

"My question was," the judge said cooly, "was there a declination memo? That could be answered yes or no without revealing anything about the substance of what's in the memo. Are you telling me that you are not permitted by somebody to answer that question 'yes' or 'no'?"

Lemons stammered. Three times he tried to start a sentence he could not finish.

Incredulous, the judge asked Lemons how, as the counsel of record in the case, he could not know whether there had been a declination memo.

Chastened, Lemons admitted that he did, in fact, know the answer.

"Is someone that you can identify for me instructing you not to answer that question?" the judge asked.

"In conversations with the office of the deputy attorney general, yes, Your Honor," Lemons replied, pointing to Todd Blanche's staff.

Lemons said he had been told his bosses had made no decision yet about whether to tell the court about the internal prosecution steps that had led to the Comey indictment. Nervous, Lemons pressed on. "I can tell Your Honor—and I don't want—I don't want— Your Honor, I don't want you to think in any way I'm trying to avoid answering your questions as directly as I can. What I can tell you is that I did seek out prior memorandums or opinions." The prosecutor seemed to decide that to survive the hearing, he needed to give ground, so he admitted that he had reviewed the internal documents, without saying much of anything about their contents.

Lemons noted that after the Comey indictment was filed, Trump denied having anything to do with it. The judge, Lemons said, should believe that denial. "Ms. Halligan was not a puppet," he said. "She was put in as a U.S. attorney, and she made independent decisions to prosecute this defendant."

Lemons had had a rough time making his argument, but it only got worse after he finished. Judge Nachmanoff asked for an explanation of how there appeared to be a two-hour gap in the grand jury transcript, starting around 4:38 p.m. that day.

Lemons said the grand jurors spent that entire time deliberating on the case without Halligan and that grand jury discussions are transcribed only when a government lawyer is present.

How was it possible, Judge Nachmanoff asked, that a second version of the indictment could be drawn up without the grand jury speaking to a prosecutor?

Lemons said it wasn't so much that a new indictment had been filed, just that the panel had voted down one count and voted for the two other counts, and eventually the prosecutor's office generated an updated version of the court papers to reflect that. "The edits to the indictment were only to reflect the voting of the grand jury and were not an actual new indictment in any way whatsoever," the prosecutor said.

Judge Nachmanoff only seemed more troubled and asked if it was correct that the filed version of the indictment against Comey "was never shown to the entire grand jury or presented in the grand jury room."

"Yes, that is my understanding," said Lemons, who'd walked away from the lectern to whisper with Halligan.

The judge decided he had had enough of Lemons's answers. "Ms. Halligan, you can come to the podium, you're counsel of record, you can address the court. It might be easier," he said. "So am I correct that—" the judge started to ask.

"No, Your Honor," Halligan said, not waiting for him to finish the question. She said the foreperson and another grand juror had come to the courtroom to hand up the indictment to the magistrate judge, and the foreperson had then explained that the panel did not indict on one count and voted to indict on the other two counts.

It was a brief but telling exchange. Halligan could have, at any time, stood up to represent the case that she had presented to the court, but she did so only when a judge specifically asked her to. And in her brief comments, she managed to convey a sense of annoyance with the judge for questioning how she had handled the grand jury.

"I just wanted to make sure," Nachmanoff said, "that the entire grand jury never had the opportunity to see the second indictment."

Halligan went back and sat down.

Dreeben seized on what seemed to be a new damning revelation about the grand jury process. The failure to show the final version of the indictment to the grand jury, he said, was another reason to dismiss the entire case. But beyond the obvious procedural missteps, there was a core issue that had to be confronted, he added. "We are here solely because the president of the United States has directed that this prosecution be brought," he concluded.

It had been only six days since the hearing before Judge Currie, and every court action had gone worse for the Trump administration than the one before. Walking out of the courthouse after the mid-November hearing, I found it hard to imagine the Comey case surviving past the holidays.

Five days later, the hammer fell. Judge Currie, who had been tasked with deciding whether Halligan had been lawfully appointed to be the U.S. attorney, concluded that she had not, and because Halligan was not really the U.S. attorney, and because she was the only prosecutor who had handled the Comey and James cases, those indictments were thrown out.

The judge found that Trump's machinations to put Halligan into the job had not followed the law and could not be allowed to stand, because if he could do that, he could keep appointing temporary U.S. attorneys who never had to get confirmed by the Senate. "It would mean the government could send any private citizen off the street—attorney or not—into the grand jury room to secure an indictment so long as the attorney general gives her approval after the fact. That cannot be the law," the judge wrote in her ruling.

The administration reacted with shock to the extremely predictable loss. Bondi vowed to use "all available legal action" to reverse the decision.

Justice Department leaders had tried to deliver the revenge sought by the president. But the U.S. court system is designed to be a fact-based, rule-based exercise, and the president's will was not enough to change the facts or the rules of the court. The arc of the Comey and James cases, however, showed how prosecutorial discretion was forced to bow to presidential decree. Blanche had pushed for the Comey indictment, and tried to kill the case against James, but such charging decisions were ultimately made by the president.

In early December, Roger Keller walked into the old federal courthouse building in Norfolk, Virginia. A career civil attorney in the U.S. Attorney's Office in Missouri, Keller had parachuted into the Letitia James case, and now the lawyer with little actual criminal prosecutorial experience was tasked with reviving the indictment against James.

He failed. The Norfolk grand jury issued a no true bill, rejecting the criminal case against James that the president had publicly insisted was so strong.

Later that week, a federal judge in Washington, DC, ruled that in the Comey case, prosecutors might have violated the rights of Comey's friend Daniel Richman, the professor whose emails and texts were key evidence in the case. Trump administration prosecutors had never bothered to get a second search warrant to examine the Richman material for evidence of possible lies by Comey to Congress, and the judge found it was possible that this could have been a violation of the Fourth Amendment. The judge ruled the Richman evidence off-limits to the Comey prosecutors, at least for the time being. Without it, the prosecutors could not even attempt a reindictment.

Desperate for a win, Keller went to Alexandria, Virginia, and in mid-December he presented the Letitia James case to a third grand jury. But like the second, this panel also rejected the case, issuing another no true bill.

The Justice Department really was in uncharted legal territory now, to use the phrase from the magistrate judge who had wrestled with the confusing Comey indictment. It is incredibly rare for a federal prosecutor to be formally rejected by a grand jury, and for generations it has been the kind of thing that could kill a prosecutor's career. Keller had managed to rack up two such rejections in the space of about a week.

Trump's quest for revenge was ending careers, destroying reputations, forcing an exodus of legal experience, and killing the credibility of the Justice Department in some courts. And in many instances, the people whose reputations it was tarnishing were not Trump's intended targets, but rather those willing to carry out his angry orders.

The department's leaders had decreed that its employees must do whatever the president wanted, or be fired. By the end of 2025, the lower courts seemed willing to say no to the president and to insist on maintaining their own standards and principles. The Supreme Court, where conservatives hold a 6–3 majority, would decide whether to side with those judges or with the president.

Ethics, Schmethics

The Adidas 2026 FIFA World Cup Pro soccer ball weighs about one pound, with a skin of polyurethane and polyester and a color scheme symbolizing the three countries—the United States, Canada, and Mexico—hosting the most-watched sporting event on earth.

Donald Trump had spent part of his first term working to bring the World Cup to the United States, and in his second term he basked in the result. The World Cup's organizers, the International Federation of Football Association, or FIFA, embraced Trump, honoring him with its first-ever peace prize, a kind of consolation gift for a president who publicly coveted a Nobel Peace Prize.

FIFA was bringing the World Cup to America after the organization had spent the better part of a decade mired in a corruption scandal. In 2015, American investigators had orchestrated a series of high-profile arrests in Switzerland over charges that the sport had been corrupted by $150 million in bribes to win the rights to broadcast FIFA competitions.

When other countries' law enforcement agencies seemed uninterested, the Justice Department had stepped in to clean up international soccer, at least at first. When indictments were announced, Loretta

Lynch, then the U.S. attorney in Brooklyn, compared the global soccer organization to a Mafia family. More than two dozen people were indicted.

One consequence of those indictments was that the bidding process for hosting the 2026 World Cup was delayed until 2017. When the winner was finally announced, FIFA had chosen a combined bid from the United States, Mexico, and Canada. Trump, halfway through his first White House term, was proud to claim the victory.

In May 2025, Trump held a press conference to discuss the administration's plan for hosting the competition. The president sat in the center of a long table of microphones. To his left sat FIFA President Gianni Infantino, whom Trump sometimes referred to as "my boy." To his right sat the vice president, JD Vance, and Attorney General Pam Bondi.

On the table in front of the president was a replica of the World Cup trophy and a limited-edition FIFA soccer ball. When the event was over, Trump pointed to the ball and asked Infantino if he could have it. The FIFA boss shrugged and said sure. Trump didn't want the ball for himself; he wanted to give it to Bondi. He walked over to her, handed it to her, and gave her a kiss on the cheek. Looking pleased, the attorney general showed the ball to an aide, who smiled.

Soccer balls are not very expensive, generally selling for $20 to $30 at most sporting goods stores. The 2026 World Cup ball, though, was billed as a limited-edition collectible, an item that sold for $150 or more.

And that's when it became Joseph Tirrell's problem. A former Navy officer and FBI lawyer, Tirrell joined the Justice Department in 2018, where he eventually became the senior official responsible for advising the attorney general and deputy attorney general on ethics questions.

Justice Department officials get gifts all the time, sometimes from visiting foreign dignitaries or when meeting with local law enforcement officials. The government ethics rules for what to do about those gifts are straightforward: Anything worth twenty dollars or less, you can generally keep; anything worth more than that usually has to be returned or thrown away.

But Bondi, the nation's top law enforcement official, wanted to keep her soccer ball. So, Tirrell ended up spending weeks in a back-and-forth with her office about it.

"The president of FIFA gave a slew of tchotchkes to the attorney general—a soccer ball, a key chain, a scarf, other things," Tirrell said. "There were problems with some of those gifts because they didn't meet the limitation, and he's not a friend of Ms. Bondi, so none of those exceptions would apply."

The ethics official's advice was straightforward: Give the ball back or throw it out. Tirrell knew that over the years, some Justice Department officials took that kind of advice as scolding from a petty bureaucrat. Bondi was not the first senior Justice official to chafe at the ethics advice she received about gifts.

But unlike other attorneys general, Bondi seemed to not want to concede the point. The argument over the soccer ball dragged on for weeks.

"It got weird," said Tirrell.

And then he was fired.

On July 11, a Friday, Tirrell got an email from someone in the Justice Department's human resources office. It included a brief letter from Bondi saying that "pursuant to Article II of the United States Constitution and the laws of the United States, your employment with the Department of Justice is hereby terminated, and you are removed from federal service effective immediately."

That language constituted the most dreaded kind of form letter in Trump's Justice Department, dismissing a veteran government lawyer without cause, a violation of civil service laws that had been followed for decades by both parties. These laws weren't meant to protect employees, though they had that effect. Civil service protections were initially drafted to ensure there was a professional workforce in the government—as opposed to the bad old system of patronage hires that tended to make government services worse.

Tirrell suspected that he was being fired not over the soccer ball, but over something he had done months earlier.

In the first Trump term, a number of administration officials found themselves in need of a lawyer while still in government—whether they were being sought as witnesses for questioning or as possible suspects themselves in a slew of congressional and law enforcement investigations. Those Trump officials often wanted to obtain free legal services—pro bono representation—but existing government regulations didn't seem to allow for this type of gift of legal representation related to the officials' government duties. So, a new regulation was created, one that allowed government officials to accept pro bono legal work connected with their government service.

Then came Jack Smith. Smith had served as the special counsel investigating and prosecuting Donald Trump from 2022 to 2024. When Trump won the election, it was clear Smith would be not only fired but investigated by the new administration. While still a government employee, he and some of his senior deputies followed the regulations and sought Justice Department approval to accept pro bono legal services from a private lawyer.

The person whose job it was to consider such requests was Joseph Tirrell. Based on the standards created for former Trump officials, Tirrell approved the requests for Smith and others on his team. "I figured I was probably putting a target on my back," he said. "My boss and I had several conversations at the time in which I said, well, maybe I will get fired for doing this."

But Tirrell had looked at the ethics rule and determined that approval was not only legal, but required.

The decision to allow Smith to receive free legal advice enraged some right-wingers. Stories and social media posts noted that Tirrell had been the official to approve the arrangement, and he spent the early part of 2025 waiting to see if he would join the ranks of the newly fired.

Months passed, and Tirrell kept doing his job. Then, in mid-July, he was fired, via email, while at home on a vacation day.

Unknown to Joe Tirrell, a much larger ethical disaster was looming for the department.

In late 2023, when Donald Trump was a four-times-indicted candidate for president, he filed a private legal claim against the Justice Department, seeking $115 million in compensation for having been unfairly subjected to an FBI and special counsel investigation over possible ties between his campaign and Russian intelligence agents. Among his claims was that the investigation had violated his civil rights, according to people familiar with the filing.

At the time it was filed, Justice Department officials in the Biden administration considered the demand a headache, but one that paled in comparison to the pitched battles in court over the two indictments filed by Smith against Trump, one for allegedly mishandling hundreds of classified documents during his post-presidency life at Mar-a-Lago, in Florida; the other for allegedly conspiring to obstruct election results, which led to the January 6 riot at the U.S. Capitol.

Then–attorney general Merrick Garland, his deputy Lisa Monaco, and their advisors largely ignored Trump's claim for compensation. Filing such a claim was a necessary step before eventually suing the government. If the department doesn't respond to a claim within six months, the claimant can then file a lawsuit in federal court.

Trump didn't sue in federal court. In the meantime, his claim sat there in a government file as a kind of marker for a future battle that might never occur.

Instead of filing a public lawsuit over the first claim, Trump's legal team filed a second private claim against the FBI and the Justice Department in the summer of 2024. Like the first, this one sought $115 million in compensation, for the alleged violation of his privacy by government agents searching Mar-a-Lago for classified documents. The new claim accused the Justice Department of malicious prosecution for charging based on the documents they had found in the search.

"Attorney General Garland, FBI Director Wray, and Special Counsel Smith's targeting, indictment, and harassment of President Trump has always been a malicious political prosecution aimed at affecting an electoral outcome to prevent President Trump from being re-elected," the filing declared.

At an earlier stage in Trump's legal fights, his twin claims might have been considered long shots or stunts. But when he filed his second claim, on August 7, 2024—just before the two-year anniversary of the FBI's Mar-a-Lago raid—he had recently scored two important court victories. In early July, the Supreme Court had significantly hobbled any prosecution of Trump for events leading up to the January 6 riot. The history-making ruling granted him broad but poorly defined immunity not just from prosecution but from investigation for official acts as president. Two weeks later, the federal judge in Florida overseeing his classified documents case, Aileen Cannon, dismissed those charges on the grounds that Smith had not been lawfully appointed to his special counsel role.

So, at the time of Trump's second claim, he was on a winning streak with the courts, and there was suddenly more reason to think his demands for money from the federal government might not be a pipe dream.

Then Trump won on Election Day.

Because Justice Department policy has long held that sitting presidents cannot be charged with crimes or prosecuted, Smith began shutting down his work and preparing to resign.

For the outgoing attorney general and his deputy, there were a million things to worry about when it came to a second Trump term, and Trump's two legal claims against the government seemed like relatively small potatoes. The Justice Department couldn't act on the claims while Smith's criminal cases were active, because courts generally keep civil lawsuits on hold until any criminal matters are resolved. That gave the Biden administration a relatively short window in which to do anything about Trump's legal demands for money during the brief period after the Trump criminal cases were dismissed and before he was sworn into office.

Nevertheless, there had been time to act. The department's leaders did not.

Officials could have formally rejected both of Trump's claims, which would have forced him to sue if he wanted money. Unlike a claim made directly to the government, a private lawsuit would have had to be scrutinized by the courts, perhaps even DC jurors.

But the Justice Department let the claims sit there, available to be picked up later by Trump's Justice Department leaders, who were also his former defense lawyers. Some former officials were upset by the inaction. To them, the decision to do nothing seemed based on a naive belief that Trump would not be so crass as to pursue the claims.

According to the Justice Department manual, settlements of claims against the department for more than $4 million "must be approved by the deputy attorney general or associate attorney general." In Trump's Justice Department, the deputy attorney general was Todd Blanche, who had served as Trump's personal criminal defense lawyer, and in that role, he had spent years making the same arguments that were in Trump's legal claims to the Justice Department. Trump's associate attorney general was Stan Woodward, who had represented Walt Nauta, the Trump valet indicted alongside his boss for allegedly conspiring with him in the classified documents case.

The legal bills for Nauta's defense were paid by Trump's political action committee, which meant Trump was effectively paying Woodward during that time.

Justice Department regulations forbid anyone from working on matters involving a former client for at least a year, meaning that, at a minimum, Blanche and Woodward should not touch the Trump claims for compensation until at least 2026.

Tirrell, the fired ethics official, said that even after that year passes, the department will still face an ethical quagmire. "Trump has made it very clear he's going to fire anyone that doesn't do what he wants them to do," Tirrell said. "Can you imagine the person who says no to Mr. Trump for $230 million isn't going to go on the firing list? And there's no one else in the entire executive branch who doesn't have the exact same issue."

Within the administration, some argued that the Trump legal claims were essentially dormant and unlikely to produce a settlement anytime soon, if ever.

Then Trump, in October 2025, alluded vaguely to the issue while speaking at a White House event with Bondi, Blanche, and his FBI director, Kash Patel. "I have a lawsuit that was doing very well, and when I became president, I said, I'm sort of suing myself," Trump said, adding, "It sort of looks bad, I'm suing myself, right? So I don't know. But that was a lawsuit that was very strong, very powerful."

Standing behind the president, Patel laughed.

After *The New York Times* published a story revealing the subterranean existence of the two legal claims, their prospective value, and the ethical morass they presented for the Justice Department, Trump was asked again about his demands for taxpayer money. "I was damaged very greatly," he said, before adding, "Any money I would get, I would give to charity." But he also acknowledged the inherent ethical problem of what he was doing. "I'm the one that makes the decision and that decision would have to go across my desk and it's awfully strange to make a decision where I'm paying myself," he said. Trump did not suggest that this would stop him. And people close to the president said that he fully expected to get paid. Eventually.

Justice Department officials have said that when it comes to the president's demand to be paid hundreds of millions of dollars in taxpayer money, they intend to follow the guidance of ethics officials.

To Tirrell, the ethics official who was fired, the situation is absurd. "I don't see a career ethics official being able to give valid advice to anyone in the department on this matter, without the explicit threat that they will be fired unless they do what's expected of them," he said.

The $230 million ethics problem was perhaps the starkest example of how far apart Republicans and Democrats were on basic questions of justice, ethics, and the rule of law.

As the Trump administration purged the ranks of the Justice Department and the FBI in 2025, some department veterans worried that the Biden administration had left the institution more vulnerable to Trump's hostile takeover. "Merrick Garland and Lisa Monaco are the worst two politicians I have ever met in my life," said one former department official. The ex-official meant it as a criticism, but Garland

and Monaco would probably take it as a semi-compliment. A former federal appeals court judge, Garland prided himself on his devotion to the independence of the Justice Department. In the Obama years, he and Monaco had both been considered as possible FBI directors, a job that ultimately went to James Comey.

Within the upper ranks of the Justice Department, some still marveled in 2025 how differently the U.S. government might look if Obama had chosen either Garland or Monaco, two people who followed procedure to a fault. Like FBI Director Chris Wray, Monaco and Garland both disliked how Comey had handled the 2016 election, particularly his decision to go solo with a public announcement of no charges against Hillary Clinton and then to publicly reopen the case shortly before Election Day.

To Wray, Garland, and Monaco, those events showed the danger of abandoning the department's rules and traditions. "Process will protect us," Wray often told subordinates. Garland and Monaco largely agreed with that approach.

During the Garland years at the department, agency leaders had obsessively enforced what was called a "contacts memo," which tightly restricted any conversations between White House officials and Justice Department personnel. The first contacts memo was written after Watergate, and many revisions had been made over the years. Over all the iterations, the memo aimed to protect the Justice Department from political interference—and the White House from scandal—by limiting interactions between staff in the two buildings.

Garland had an almost religious faith in the importance of such limitations. One senior official recounted having to forward an email to a department employee who had been on temporary duty at the White House. The email itself was innocuous—notifying the employee that the open enrollment period for them to select their health care benefits had begun—but the department was so scrupulous about the contacts policy that the open enrollment email was also sent to a slew of senior lawyers at the White House and the Justice Department.

That devotion to rule-following seemed all the more farcical when the

Trump administration came into power and immediately discarded the old contacts memo, ushering in an era when communication between the Justice Department and the rest of the administration was more or less a free-for-all. The lines blurred so quickly that at one point in 2025, two career prosecutors in relatively low-level positions at U.S. attorney offices were fired not by their Justice Department superiors, but by personnel officials at the White House.

Trump had little use for many of the department's rules, not in how Justice communicated with the outside, not in how it hired and fired, and especially not when it came to high-profile cases that the president cared about. All he cared about was results.

In early 2026, dozens of U.S. attorneys from around the country gathered at the White House to meet the president. Such meetings were mostly ceremonial affairs, a moment for a group photo and an encouraging word from the commander in chief. At a similar event years earlier, when Barack Obama was president, Obama pointedly told the prosecutors, "I appointed you, but you don't serve me. You serve the American people. And I expect you to act with independence and integrity."

Trump's remarks were altogether different. He complained the U.S. attorneys were weak, and "not doing anything" about cases he cared about.

He singled out a few prosecutors for criticism, but aimed most of his anger at one U.S. attorney in particular, Kelly Hayes of Maryland. Months earlier, Hayes had been given the mortgage fraud case against Adam Schiff and still had not filed criminal charges against the senator. Within the Justice Department, career prosecutors saw the Schiff case as woefully weak, but Trump, Pulte, Martin, and others refused to accept that.

Hayes, the president said in front of everyone, was a "huge disappointment."

Trump's disgust with lawyers was not limited to the ones who worked at the Justice Department. He and his aides often complained that much of the legal profession was biased against him and his supporters. Just as he had in his attacks on the media and higher education, he aimed to make the law firms pay.

In late February 2025, barely a month into the new administration, President Trump signed a memorandum suspending the security clearances of any lawyers at the firm of Covington and Burling who had provided legal assistance to Jack Smith, the former special counsel. Trump also ordered government agencies to "terminate any engagement" they may have had with the firm.

Weeks later, he issued an executive order targeting the law firm of Perkins Coie, on the grounds that it had represented Hillary Clinton's 2016 campaign and had paid for the research work that led to a "dossier" of unsubstantiated accusations against Trump. The order suspended security clearances for employees of the firm, restricted the firm's access to government buildings, and shut down government contracts with the firm. More such orders would follow, targeting other law firms that Trump blamed for what he claimed was unfair treatment of him and his allies.

The potential damage to big firms was tremendous. If a major corporation's law firm could not represent its interests to government agencies, the corporation might simply fire the firm.

Not surprisingly, some of the firms targeted by Trump quickly sued, and won restraining orders against the administration. In the first day of such court hearings, the lone administration lawyer assigned to defend the president's orders struggled to articulate a legal basis for any of it.

At many other law firms, however, the fear and panic caused by the president's orders had the desired effect. The first law firm to strike a deal with the president for protection was Paul, Weiss. The firm's chairman, Brad Karp, quickly agreed to provide the administration $40 million in free legal work in order to get Trump to revoke his March 14 order targeting the firm. Soon after, an even bigger, richer firm, Skadden, Arps, Slate, Meagher and Flom, agreed to provide $100 million in pro bono work to the administration, as long as it in turn agreed not to try to drive the firm out of business.

The settlements sparked a deep split inside the legal profession, as many lawyers thought that cutting a deal with the Trump administration amounted to abandoning the first principle of being a lawyer—advocating for a client.

The deals, though, also reflected a truth about Big Law. Many of the law firms were large corporations unto themselves and were in the business primarily of negotiation and settlement, so to the leaders of some of those companies, it made more sense to negotiate and settle than be blacklisted by a vengeful president.

There was another, unspoken reason for the big firms to strike deals, as long as too many clients or employees didn't walk away. Ethics and bar rules for lawyers in Washington, DC, made it incredibly unlikely that the firms would ever have to provide anything like the millions of dollars of pro bono legal work to the Justice Department that was promised. The Trump administration certainly needed all the legal help it could get, as its policies and treatment of employees had caused thousands of people to quit the department.

The administration knew full well it faced a huge brain drain, one that would hamper its agenda if it didn't find more lawyers as quickly as possible. Unknown to many senior officials, however, the rules for lawyer conduct and potential conflicts are strict, making it extremely difficult for anyone but federal employees to do most kinds of legal work for the federal government. In effect, the administration had gotten IOUs from law firms that the Justice Department could not cash.

In the spring of 2025, the issue came to a head as Blanche and Bondi's staff desperately wanted to get help navigating the sea of new cases being created by Trump's frequent disregard for established case law, regulations, and past practice.

The Justice Department office that handles human resources questions was stumped on how to bring those Big Law bodies or dollars aboard. Told in no uncertain terms by the department's leaders to figure out a way to use this pledged law firm money, they could not come up with one.

For one thing, it was very unlikely that Big Law attorneys would take the significant pay cut involved in joining the government. For another, even if private firm lawyers were paid their regular corporate rate to help the government, a federal regulation effectively bars lawyers from working on anything for the U.S. government that involves the firm where they are employed.

In order to resolve potential conflicts of interest by using corporate lawyers to work at the Justice Department on government cases, the government would have to spell out what the potential conflicts were, revealing what companies were under investigation. The corporate clients would also have to waive any potential conflict from a law firm whose personnel were in theory working on two different sides.

In other words, adherence to ethics rules could essentially kill the secrecy around almost any Justice Department investigation of a major company and might still lead to a situation in which the client corporations refused to waive the potential conflict.

The whole issue came to a head in the spring of 2025, when officials at the department's Justice Management Division tried to figure out a way to meet the demands of Bondi and Blanche for private firm lawyers to beef up their dwindling ranks of attorneys. The officials tried repeatedly to come up with some way to give the administration what it wanted, but they were frustrated to discover there was very little they could do without changing federal laws or bar rules. And without changing those, it seemed highly unlikely that any well-paid private-sector lawyer was going to risk his or her long-term career or bar license to help the Justice Department deport immigrants or sue U.S. cities or investigate claims of reverse racism on college campuses.

Law firms like Paul, Weiss had taken a reputational beating for caving to Trump, and some of their best lawyers were so upset they left to work elsewhere. But the firm had made a largely empty promise of future money or services, in exchange for what may prove to be a similarly empty promise from the administration of no vengeful punishment.

There remains the possibility that some other government agency—say, Commerce or the State Department—might find a way to derive some meaningful legal work from the firms. But the federal government's lawyers are concentrated in the Justice Department for the obvious reason that that is where most of the government's legal work is done. And the people running the department during the Trump administration were slow to realize the promised legal help wasn't coming.

By late 2025, it was increasingly clear to career lawyers at Justice that the administration's failed plan to use rich law firms to fix their self-created staffing problem was just another way in which the basic functions of the department were breaking down.

Nine law firms had decided to surrender and strike deals with Trump. Four major firms chose instead to sue to defend the most basic principle of the profession. All four were winning when, in early 2026, the administration filed papers seeking to abandon the effort. A day later, however, the president ordered the Justice Department to go back to court to keep fighting the cases—an embarrassingly rapid reversal.

The president was still unwilling to retreat from his war on the legal profession, as battles raged on in the courts, state bars, and the Justice Department itself.

CHAPTER 12

Message in a Bullet

Wearing a white shirt that read FREEDOM in black letters, Charlie Kirk sat in a chair with a microphone in the middle of Utah Valley University campus, as he kicked off his newest tour of American colleges, dubbed "the American Comeback."

Kirk, the thirty-one-year-old co-founder of Turning Point USA, was a right-wing political activist who had built a national following by challenging liberals, often students, to defend their views. In an age when political activists of all stripes frequently lived in walled-off echo chambers and ideological bubbles, Kirk was different. He spent much of his time specifically talking to those he disagreed with. He had made a successful political career out of "owning the libs," even if many of those liberals viewed his message as disturbingly xenophobic, racist, and backward.

September 10, 2025, began with a typical example of Kirk-style politicking. Speaking under a shade canopy that dared people to PROVE ME WRONG, Kirk debated and sparred with student questioners. He sat in a kind of outdoor stage, at the bottom of a bowl of terraced lawns surrounded by concrete school buildings.

About twenty minutes into the event, a student asked Kirk how many transgender people had committed mass shootings in the past ten years.

"Too many," Kirk replied, echoing an accusation increasingly popular on the right, that transgender people were responsible for an outsize number of mass violence events.

"Five," the questioner replied, then asked Kirk how many mass shooters there had been overall in the United States in the same period.

"Counting or not counting gang violence?" Kirk responded, still eager to debate the sources of violence in America.

The crack of a rifle shot ended the back-and-forth. The sound traveled around the concrete walls of the campus buildings ringing the event, making it hard for some in the crowd to tell where the shot had come from. The bullet from a .30-06-caliber rifle slammed into Kirk's neck, causing a sickening sideways lurch as he collapsed.

Kirk's killing was a tragedy—a devastating loss for his young family and a horrifying replay of the kind of violence that had nearly killed Trump during the 2024 campaign. The murder also became a rallying cry on the right for a crackdown on leftist groups and a lens through which to see how drastically Trump, Bondi, Blanche, and others in the administration wanted to change seventy years of civil rights enforcement in America.

Tyler Robinson, a twenty-two-year-old Utah man who despised Kirk's politics, confessed to killing him in a text conversation with the roommate he was dating, who had begun transitioning from male to female, according to court filings.

Robinson, police determined, had used an old bolt-action rifle that once belonged to his grandfather to kill Kirk, according to court papers, which said he had also left a note under his computer keyboard that read, "I had the opportunity to take out Charlie Kirk and I'm going to take it."

Robinson messaged his roommate on the day of the shooting, "I had hoped to keep this secret til I died of old age."

"You weren't the one who did it right????" the roommate typed back.

"I am, I'm sorry," Robinson replied, according to court records. "I had enough of his hatred. Some hate can't be negotiated out."

Police who discovered Robinson's rifle in nearby woods found video game and internet memes etched onto the bullet shell casings. One read, "hey fascist! CATCH!," near a series of arrows used in a video game called *Helldivers 2*.

Days after Kirk's death, Stephen Miller was interviewed by Vice President JD Vance for an episode of Kirk's podcast. Miller pledged to go after liberal activist networks that he called terrorist conspiracies. "The organized doxing campaigns, the organized riots, the organized street violence, the organized campaigns of dehumanization, vilification, posting people's addresses, combining that with messaging that's designed to trigger, incite violence in the actual organized cells that carry out and facilitate the violence: It is a vast domestic terror movement."

Kirk's killing, Miller argued, was a wake-up call to the government to go after those people more aggressively. "With God as my witness," he vowed, "we are going to use every resource we have at the Department of Justice, Homeland Security and throughout this government to identify, disrupt, dismantle and destroy these networks and make America safe again."

Few people knew it at the time, but when Miller complained about doxing campaigns and "dehumanization," he was talking about not just the wider world, but also his own life. He, his wife, and their young children lived in Arlington, Virginia, a county of about a quarter million people who had voted nearly 4–1 for Kamala Harris over Trump in 2024. DC residents often refer to Arlington, with some justification, as the "sleepy suburbs," but for some high-profile government figures, the anger and drama at work followed them home.

In January 2024, a group of local liberal activists began protesting outside the Arlington house of Antony Blinken, President Biden's secretary of state. Unhappy with U.S. policy when it came to the Israeli military campaign in the Gaza Strip, the protesters set up on the road outside Blinken's house, demanding a ceasefire.

The protesters, a rotating group that included a sixty-five-year-old retired academic and peace activist named Barbara Wien, built a small encampment of tents and signs and remained on the side of the road for six months—at which point, Virginia officials declared the protest a safety hazard for motorists and pedestrians and cleared out the encampment. The regular protests, however, continued, just without tents. Sometimes a caravan of cars would slow-drive past Blinken's house, waving signs and shouting support for Palestinians.

The following year, the group that had carried out the Blinken protests, Arlington Neighbors United for Humanity, began protesting outside Miller's Arlington home. The protests were spotty, often fewer than a dozen people, and frequently involved writing in rainbow-colored chalk on the sidewalk. STEPHEN MILLER IS DESTROYING DEMOCRACY, read one chalk message. WE ♥ IMMIGRANTS, read another. NO WHITE NATIONALISM.

On August 4, local Arlington police, responding to a call, arrived at a park near the Millers' home, where Katie Miller was waiting for them. When the officers arrived, she was removing a flyer about her husband from the back of a county sign. The flyer showed Stephen Miller's face inside a circle and a diagonal line, like a No Smoking sign, and the words NO NAZIS IN NOVA, using the common acronym for Northern Virginia. The flyer described Miller as the "architect of Trump's immigration policies," and a "known white nationalist & 'totalitarian toady.'" It also listed his home address.

"Scan the QR code to demand a congressional investigation," it read.

The Arlington Police Department, accustomed at this point to the group's protests and seeing nothing criminal in the activists' behavior, did not take any action against them.

About a month later, on September 10, came Charlie Kirk's killing. Gates McGavick, a Justice Department spokesman who idolized Kirk, was sitting near Bondi on a plane heading back to Washington, DC, from Illinois when he saw the gruesome video of Kirk being shot.

Overwhelmed, McGavick showed his boss the news on his phone. "You have to see this," he said, unable to describe it.

The next morning in Arlington, a black Toyota Prius pulled up to the Millers', and Barbara Wien, the elderly activist, got out of the car. Katie Miller, sitting on her front porch talking on her phone, later told police she watched Wien walk to her neighbors' front door, apparently to leave an envelope of flyers in their mailbox.

Walking back to her car, Wien looked at Miller, pointed her index and middle finger at her own eyes, and then pointed the same fingers at Miller, seemingly to say "I'm watching you." According to court documents filed later, Miller told police she perceived it as a threatening act "intended to intimidate or harass her."

After Kirk's death, Katie Miller was afraid to walk in the neighborhood with her kids. The Miller family had Secret Service protection outside their home. But the Millers wanted more, and that week, the FBI was summoned to their home, along with Erik Siebert, the U.S. attorney, and the Virginia State Police.

Sitting in the their living room, Katie described her concerns and her desire for a full-fledged federal investigation of Wien, her group, and any others. The Millers feared that the doxing flyers on their neighborhood street weren't all that had happened. They suspected activists were following their family around the neighborhood while they did errands and went about their lives.

The Millers wanted the FBI to launch an undercover investigation; specifically, Katie wanted a covert FBI agent to do immediate undercover work, both in person and online, to investigate the protesters, even going so far as to offer the agents the use of a preexisting account to monitor the activists' online conversations. The agents listened patiently and then explained to the couple that it would be very difficult, if not impossible, to launch on short notice an undercover operation like the one they described, according to people familiar with the conversations. FBI undercover operations require multiple layers of approval, scrutiny, and legal discussion before being launched. It is incredibly rare to launch and execute one in a single night or two.

And that didn't even get into the question of whether such an investigation would be lawful. Within the FBI, numerous agents and supervisors didn't believe it was, even if the request was coming from someone with tremendous sway in the administration. Senior FBI officials had watched Miller successfully push for the firing of veteran agents with decades of experience. Saying no to him, some agents thought, would be very risky for the FBI.

The agents told the Millers that for a host of reasons, including the First Amendment, they could not deploy an undercover agent, infuriating the couple, according to people familiar with the conversation.

By the end of September, the investigation of Wien and the other activists included the police departments of Arlington and adjoining Fairfax County, the Virginia State Police, the FBI, and the Secret Service. Fairfax investigators uncovered an April message from Wien to others in which she called Stephen Miller an "evil fascist," noted that he had moved to Arlington, and asked others to let her know if they would like to join her effort.

"His wife sits their [*sic*] smugly swilling wine on their patio, while her husband orders the arrest of more and more of our Muslim, Arab American, and Hispanic brothers and sisters," Wien wrote in a group chat. "My Showing Up for Racial Justice (SURJ) chapter in N. Virginia intends to make his life hell."

That statement in particular struck Virginia State Police officials as justification to investigate Wien. Virginia state law made it a misdemeanor to publish a person's name or photograph along with their home address "with the intent to coerce, intimidate, or harass another person." A federal statute makes it a crime to publicize information like a home address of a government official, but only if the intent behind the disclosure is to "threaten, intimidate, or incite the commission of a crime of violence," or with the knowledge that the information will be used to do so.

Wien had been protesting and practicing non-violent protest for years, and Arlington authorities did not see her as a threat. On September 14, an Arlington police officer responded to the Millers' street, where the officers watched about a dozen protesters write in chalk on the sidewalk. "The messages were non-threatening and alluded to political issues such as immigration, transgender rights, DEI and white supremacy," the police report later noted.

Two weeks later, the Virginia State Police sought a search warrant for Wien's phone, and a local judge signed it. When the state investigators showed up at her home to execute the warrant, they brought with them FBI and Secret Service agents. The FBI interviewed Wien, who eventually turned over her phone to the state investigator. The next day, her lawyer, Bradley Haywood, began fighting the warrant and the entire investigation, arguing that it was an abuse of government power and a violation of Wien's First Amendment rights to protest and speech.

In two decades as a lawyer, Haywood had never seen a case like this one. "The Secret Service knows who Ms. Wien is, they know she has never been convicted of any crime, they know her background in academia and that she's now retired, they know why she is active in civic affairs, and they know she has no intention of harassing, coercing, or intimidating anyone. Most of all, they know that she merely aims to exercise her First Amendment rights," Haywood wrote in a court filing fighting the search warrant.

As the lawyer saw it, a senior White House official with tremendous pull inside federal law enforcement agencies had engineered a criminal investigation into local residents engaged in peaceful protest. The state police, it turned out, had gotten involved only after a specific instruction from the governor, Republican Glenn Youngkin.

The Millers wanted more than security. They wanted a complete criminal investigation, including the names of those involved with Wien and the flyers that displayed their address.

After the state police and federal agents went to Wien's house to get her phone, the local prosecutor became concerned that her office had been misled about the full scope of the investigation. Parisa Dehghani-Tafti, a Democrat, served as the commonwealth's attorney in Arlington—Virginia's version of district attorneys. It is exceedingly rare for prosecutors to argue against a search warrant, but in this case she decided to ask the judge to limit what kinds of data would be searched on Wien's phone. "Our office was assured," she wrote to the judge who had signed the warrant, "that the investigation was local and the purpose of the search was related to local charges only."

The fight over Wien's phone quickly became a mess. After the local prosecutor sought to scale back the search of it, Virginia Attorney General Jason Miyares, a Republican, filed his own counterargument, arguing in favor of the initial search warrant and against Dehghani-Tafti's motion.

The Wien investigation ground on but accomplished little. In December 2025, two of Wien's friends were questioned by the FBI about her, but despite all the pressure from the Millers, the Justice Department seemed no closer to charging her with anything. The case was a study in miniature of how the Trump administration wanted to take an aggressive new approach to investigating possible conspiracies on the left.

In their quest to counter what they called "weaponization" by the previous Democratic administration, Miller and others in the Trump administration wanted aggressive investigations of liberal activists who they claimed were primed to commit violence. Two weeks after the Charlie Kirk killing, the senior Justice Department official Aakash Singh pushed more than a half dozen U.S. attorney offices around the country to pursue investigations of the Open Society Foundations, the umbrella organization of liberal, anti-Communist, and pro-democracy groups funded by George Soros and his family. Singh's instruction said the prosecutors should consider charges of racketeering, arson, wire fraud, and material support for terrorism.

But more than the mere existence of liberal groups, it was their public protests that seemed to especially enrage the Trump administration. From the president to Miller to Bondi, senior officials sought to paint protests against Trump policies as uniquely dangerous—and kept claiming without evidence that they were somehow fake gatherings of people paid to feign outrage.

Weeks after the Kirk killing, Trump signed an executive order designating antifa a domestic terrorist organization, which the president blamed for "coordinated efforts to obstruct enforcement of federal laws through armed standoffs with law enforcement, organized riots, violent assaults on Immigration and Customs Enforcement and other law enforcement officers, and routine doxing of and other threats against political figures and activists." He also issued National Security Presidential Memorandum 7, a sweeping directive for federal law enforcement agencies to investigate "terroristic activities under the umbrella of self-described 'anti-fascism.'"

The "anti-fascist lie," Trump's directive read, is animated by "anti-Americanism, anti-capitalism, and anti-Christianity; support for the overthrow of the United States Government; extremism on migration, race, and gender; and hostility toward those who hold traditional American views on family, religion, and morality."

The president ordered the FBI to aggressively investigate as domestic terrorism broad categories of crime, including "organized doxing campaigns, swatting, rioting, looting, trespass, assault, destruction of property, threats of violence, and civil disorder."

The Trump administration's ambitions for NSPM-7 are staggering. Officials envision a standalone FBI unit that uses a host of investigative techniques to build criminal cases against leftist activists and organizations, and expect it to be operational well before the November 2026 congressional elections.

In the first half of 2025, the Trump administration used the word *terrorism* to describe a wide swath of drug crime. In the second half of the year, they stretched that definition even farther, to include all manner of unrest. Using the word *terrorism* wasn't simply a rhetorical flourish—it affected how law enforcement arrested and charged people in Chicago, Los Angeles, and Minneapolis, where large groups protested federal actions, and some clashed with officers. Trump's directive demanded the maximum charges, and the Justice Department set out to file them whenever possible, even if judges or juries often balked.

When it comes to tracking threats of violence, it was becoming harder for law enforcement and the public to distinguish internet noise from real danger, in part because hoaxes were pulsing in all directions. Politicians thought they were unique in the quantity of threats they faced, but that wasn't true. The internet had made it incredibly easy to anonymously lodge a pipe bomb threat against a school, or against dozens of schools, all before the lunch bell. Schools, hospitals, and businesses faced a tremendous spike in threatening messages, most of them belligerent nonsense designed to scare people, but law enforcement officials often had to make snap decisions about which threatening email or phone call or text to take seriously and which to ignore.

Months before Kirk's killing, a Democratic lawmaker in Minneapolis and her husband were assassinated by a man pretending to be a police officer. Authorities charged the same man with shooting and nearly killing another Democratic lawmaker and his wife that same night. When he was captured, the gunman was in possession of a list of dozens of people, most of them Democratic politicians and abortion-rights advocates or abortion providers, according to officials.

After the Minneapolis killings and the Kirk shooting, politicians and high-profile government officials were increasingly unnerved and fearful about the threat matrix. Five days after Charlie Kirk's murder, Attorney General Pam Bondi appeared on Katie Miller's new podcast. "There's free speech, and then there's hate speech," she said. "We will absolutely target you, go after you, if you are targeting anyone with hate speech, anything, and that's across the aisle . . . We're seeing people online posting hate speech, they should be shut down."

As legal analysis by the nation's top law enforcement official, Bondi's comments were nonsensical. The United States does not criminalize hate speech, which, however awful, is protected by the First Amendment. What *is* illegal is making true threats.

Even conservatives were aghast at Bondi's claims, given that many of them had spent recent years arguing against the stifling of right-wing rhetoric by social media companies. The attorney general, observed conservative radio host Erick Erickson, "is apparently a moron."

Bondi later tried to clarify what she meant, posting on social media that hate speech "that crosses the line into threats of violence is NOT protected by the First Amendment"—which was an accurate statement, but one with little relationship to what she had said in the first place to anger people on the left and right. She also added, in another inaccurate description of the law, "You cannot dox a conservative family and think it will be brushed off as 'free speech,'" seemingly a reference to the Millers and Barbara Wien.

There are anti-doxing laws, but the mere act of posting someone's address on a neighborhood flyer is not a crime, unless investigators can show criminal intent behind that action. It would make little sense, for example, to criminalize real estate listings or the myriad other ways people's home addresses get posted online. What makes posting an address a crime under federal and state law is if the intent of the act is to harm, threaten, or intimidate someone.

Bondi's public statements about hate speech, while inaccurate and ham-handed, did capture a growing sentiment in America, one fueled by the expectation of anonymity in many online interactions. That expectation, however, is mostly a modern concept. American life and law have long assumed that people's addresses, including the addresses of famous or powerful people, are findable to those willing to look hard enough through public records. The internet's frequently false promise of anonymity, however, has led many Americans to believe such information is or should be private. But it rarely is.

And when it came to liberal activist groups, the Trump administration had decided well before Charlie Kirk's assassination that it wanted to gather lists of suspected subversives to investigate. The September killing wasn't the spark for that effort; it was fuel to push the effort faster and further.

In the weeks and months that followed, Trump administration officials pushed for federal hate crime charges to be filed against Kirk's accused killer, Tyler Robinson. Robinson already faced a possible death sentence in state court, but the Trump administration, according to people familiar with the discussions, pressed prosecutors in the Civil Rights Division to try to make a federal hate crime case against him on the theory that Kirk was killed because he was a Christian.

Federal hate crime laws were written to prosecute crimes motivated by bias against a person's "race, religion, disability, sexual orientation, ethnicity, gender, or gender identity." Those laws do not include a category for killing someone over their political views, and Justice Department lawyers and FBI agents told their bosses in late 2025 that the evidence of Robinson's motive made it a poor fit for a federal hate crime case.

The Trump administration's reaction to Kirk's killing was not the beginning of its effort to change civil rights enforcement in the United States. By September 2025, senior administration officials had spent months dismantling the Justice Department's Civil Rights Division in order to fundamentally change which Americans, and which rights, would take priority.

CHAPTER 13

Our Rights Versus Their Rights

Within the Justice Department's eight divisions, none faced more turnover in 2025 than the one whose lawyers enforced the nation's civil rights laws. In some ways, the Civil Rights Division was the least prepared for the second Trump term.

Established by the historic 1957 Civil Rights Act, the Civil Rights Division was initially founded to protect voting rights, particularly for Black Americans in the South. In the years that followed, other laws passed by Congress added to the lawyers' duties, such as prosecuting hate crimes and police abuse of citizens, and fighting against housing discrimination, religious discrimination, and lack of access for people with disabilities.

The division's mission was to uphold the Constitution's promise to all Americans of equal protection and due process under the law, and that generally meant protecting minorities and other marginalized groups. By the end of the Biden administration, the division's staff numbered more than six hundred people, most of them lawyers. Many of those lawyers had also worked there during the first Trump administration, during which they experienced the kind of policy changes typical of a change from a Democratic to a Republican administration. For most lawyers in the division, that did not greatly affect their work, and at the start of 2025 many were cautiously optimistic that the same pattern would prevail in the second term.

Stacey Young was firmly in the camp of Civil Rights Division lawyers who thought otherwise. "Many people inside the department told me, 'We lived through the first one, and we'll do it again,'" she said. "They didn't believe all the campaign rhetoric would be executed."

To Young, the department and the Civil Rights Division were vulnerable in part because they were so unlike the "deep state" caricature used by Trump supporters. Rather than a vast conspiracy of political-minded schemers, many in the Justice Department workforce were, in truth, nerds intently focused on the law, often to the exclusion of the political currents dominating the rest of Washington.

Shortly before Trump was sworn into office, Young wrote an op-ed in *The New York Times* warning of what was about to happen to her coworkers. "The incoming leaders of the government have told us in aggressive terms that they want us either gone or miserable," she wrote. Her message was not a call to arms for those inside the department, but rather an appeal for members of the public to help protect the nonpartisan government workforce.

Young, who had already spent years as an in-house advocate for gender equality at the Justice Department, understood that the public missive would probably mean the end of her Justice Department career. Twelve days later, she resigned from the department, not waiting for officials to fire her. She then launched an outside organization to do precisely what she had urged—support current and former Justice Department workers. Her group, Justice Connection, would become a kind of self-defense training program for department employees, and one of the earliest and loudest critics of the sweeping changes being wrought by the Trump administration.

It took many of Young's former coworkers a couple more months to realize just how different this Trump administration would be. The first lesson came in the form of orders to combat "illegal diversity, equity, and inclusion" programs, known as DEI. In early 2025, Civil Rights Division lawyers were told to draw up plans to withdraw federal funding immediately from any universities, colleges, or schools found to still be supporting DEI.

One problem loomed large for the civil rights lawyers given the assignment. What was "illegal DEI," exactly? The administration was rushing to impose multimillion-dollar punishments on schools and other institutions for diversity practices the administration could not yet define. Many lawyers in the division feared that whenever their political bosses produced such a definition, the instructions would be glaringly at odds with long-standing civil rights laws. If the purpose of the Civil Rights Division was to safeguard due process and equal protection under the law, how did that square with an effort to rid higher education, law firms, and all manner of American institutions of "diversity, equity, and inclusion"?

Even without a definition for what they were supposed to be investigating and punishing, many lawyers in the division came to see the directives as having one overarching theme. The Trump administration appeared to have decided that the most pressing civil rights issue of the modern era was protecting white men.

It was a message that was expressed subtly in the early days of the administration, but by the end of 2025, it had adopted the tone of billboard ads for accident liability lawyers. "Are you a white male who has experienced discrimination at work based on your race or sex? You may have a claim to recover money under federal civil rights law," the head of the Equal Employment Opportunity Commission, Andrea Lucas, said in an online video, urging such men to file claims with the commission.

Lucas's EEOC was not part of the Justice Department, but it shared a message and a goal: to repurpose a host of government agencies that had been created and that operated to protect minorities and women in order to significantly expand efforts to protect the rights of white people generally and white men in particular.

Trump put it bluntly in an interview with *The New York Times* in early 2026, when he was asked about the effects of civil rights laws. "White people were very badly treated, where they did extremely well and they were not invited to go into a university, to college," he said. "I think it was also, at the same time, it accomplished some very wonderful things, but it also hurt a lot of people, people that deserve to go to a college or deserve to get a job were unable to get a job. So it was, it was a reverse discrimination."

Justice Department lawyers get memos every day, but they couldn't recall ever seeing a memo like the one Pam Bondi sent on February 5, 2025, part of a flurry of directives issued on her first day in the job. Months later, Justice Department employees could still recall where they were when they read Bondi's memo on "zealous advocacy." "The responsibilities of Department of Justice attorneys include not only aggressively enforcing criminal and civil laws enacted by Congress, but also vigorously defending presidential policies and actions against legal challenges on behalf of the United States," she wrote. Lawyers may not "substitute personal political views or judgments for those that prevailed in an election."

It's difficult to overstate the significance of Bondi's memo and the internal reaction to it. For generations, Justice Department lawyers had been taught that a critical part of their job was to work not necessarily to please the government of the United States, but to serve the United States and do justice. Bondi's one-page instruction seemed to throw all that aside and replace it with the argument that their oath to uphold the Constitution now meant a kind of sworn allegiance to whatever the president wanted. Dissent and disagreement were forbidden. This was anathema to most Justice Department lawyers. Disagreements were a normal part of how prosecutors and agents operated and a critical ingredient of their decision-making process. When handling tricky cases for the government, it was often the internal disagreements that led the department to craft a stronger position or legal strategy.

If some Justice Department lawyers still thought they could do business the old way, Bondi's memo was clear: Insubordinate employees would be fired. Any Justice Department lawyer who "because of their personal political views or judgments declines to sign a brief or appear in court, refuses to advance good-faith arguments on behalf of the administration, or otherwise delays or impedes the department's mission will be subject to discipline and potentially termination," Bondi wrote.

At other federal agencies, Elon Musk's Department of Government Efficiency drove much of the firing and cost-cutting effort. But the Justice Department was mostly spared from DOGE-style cuts. Instead, more than 6,000 employees out of the more than 110,000-person Justice Department workforce were driven out by the new conditions of their employment—orders to launch investigations they considered unjustified and possibly unlawful, like the mortgage fraud cases against Letitia James and others; demands to drop cases they believed were righteous and necessary, like the charges against New York City's mayor; and behind the relentless stream of new orders and directives, the implicit threat that any disloyalty would result in their removal, like Erez Reuveni's being fired after he refused to lie.

In early March, Emil Bove ordered the Civil Rights Division to investigate student protesters at Columbia University in New York City. Amid growing concerns that Jewish students were facing threats and harassment, Trump had promised during his presidential campaign to crack down on campus protests against Israel.

On February 26, protesters at Columbia's Barnard College building pushed past a security guard and occupied a hallway, demonstrating against an earlier decision by the school to expel students accused of disrupting a History of Modern Israel class. School officials said at the time that the guard was assaulted and taken to the hospital for minor injuries.

Bove ordered an investigation into Columbia University Apartheid Divest, a group behind that protest and others. CUAD was a coalition of student groups involved in pro-Palestinian demonstrations. Bove wanted prosecutors to gather a membership list for the group, prosecutors were told, so it could be shared with immigration officials. The prosecutors refused to compile such a list, fearing it would be used to conduct unjustified and possibly unlawful deportation efforts. That same month, immigration agents arrested Mahmoud Khalil, a recent Columbia graduate, and began proceedings to deport him. Khalil, who was born in Syria but had a green card, had been a prominent figure in CUAD's protests, and his lawyers argued that he was being targeted for deportation solely for his constitutionally protected activism.

When prosecutors refused Bove's demand for a CUAD membership list, he ordered them to apply for a search warrant for the group's Instagram account, in order to get the non-public information about who used and followed the account, according to people familiar with the matter. Bove argued that whoever operated the social media account had posted graffiti on the wall of a building where the school's president lived, and that the graffiti constituted a threat. The graffiti featured splashes of bright red paint, the words FREE THEM ALL, and a triangle pointing downward. That triangle, federal prosecutors argued, was a threatening Hamas symbol comparable to the burning of crosses.

Magistrate Judge Sarah Netburn found that argument unpersuasive, and three separate times she rejected the prosecutors' application for a search warrant. Such rejections by a federal judge were rare but not unprecedented. The judge's denial of the warrant seemed to validate the original concerns of federal prosecutors assigned to the case, that the Civil Rights Division was now being used to try to violate the First Amendment rights of students and protesters.

The Trump administration pressed ahead, appealing Judge Netburn's decision to a federal judge in Manhattan, John G. Koeltl. Judge Koeltl also shot them down. "Although the writing on the wall was reprehensible, there are statutes that cover such vandalism," he ruled.

Bove tried other ways to shut down the protests at Columbia. He ordered FBI agents on the Joint Terrorism Task Force in New York to put on raid jackets, go up to the campus in large numbers, and stand around protesters as a show of federal force. Managers at both the FBI and the Civil Rights Division thought the instruction was highly improper—a blatant attempt to use agents as an intimidation tactic against protesters. The FBI refused to do what Bove wanted.

The Columbia investigation was an early window into how Trump's Justice Department planned to deal with protesters. The bar for investigating advocacy groups on the left would be lowered, by the same officials who argued that the Biden administration had improperly lowered the bar for investigations of right-wing groups.

Harmeet K. Dhillon, Trump's pick to lead the Civil Rights Division, arrived at the Justice Department in April and wasted little time making sweeping changes. Dhillon, a California lawyer whose civil rights firm championed conservative causes, had publicly claimed to have evidence of fraud in the 2020 election that Joe Biden won. "We already have a lot of evidence of fraud that's been filed in court," she said on Fox Business News a week after the presidential vote.

As a government lawyer and civil rights chief, Dhillon liked to announce new investigations and initiatives on Elon Musk's X social media platform. Being perpetually online also meant she had a tendency to get into public spats with random people. At one point, frustrated over conservative influencers attacking her boss Pam Bondi, Dhillon called such criticism "bullshit" and said, "You are earning money to spread misinformation. You are hoes."

In her first month at the Justice Department, Dhillon took aim at one of the Civil Rights Division's signature issues, police misconduct. For decades, the division had conducted "pattern or practice" investigations into police departments, often after a high-profile killing or abuse case. Pattern or practice investigations were designed to probe the work culture of an entire department to look for systemic problems of racism, mistreatment of suspects, or excessive force.

Pattern or practice investigations were opened with an eye toward eventually reaching a settlement with the department being investigated. Those settlements, called consent decrees, grew in part out of the 1992 rioting that convulsed Los Angeles after an all-white jury acquitted police officers for beating motorist Rodney King.

Such consent decrees were not a miracle cure for problems of police misconduct. As decades passed and some police departments faced multiple pattern or practice investigations, the effectiveness of such consent decrees was sometimes debated within law enforcement circles. To President Trump, there was nothing to debate. In his first term, he joked publicly about cops roughing up people when placing them in police cars. He also complained that laws "protect the criminal" instead of officers.

In contrast, the Biden administration had been committed to police reform and seen the Justice Department's consent decrees as an effective way to professionalize and modernize police departments. The Biden administration, however, moved painfully slow with their pattern or practice cases. Years passed without their striking consent decree settlements with police departments.

The Justice Department finally reached a settlement in December 2024 with Louisville, following the police killing of Breonna Taylor in her home by officers executing a warrant. In early January 2025, the department reached a consent decree with Minneapolis, the city where a police officer murdered George Floyd in 2020 by kneeling on his neck for nine minutes and twenty-nine seconds. Both deals were struck more than four and a half years after the killings that spawned them and weeks before the Trump administration took control of the Justice Department.

To many current and former Justice Department civil rights lawyers, including those who believed that much good could come from consent decrees, the Louisville and Minneapolis settlements had taken too long and accomplished little, because everyone understood on the day they were announced that the Trump administration would immediately retreat from them—which they did.

In the spring of 2025, Dhillon announced that the department was abandoning efforts to oversee or investigate nearly two dozen police departments accused of civil rights violations, including in Minneapolis and Louisville, where the settlements the Biden administration struck months earlier were dismissed by the courts.

Instead of investigating those police departments, Dhillon's division launched an investigation into Los Angeles County officials for what she said was a pattern or practice of limiting residents' rights to carry concealed firearms. The Los Angeles area was also a target of the Justice Department for a different reason: The Trump administration wanted to quickly investigate and punish the University of California system over claims of on-campus anti-Semitism.

Ejaz Baluch Jr., a lawyer in the Civil Rights Division who worked on employment discrimination, was assigned in the spring of 2025 to help in the California investigation. It quickly became clear to the lawyers on the case that the administration already knew what it wanted and that their assignment was not to ask questions and find out facts, but to build a case to support conclusions their bosses had already reached.

Michael Gates, who was directing the investigation, told the team they had thirty days to investigate—and draft a complaint against—the California university system. "That turns the process completely upside down. You are supposed to start with a question and then find an answer. He gave us the answer and told us to reverse-engineer the questions," said Baluch. "We were all appalled."

As the investigation proceeded, the lawyers sent regular updates to Gates, explaining that on most of the California campuses, there simply was not enough evidence of the kind of anti-Semitism he wanted them to find. Eventually, Gates became so frustrated with the evidence they were gathering that he suggested they base their lawsuit instead on public reporting. "Can't we just rely on that?" he asked the team.

Lawyers who had been trained to meticulously gather their own evidence were again shocked by Gates's approach to the work. No, they explained, they couldn't just rely on news articles or social media posts as evidence.

The more Gates pushed, the more absurd the assignment seemed to the lawyers working under him. And as the investigation continued through the spring, the exodus of lawyers from the division started to have more of an impact. Baluch's practice group, which had once had nearly forty attorneys, dwindled to just seven.

Gregory Brown, one of the new bosses in the division, told the civil rights lawyers in one meeting, "We're getting a lot of pressure to bring this case." Brown was part of the new Trump team, so the lawyers inferred that if he was under pressure, that likely meant the pressure was coming from the White House.

"That's when I knew the game was rigged," said Baluch.

As he worked on the case in May, Baluch thought there had been at least some evidence of anti-Semitism on the UCLA campus. In one interview, he listened to a heartbreaking account from a Jewish professor. "Some of them had groups of students come up to them in a dark parking lot and yell at them; it was pretty bad harassment," Baluch said. "In one interview a professor started crying describing his experiences. In that moment I felt sick to my stomach, because here are these professors who faced genuine harassment, and they are crying while telling their stories to us, but I knew this Justice Department would not actually do anything to solve the problems they are describing."

To Baluch, the real problem was that it was already clear that the investigation ordered by political leaders was a sham. The administration, it seemed clear to him, was using concerns about anti-Semitism to try to extract promises of political loyalty, as well as astronomical sums of money, far more than it had sought in similar cases about discrimination and mistreatment. "I felt like I was part of an apparatus that was using their very real pain only for political gain, and it made me sick to my stomach," he said. That was the moment he realized he could not in good conscience continue to work on the case.

Things got so bad inside the Civil Rights Division that Baluch was relieved when he was transferred down to a grunt work legal assignment. But then Dhillon's office realized they were so short-staffed that they needed Baluch to keep working on the California investigation.

He chose to resign instead and was gone by June.

In August, the Trump administration announced that it was suspending more than half a billion dollars of grant money for UCLA and seeking a one-billion-dollar settlement from the school—confirming Baluch's worst fears that the purpose of the investigation was never to fight anti-Semitism, but to exact a steep price, politically and financially, from a perceived liberal bastion.

The Civil Rights Division, he said, "is unrecognizable" from what it was prior to January 20, 2025.

Baluch said that civil rights laws had long protected marginalized communities, but the Trump administration had abandoned that work and instead chosen three specific groups to protect: white men, Christians who claim to have suffered from anti-Christian bias, and Jewish people who suffer from anti-Semitism but only in one narrow sense, which is being on a campus where there are pro-Palestinian protests.

The new kind of civil rights enforcement drove away a staggering 75 percent of the lawyers who worked at the Civil Rights Division. The division began 2025 with more than six hundred lawyers and other staff. By the end of 2025, roughly four hundred people had quit. Dhillon publicly praised the exodus. "Over 100 attorneys decided that they'd rather not do what their job requires them to do, and I think that's fine," she told conservative commentator Glenn Beck.

The Trump administration struggled mightily to fill the vacancies. After attacking law schools, firing more than two hundred of its personnel, and driving away thousands more, the Justice Department was no longer a particularly attractive place to work for many young lawyers.

For generations, lawyers who joined the department understood that there was a trade-off in working there: They would never earn the same kind of money as their classmates who went to big corporate firms, and they would probably never be able to afford that second vacation home. But they took pride in the belief that their work was more rewarding, because their mission was to achieve a just outcome for the nation. Justice Department lawyers also consoled themselves that as civil servants, they had the kind of job security the private sector could never promise.

That sense of purpose was stripped away from many of the department's lawyers and staff in 2025, making it more difficult to recruit new lawyers to what suddenly seemed like a low-paying, unstable, and unrewarding assignment.

Outwardly, the Civil Rights Division was never busier. Dhillon regularly announced new investigations on social media, firing off letters to city officials demanding immediate answers to her questions. But she was the captain of a hollowed-out ship, a vessel racing into uncharted territory with a skeleton crew who had to hope and pray they would not have to actually litigate all the cases their boss had started.

The Civil Rights Division saw the biggest exodus, but there were significant departures affecting the entire agency. U.S. attorney offices saw an exodus, too: In New Jersey, Texas, Colorado, and elsewhere, they lost 30 percent or more of their staff. There was a host of reasons, including the general uncertainty surrounding a new administration that seemed to declare a fresh crisis almost every week and the sudden, nagging lack of job security.

But there were targeted firings, too, and they had an outsize effect on those who remained. In 2025, roughly two hundred people were fired outright—again, a small figure relative to many other agencies, but the firing of those prosecutors and agents, often for having worked on cases related to Trump or his supporters, instilled fear in many of those who remained.

Peter Carr, a longtime Justice Department spokesman, was fired in April 2025. Carr was walking down a first-floor hallway one Friday when he happened to pass by Todd Blanche, the deputy attorney general, getting coffee. Before that moment, Carr and Blanche had seen each other only in court—Carr because he had served as the spokesman for Special Counsel Jack Smith, and Blanche because he was the lead defense attorney for Trump. The two men briefly locked eyes before continuing on their way. Hours after their silent, odd reunion, deputy marshals delivered a letter to Carr from Blanche. He was out.

Carr, who had served as an aide to a Republican senator from Utah before spending more than a decade at the department, was given an hour to pack up his office and leave for good. Weeping coworkers helped him gather his things, and he walked out of the building carrying several shopping bags stuffed with belongings. Weeks later, he joined Stacey Young's group Justice Connection, which advocates on behalf of Justice Department workers.

By August 2025, Barbara Schwabauer, a lawyer in the Civil Rights Division, had had enough. Schwabauer's belief in civil rights work was rooted in her Catholic upbringing and Jesuit education. In leaving the department after fifteen years, the appeals lawyer penned a passionate departure letter that stood out even in a year of fiery Justice Department resignation letters. The agency's leadership, she wrote, is "based on a fundamental lack of kindness and reliance on a lazy playbook with just three tactics: divide, erase, and insult." She also singled out those colleagues who had decided to embrace the administration's changes. "Your legacy will be how eagerly you got in the passenger seat of the bulldozer that destroyed our hard work (including your own), our decades-long careers, and the division's respectability as a beacon for civil rights. May your ambition be worth the cost you've accepted."

As Dhillon and the Trump administration worked to redefine civil rights work in the United States, they were focused on tackling the target looming ahead of them in 2026: the midterm elections.

CHAPTER 14

Election Daze

On the morning of November 6, 2024, Election Day, the chief of the Justice Department's Public Integrity Section, Corey Amundson, was inside the Strategic Information and Operations Center, a 24/7 global command post at FBI headquarters where dozens of agents, prosecutors, and analysts had gathered to track any threats to the democratic process.

For about a week leading up to the election, federal agencies had been staffing the election protection effort, ready to respond with legal advice, resources, and whatever help was needed as voters in fifty states went to the polls to pick either Donald Trump or Kamala Harris to be the next president.

All day and night, prosecutors in Washington worked as a kind of legal advice hotline for FBI agents tasked with investigating potential threats to election safety and security: A random social media post declaring an intention to kill someone if this or that candidate were elected. A threat made to a specific candidate. A bomb hoax targeting a polling place.

The irony of the prosecutors' work was that if it went well, the public wouldn't know anything about it. A relatively quiet, peaceful election was the goal and the measure of success.

That morning, Amundson sent an email rallying his section for the last big push. "Thank you to all those who have helped and are helping in handling the hundreds of election-related consultations that have flooded SIOC over the last few days," he wrote. The Public Integrity Section's "reputation as a non-partisan overseer of the Department's election-related policies and election crime portfolio has been evident throughout this cycle."

Amundson reminded his staff not to get caught up in their own opinions about the election, whatever they were. "We set those views aside when doing our important work. To do otherwise would be to betray our very mission."

By November 2025, Amundson's email read like a time capsule from another era, one in which career Justice Department lawyers aggressively investigated corruption in politics, helped protect free and fair elections, and believed they were not just authorized but required to do so. Less than three months after the 2024 election, Amundson would be forced out of the department amid the Trump administration's purge of senior officials.

His group of roughly thirty anti-corruption lawyers, confronted by Emil Bove with an impossible choice over the case against New York City Mayor Eric Adams, would be effectively dismantled. Amundson's successor, Ed Sullivan, went on to lead a section with almost no people working in it—so diminished that even Sullivan's job was deemed temporary.

The Justice Department's work to keep American elections safe, secure, and trusted by voters underwent significant changes as the Trump administration prepared for a high-stakes political contest in 2026 for control of Congress. If the Democrats were to take back the House or Senate or both, they could challenge Trump's ever-expanding presidential power.

Justice Department officials began planning for the midterm elections in late 2025. No longer, the administration decided, would agents and prosecutors around the country call a central hub in Washington to consult with prosecutors on how to handle emerging election cases or threats. In 2026, U.S. attorney offices would handle that work on their own.

Each U.S. attorney's office and each FBI field office has assigned election prosecutors and agents. But some Justice Department veterans thought it risky to give rapid-fire decision-making authority over sensitive election issues to U.S. attorney offices. There was a potential upside, in that decisions made inside those offices might come quicker because less time was spent seeking input from Washington. But those delicate and sometimes consequential decisions would now rest with the U.S. attorneys, a group that included Sigal Chattah, the U.S. attorney in Nevada who had long pushed unfounded claims of mass voter fraud.

The change could also significantly affect the way agents and prosecutors functioned on the ground. The degree of in-house election expertise varied greatly among U.S. attorney offices; many of the prosecutors given the assignment tended to have little experience in such work. And FBI agents in the field were in the habit of rushing out and responding to whatever threat or tip they got. That can sometimes be the wrong move in a nascent election case, where an official government response may bring more public attention to false claims, or may make it look like the government is taking sides in a political contest. Not every social media rant required a federal agent's attention, and not every internet hoax deserved the oxygen of a government inquiry.

In 2024 and other election years, a lot of the advice coming from prosecutors in Washington to agents in the field amounted to essentially this: Calm down, slow down, and don't overreact. The Public Integrity lawyers often reminded agents and prosecutors in the field that plenty of cases could and should be investigated after the election, without any risk to people or evidence. Other times, they had to explain to investigators where the line was between First Amendment–protected speech and true threats under criminal law. Some agents also needed to be reminded that federal law prohibits armed federal personnel at any location where an election is being held, including facilities actively receiving ballots. In the days surrounding the 2024 election, prosecutors in Washington provided more than a thousand consultations with investigators and prosecutors around the country.

Two years later, as the U.S. attorneys were told to figure it out for themselves in 2026, there was less reason to expect such careful advice would be forthcoming. There was also less reason to expect senior officials in Washington to react cautiously to election season alarms or jitters. On her social media feed, Harmeet Dhillon, the head of the Civil Rights Division that was responsible for a host of election issues, sometimes angrily sparred with the administration's critics.

As the administration prepared for the midterm elections, there were plenty of indications that a president who still angrily refused to accept losing the 2020 election might also reject the 2026 results if they didn't go his way. By early 2026, Dhillon's Civil Rights Division had filed lawsuits against roughly half the states in the country—cases that could become grist for future fights over the results of the congressional midterms.

The Justice Department's Civil Rights Division has played an important role over the decades when it comes to enforcing voting rights, but that role was always deliberately limited. The prosecutors who did the hotline work at FBI headquarters were not managing or supervising the election—that job had long been left to the states, with only limited input from the federal government. The job of the FBI and Justice Department in elections is largely to investigate, apprehend, and stop anyone engaged in crimes surrounding an election.

Historically, the feds have focused more on making sure people are able to vote without interference, intimidation, or unfair treatment, and less on tabulating votes and maintaining voter rolls. Dhillon set out to change that. In 2025, she sued more than twenty states and the District of Columbia, demanding access to their non-public voter rolls as part of an administration effort to see if illegal immigrants had committed mass voter fraud.

The voter roll lawsuits were another measure of how different the second Trump term would be from the first. While Trump had attempted something roughly similar with his Presidential Advisory Commission on Election Integrity, he abandoned it in 2018 after efforts to acquire voter roll data ran into a wall of resistance from Republican and Democratic state officials. In the second term, the administration has not given up so easily.

Dhillon insisted there was nothing untoward about making sure states followed laws about keeping careful voter data records. Nearly two dozen states, however, challenged the presumption that the federal government needed the private, personal information of millions upon millions of Americans to determine if the states were following data regulations.

Critics of Dhillon's approach called it wildly inappropriate, a violation of federal privacy laws, and a possible pretext for future challenges to 2026 election results. The effort to establish something akin to a national voting database raised alarms among state voting officials and voting rights experts, partly because it had never been done before and partly because the effort was led by allies of the president who in 2020 had championed bad data, faulty assumptions, or pretzel logic to claim the 2020 election was stolen from Trump.

"No Republican administration or even Democratic administration did voter roll litigation before," Dhillon proudly announced on the *Charlie Kirk Show* podcast at the start of 2026. "There was a lot of hedging and hawing, including from red states, a lot of back-and-forth and then outright refusal to cooperate from many states."

Under Dhillon, the Civil Rights Division also began relitigating the 2020 election that Trump lost. After the defeat, Trump had urged Georgia officials to "find" enough votes for him to win the state. A manual recount in the county ultimately confirmed Biden's victory, but Trump and many of his supporters have refused to accept that. In December 2025, more than five years after the 2020 election, the Justice Department filed a lawsuit against Fulton County, Georgia, seeking to seize and inspect old ballots from that contest. As a private lawyer, Dhillon had raised the specter of voter fraud in Pennsylvania immediately after the 2020 election. In late 2025, as the top civil rights official in the country, she suggested something was seriously amiss in Fulton County's five-year-old results.

After the Fulton lawsuit was filed, she said, "news came out about hundreds of thousands of improperly recorded votes with inappropriate chain of custody and other indicia in Georgia." Dhillon was referring to a problem in which precinct workers had not signed tabulation tapes for about 315,000 votes. But that wasn't fraud; it was sloppy paperwork: There was other documentation indicating the validity of those votes. Yet conservative social media voices quickly trumpeted the idea that hundreds of thousands of fake votes had been cast in Georgia. If that were true, it would certainly call into question the results. But that's not what the evidence showed.

In her comments, Dhillon was still somewhat circumspect, implying, but not actually saying, that the hundreds of thousands of votes were fraudulent. Treading carefully, she skirted around any outright accusations of voter fraud. Current and former lawyers inside the Civil Rights Division saw that as a dangerous kind of game, one where the reality-warping rhetoric could easily be dialed up as election season approached, particularly if Dhillon and other Justice Department leaders faced pressure from the White House or its allies, as Attorney General Bill Barr did when he was pressured by Trump in 2020, causing an irreparable break between the two men.

Those concerns were only amplified by Dhillon's hiring of Eric Neff, a California lawyer with his own checkered past, to be the acting head of the Civil Rights Division's Voting Rights Section. In that job, Neff had a key role in the Justice Department lawsuit against Fulton County. In 2022, when he was working as an assistant district attorney in Los Angeles, Neff had brought criminal charges against an election management software company based in Michigan, accusing the company and its owner, Eugene Yu, of illegally storing data about poll workers on computer servers in China. The criminal charges claimed not actual election fraud, but rather contract fraud by an election services provider. Nevertheless, the case produced the kinds of headlines that

Trump and many of his allies loved, and the former president eagerly embraced Neff's case.

Six weeks after the charges were filed, the district attorney's office dropped them completely. The DA also filed court papers declaring Yu innocent and agreeing to pay him a five-million-dollar settlement.

The *Los Angeles Times* later reported that Neff was the subject of an internal investigation because supervisors in the DA's office had grown concerned that he had hidden the role that a group called True the Vote had played in building the case against Yu. Before and after the 2020 election, True the Vote promoted sensational election fraud claims that were later widely discredited. Neff has filed a lawsuit against the district attorney, denying he did anything wrong.

Even after leaving his job as a prosecutor, Neff seemed drawn to cases involving scurrilous claims of voter fraud. He also represented Patrick Byrne, the former CEO of Overstock, who made a second career out of championing a wild array of unsupported claims about voter fraud, claims that got him sued by both Dominion Voting Systems and President Biden's son Hunter.

As the midterm campaign year began, one of the most pressing questions for the Justice Department was how much it would act as an amplifier and enforcer of unfounded claims of voter fraud—seeking to discredit particular state and county voting systems in accordance with the president's wishes.

The current and former Civil Rights Division lawyers who worried about Trump's Justice Department boosting false claims saw some of their fears realized in early 2026. In January, Trump publicly vowed much tougher action against 2020 election officials, in order to get the kind of election he wants. "It was a rigged election, everybody now knows that, they found out," Trump said. "People will soon be prosecuted for what they did." And if the midterm results failed to please him, more people could be in his line of fire.

A week after those comments, FBI agents descended on an election office building in Fulton County, Georgia, armed with a search warrant to seize all paper ballots, voter rolls, and other data from the 2020 election. The Justice Department was escalating, under the direction of the president, who ordered Tulsi Gabbard, the director of national intelligence, to go to Atlanta to oversee in the search. Her presence at the search, along with that of FBI Deputy Director Andrew Bailey, was far out of step with how their agencies normally operated—the heads of agencies do not participate directly in investigative actions. But presidential discretion once again prevailed. The FBI agents seized hundreds of boxes of paper ballots, a haul of evidence so huge it had to be taken away in trucks.

After the seizure, Gabbard visited with some of the FBI agents, and while she was with them she called the president. At first, he didn't pick up, but he quickly called her back, and Gabbard put Trump on speakerphone to talk to the agents. For many FBI veterans, it was a deeply disquieting moment, one that undermined any pretense of political impartiality to the investigation. And it was a particularly ominous sign, given how much more the Trump Justice Department might do with eight months until the congressional election.

Shortly before the search, Paul W. Brown, the head of the Atlanta FBI office, told officials in headquarters that there was not probable cause to justify a search of the Fulton County offices. Days later, he was told to retire. Brown, a longtime counterterrorism agent who once ran the FBI's high-value-detainee interrogation group, became another casualty in the rolling purge of senior FBI agents deemed disloyal to the Trump administration. He was far from the last.

January 2026 saw Dan Bongino depart his job as deputy director of the FBI and return to his career as a right-wing podcaster. Trump, appearing on Bongino's show days after the FBI search in Fulton County, laid out his intentions for the coming election. "The Republicans should say, 'We want to take over,'" the president said. "We should take over the voting, the voting in at least many— Fifteen places. The Republicans ought to nationalize the voting."

CHAPTER 15

Playing Favorites

The Justice Department's Tax Division had built what prosecutors thought was a slam-dunk case against Roger Ver, known on the internet as Bitcoin Jesus, for his evangelizing for the groundbreaking crypto currency. The prosecutors had gotten significant help in building the case against Ver—from the Messiah himself.

In 2016, Ver had spoken at a conference in Acapulco called Anarchapulco, an annual gathering of what organizers liked to call "self-sovereignty" enthusiasts. Part of Ver's speech succinctly summarized the appeal of the cryptocurrency. "Bitcoin completely undermines the power of every single government on the entire planet to control the money supply, to tax people's income, to control them in any way," he said, "because it makes it so incredibly easy for people to hide their income or evade taxes."

Ver then laughingly described how some of his friends, once they had made money in Bitcoin, asked him for advice on how to conceal that money from the government. "I need your help," he described one friend telling him. "I need you to show me how to hide my Bitcoin so I don't have to pay taxes on it."

When building a case for criminal tax evasion, it helps to have the suspect describe it to a roomful of people. And record it. And post that recording online.

Around 2011, Ver had made hundreds of millions of dollars as an early Bitcoin enthusiast, but his passion against the government went back further. In 2002, he had pleaded guilty to illegally selling explosives online, having used eBay to sell a kind of firework that would soon be outlawed as too large and dangerous. Facing the possibility of being convicted at trial and serving five or more years in prison, Ver took a plea deal for ten months at the Lompoc federal correctional institution in California. When he got out, he ran a company that sold computer equipment and began buying Bitcoin, which jumped so high in value that it was worth hundreds of millions of dollars.

Ver's tax odyssey began in 2014, when he renounced his U.S. citizenship. Giving up citizenship doesn't absolve ex-Americans of their tax obligations arising from when they were Americans. Even though he was no longer a U.S. citizen, Ver was still required to file certain tax forms and to pay taxes on the capital gains of his assets, including Bitcoin. In 2017, he sold roughly $240 million worth of his previously acquired Bitcoin, but never reported it to the IRS.

It took the taxman a long time to catch up, but in 2024, Ver was arrested in Spain on criminal charges of evading U.S. taxes, mail fraud, and filing false tax returns. He was charged with failing to pay $48 million on his cryptocurrency holdings.

Soon after Trump was sworn back into office, Ver publicly appealed to him for help with his case. "Mr. President, I am an American, and I need your help," he posted on social media. "Only you, with your commitment to justice, can save me." Ver said that he, like Trump, was a "victim of lawfare."

In early 2025, the new leaders of the Justice Department were deeply skeptical of the Tax Division. Ketan Bhirud, who worked in Deputy Attorney General Todd Blanche's office, frequently told Tax Division lawyers who handled criminal evasion cases that he didn't believe in what they were doing, despite the fact that he was the person responsible in

Blanche's office for overseeing the division. "I don't give a shit about tax enforcement," Bhirud said more than once. "I don't think it should be a crime."

The Trump administration seemed to agree with him. Of the Justice Department's seven litigation divisions, the Tax Division was the only one singled out in 2025 to be eliminated entirely.

The Tax Division existed for two specific reasons. First, to enforce the tax laws of the United States, a role that brought in many times more revenue than it cost to staff the division. Unlike most parts of the federal government, the Tax Division paid for itself and then some. The second reason the Tax Division at Main Justice was critical was that it forced the government to follow a nationwide standard for tax enforcement so that a tax cheat in Alabama wouldn't be treated significantly differently from one in Alaska. Similar to how the Public Integrity Section once oversaw public corruption cases around the country, the Tax Division in Washington existed to ensure consistency across the country.

The Trump administration decided to throw that away. In the spring, a memo from Blanche called for the elimination of the Tax Division, with its responsibilities divvied up among U.S. attorney offices around the country. It was a recipe for uneven enforcement, and the veteran tax lawyers in the division tried to change their bosses' minds. They half succeeded.

Blanche eventually decided that the Tax Division would still die, but rather than cut it up into tiny pieces, he sliced it in half. Criminal tax enforcement work moved over to the Justice Department's Criminal Division, and civil enforcement was shipped off to the Civil Division.

Since the Watergate era, the Tax Division had been allowed to operate largely on its own, walled off from interference by bureaucracy and by a section of federal law that expressly forbids the unauthorized sharing of taxpayer information and carries criminal penalties for anyone who does. The law was necessary because the Nixon administration had expended great effort to use the Internal Revenue Service against their political opponents, with Nixon's chief of staff, John Dean, complaining in a memo that changes were needed because he had been "unable to obtain information in the possession of the IRS regarding our political enemies" and "unable to stimulate audits of persons who should be audited." Dean's memos were blunt and got straight to the point, with one helpfully titled "Dealing with our Political Enemies."

After Nixon resigned in disgrace, Congress passed a new law, called 6103, making it a crime punishable by up to five years in prison if one makes an unauthorized disclosure of federal tax information. In that way, the Tax Division was unique among many other parts of the department. The 6103 language made it very difficult for the Trump administration to use the Tax Division to get revenge or engage in retribution campaigns against President Trump's enemies the way other parts of the Justice Department were used to publicly attack Trump's perceived enemies.

Large sections of the Justice Department had always relied on men and women of good character to make good-faith decisions and to subject themselves to meaningful ethical standards. But those were not codified in any way, so when the Trump administration decided to kill the charges against New York's mayor in the hope that Adams might help them with immigration enforcement, there was little on the law books to stop them.

The Tax Division, however, did have a law: 6103. And not even the attorney general or the deputy attorney general could erase it from the law books. But if the administration couldn't use the Tax Division in 2025 to punish their enemies, they could at least use it to help their friends. And they had a friend in Bitcoin Jesus.

Roger Ver hired an ex-Trump lawyer, Christopher Kise, to make his case to the Trump administration. Kise had stayed out of the government when other Trump lawyers like Blanche, Bove, and Sauer had gone in. That decision helped make him one of the most sought-after, and highest-paid, lawyers seeking to end or weaken criminal cases against their client. Kise also did a brisk, lucrative business in seeking pardons for his clients.

When the Trump administration came into power, the Tax Division lawyers handling the Ver case slowly realized that Kise had begun negotiating directly with Bhirud and others in Blanche's office.

Justice Department leaders who had once agreed that the case against Ver was a slam dunk now pressed the prosecutors to settle it on terms very favorable to Kise. At times, it seemed like the senior officials negotiating the deal were most interested in crafting one that kept Kise happy.

Negotiating with Kise proved difficult. He insisted that his client not serve any prison time, a condition that violated the department's basic objective of pursuing large tax evasion cases as criminal matters deserving time behind bars. Even more alarming than the terms under negotiation was who was doing the negotiating for the department. For decades, the Justice Department's political appointees generally gave the tax division a wide berth to handle criminal cases, lest they be accused of political interference and unethical conduct. But the Ver case was entirely different, as the negotiations were taken over by Blanche's office. Bhirud seemed determine to cut a deal that would allow Ver not only to go free, but to pay only what he owed, and also one that didn't explicitly accuse him of fraud.

As the two sides got closer to a sweetheart deal with no prison time for Ver, Bhirud and others pressed for language in a deferred prosecution agreement that would ensure Ver didn't talk about how he had bested the Justice Department. The administration was willing to give Ver a very generous deal, but they didn't want him bragging about it.

Ver got his settlement in October 2025, agreeing to pay nearly $50 million to have the indictment dismissed. Inside the Tax Division, it was a demoralizing result, one that even senior Justice Department officials seemed to realize was potentially damaging to their reputations. Aaron Henricks, another lawyer working in Todd Blanche's office, remarked at a meeting that the department was starting to get pushback from Republicans in Congress about the appearance of favoritism in how they were handling tax cases. Karen Kelly, a veteran Tax Division lawyer not known for holding her tongue, said pointedly, "The appearance of favoritism? No. We're talking about actual favoritism, plain and simple."

She left the Justice Department soon after.

In a bureaucratic sense, the tax enforcers at the Justice Department lost the war in 2025: They saw their division dismantled. But they also were able to preserve some of the important work the division does, largely because tax enforcement had a more rigid set of not just policies, but also rules and laws guiding their work. When a senior official in Blanche's office asked tax enforcers if they could launch tax investigations into activists who may have provided anti-Trump protesters with protective riot gear, they were rebuffed by the career lawyers, and the senior official dropped the matter.

President Richard Nixon was in a bad mood on the afternoon of April 19, 1971, and he dispensed quickly with the formalities in his phone call to Richard Kleindienst, his deputy attorney general at the Justice Department. Fortunately for historians, this moment in presidential corruption was preserved on tape.

"I want something clearly understood," Nixon growled, as he started to complain about the head of the department's Antitrust Division, Richard McLaren. "And if it is not understood, McLaren's ass is to be out within one hour," the president said.

Nixon was calling about a delicate antitrust case involving International Telephone and Telegraph. IT&T had pledged $400,000—the equivalent of $3.2 million in 2025 dollars—to help pay for Nixon's 1972 Republican Convention. An internal company memo said the payment was part of a deal to get the Antitrust Division to drop its opposition to IT&T's acquisition of the Hartford Fire Insurance Company.

Nixon ordered the Justice Department to abandon the case and clear the way for the deal. "The IT&T thing, stay the hell out of it. Is that clear? That's an order," he snapped.

Kleindienst started to ask, "You mean your order is to—"

"The order is to leave the goddamned thing alone. Now, I've said this, Dick, a number of times and you fellows apparently don't get the message over there. I do not want McLaren to run around prosecuting people, raising hell about conglomerates, stirring things up at this point. Now you keep him the hell out of that. Is that clear?"

Kleindienst tried to answer, but Nixon kept going.

"Or either he resigns," the president said, referring to McLaren. "I'd rather have him out anyway. I don't like the son of a bitch."

Kleindienst tried to bring up a court deadline looming over the case, but Nixon was having none of it.

"I know all the legal things, Dick. You don't have to spell out the legal—" the president started again, but now it was Kleindienst's turn to interrupt.

"The brief has to be filed tomorrow," the deputy attorney general said.

"Don't file the brief," Nixon shot back.

"Your order is not to file a brief?" Kleindienst asked, seemingly confused by Nixon's cut-to-the-chase corruption.

"My order is to drop the goddamn thing. Is that clear?" Nixon barked.

"Yeah, I understand that," Kleindienst finally conceded.

"Okay," Nixon said, hanging up with a note of exasperation that the seventy-one-second conversation had taken even that long.

When it was revealed, the conversation ultimately led to Kleindienst pleading guilty to withholding information from Congress when he had denied there had been any political pressure in the case.

Mostly forgotten now amid the larger, more memorable scandal of Watergate, the IT&T scandal gained sudden new relevance in 2025, when allegations of unsavory backroom dealmaking set off a fratricidal fight within the Trump administration and the Justice Department.

That Nixon-Kleindienst conversation, and the settlement the Nixon Justice Department later struck with the company, also led Congress to pass a law called the Tunney Act, which provides a level of judicial and public scrutiny to antitrust settlements. When the Antitrust Division settles a merger case, or any other civil antitrust case, the Tunney Act allows judges to scrutinize the deal to make sure nothing inappropriate is done against the public interest.

Since its creation during the Great Depression, the Justice Department's Antitrust Division has sought to enforce federal laws like the Sherman and Clayton Antitrust Acts, which try to prevent monopolies or a concentration of economic power. Beginning with the railroads in the 1800s, Americans had grown increasingly worried about big businesses becoming so dominant that they would gouge consumers with high prices, or treat workers unfairly by suppressing wages. The goal of the Antitrust Division is to ensure enough genuine competition in the marketplace that companies must vie for consumers in a race with one another for business.

To try to maintain healthy competition, the division focuses on a few types of activity: corporate mergers, price-fixing, and monopolistic behavior by megacompanies. In recent years, much of the Antitrust Division's focus has been on tech companies, as firms like Google and Apple have become not only national but global behemoths.

In December 2024, many lawyers at the Antitrust Division were cautiously optimistic about the new administration, particularly when Trump announced that his nominee to run the division, Gail Slater, would take on Big Tech, which he complained had "run wild for years." While Trump was a business-loving CEO who prided himself on the "art of the deal," as a politician, he had a decidedly populist bent and a base of support among corporation skeptics within the Republican Party.

For decades, the GOP had been a pro–big business party and generally considered antagonistic to the kind of aggressive antitrust enforcement favored by some Democrats. But Trump liked to pick fights with big companies, and the populist branch of the Republican Party usually cheered tough antitrust enforcement of tech companies. Many of Trump's MAGA supporters followed his lead in accusing social media companies of censoring conservatives and boosting liberals, particularly when it came to the public health arguments surrounding the Covid-19 pandemic.

Inside the Antitrust Division, lawyers had a general sense that the new Trump administration could be a nightmare for other parts of the Justice Department, but that they themselves might be spared.

Big corporate mergers involved billions of dollars, and government approval of such mergers was worth a fortune to those companies. For that reason, corporations seeking approval for mergers were uniquely vulnerable to pressure from the government, and that vulnerability meant huge opportunities for Trump allies outside government—lobbyists, lawyers, or even just well-connected social media influencers—to get paid.

Antitrust, one Justice Department veteran observed, was an ideal spot for lobbyists to plant a tollbooth on corporate deals and rake in millions of dollars. It's also a relatively niche corner of the legal landscape, one that doesn't attract much public attention most of the time. Antitrust could also be lucrative work for the law firms specializing in it, helping companies with cutting-edge computer technology and global business practices to navigate laws that were first written for the age of steam engines.

About a month after the 2024 election, Antitrust officials held what they call a "last-rites" meeting, with lawyers and executives for Hewlett Packard Enterprise, which had announced earlier that year a $14 billion takeover of Juniper Networks. The combined company would end a rivalry in the wireless networking industry, which provided wireless technology systems to business clients like corporations, hospitals, and universities. Biden administration officials had been reviewing the deal for months, but the imminent arrival of the second Trump term put a deadline on a decision by the government.

At the division, a last-rites meeting is meant to be the final, most serious conversation before the government decides whether to file a lawsuit to block a planned merger or accuse a corporation of misconduct. It's a moment when, after a phalanx of lawyers have spent months discussing the intricacies of a corporate deal, the top officials on the government side and the corporate side sit down and look each other in the eye to see if they are going to fight in court. It's not an exaggeration to say billions of dollars can be at stake.

In late 2024, many in the Biden administration were running on fumes, finishing as much of their to-do list as they could before the

Trump team took over. The views of the Antitrust Division's experts who had analyzed the HPE-Juniper deal were decidedly mixed on it.

On the one hand, there were real problems in turning a marketplace of three major competitors into just two. This was the kind of near-monopoly condition the Antitrust Division had been built to stop. However, there was also a sense within the administration that the agency did not have the resources or the personnel to pursue the case in court, so it might be better off to simply save their lawyerly ammunition for a larger, more important issue down the road.

But given the timing of the last-rites meeting, it was unclear how much the Biden administration's opinions even mattered. As the sides sat down, everyone understood the company could simply push back the agreed-upon December 24 deadline for a decision and wait to see if they got better treatment from the Trump administration.

At the end of the meeting, Hewlett Packard Enterprise chose to extend its own deadline into 2025. So, the last-rites meeting ended up being a second-to-last-rites meeting. In late January 2025, just days into the new Trump administration, the two sides met again. This time, the government side was led by the new, temporary head of Antitrust, Omeed Assefi.

Assefi had worked in the U.S. attorney office in Washington for years before he arrived at the Antitrust Division in mid-2024 to serve as a criminal trial attorney. His selection to run the entire division while the department awaited Slater's Senate confirmation came as a complete surprise to the Antitrust staff. He clearly had connections. During the first Trump term, he had worked at the White House handling the Robert S. Mueller III special counsel investigation.

At Antitrust, he was suddenly supervising people with decades more experience than he had. Wearing cowboy boots with a Trump logo on them, he brought what colleagues described as a "bro" vibe to meetings. He was also close with Ed Martin, the wrecking ball of a U.S. attorney in DC who had fired prosecutors, tried to charge Senator Charles Schumer with crimes over a weekend, and operated as Trump's "weaponization" general inside the Justice Department.

HPE's pitch in late January for merger approval had changed drastically from the previous last-rites meeting. The company's slideshow featured a gauzy quote from Marco Rubio, Trump's new secretary of state. And the core argument suddenly emphasized that the merger would benefit national security, because America needed a tech company to compete with the Chinese behemoth Huawei. The government lawyers were skeptical on that point, given that Huawei was banned from competing in the U.S. market.

The government talked tough in the last-rites meeting, but privately, staff lawyers at Antitrust had already recommended against filing a lawsuit to stop the merger. Assefi, their new temporary boss, thought differently and ordered them to file the suit.

The 180-degree turnaround on a huge merger surprised many of the staff, but the new administration's handling of the case only got stranger. Mike Davis, an influential Republican activist who leads a group called the Article III Project, initially opposed the merger, posting on social media, "3 into 2? You must sue," a reference to the concerns about the consolidation of major players in the industry. Then HPE hired Davis to fight in favor of it.

Davis held unique sway in Washington in 2025. He had previously worked as the chief counsel for nominations for Senator Charles Grassley, the Republican chairman of the Senate judiciary committee, and his Article III Project was a major player in selecting Trump nominees for judicial positions and some Justice Department positions. In Republican circles, Davis was generally viewed as having the power to kill a judicial nomination.

But he didn't necessarily have the juice or the legal arguments to convince the Antitrust Division. Having already decided to sue to stop the HPE deal, officials there were not swayed by the new arguments about letting the deal go through to counter Huawei. Slater, now confirmed by the Senate as the head of the Antitrust Division, shared the view of two of her top aides, Roger Alford and Bill Rinner, that there was little reason to change their analysis of the basic competitive issues.

In the spring, Davis proceeded to negotiate on HPE's behalf with

Chad Mizelle, the chief of staff to Pam Bondi, and with Stan Woodward, who had been nominated to the number three position at the Justice Department. There were reasons those two people might be more susceptible to pressure from Davis than most other Justice Department officials. Mizelle's wife was widely known to be under consideration for a federal appeals court nomination—a nomination that Davis could spike if he chose to. Woodward was a nominee waiting for a Senate vote. Angering Davis could spell disaster for both prospects.

By going above the Antitrust Division lawyers to negotiate directly with the department's political leaders, Davis was taking an unusual step that disregarded how such negotiations normally worked. Traditionally the political leaders of the department are not part of such discussions. But at both the Tax and Antitrust Divisions, career lawyers found high-stakes negotiations on sensitive cases were brusquely taken over by political leaders of the department.

As Davis went around Slater and her team, tensions mounted inside the department. Slater and Davis were good friends and worked together years earlier on conservative issues surrounding social media companies, but suddenly they were at odds.

In June, Mizelle announced that the Justice Department had reached a settlement to withdraw the lawsuit. HPE got its merger approval, making only a minor concession. The deal was signed by political appointees, not a single career staffer, which was a remarkable admission of how much the career lawyers at the department disagreed with the result.

The settlement, however, did not end the battle inside the department. Privately, Davis threatened to have Justice Department lawyers fired for their obstinance—a remarkable flex of the power he seemed to wield in the Trump administration. About a month after the HPE settlement, Slater's deputies, Alford and Rinner, were called into a tense meeting with Mizelle and put on administrative leave. Their bios were also wiped from the Justice Department website, leading many of their colleagues to believe they had been fired. Days later, they were dismissed, purportedly for insubordination.

Alford returned to his law professor job at Notre Dame, and in August he gave a speech at a tech conference to call out what he saw as a corruption of antitrust law enforcement work by lobbyists. "Chad Mizelle and Stanley Woodward perverted justice and acted inconsistent with the rule of law," Alford said. "I am not given to hyperbole, and I do not say that lightly."

Alford was a Republican who believed antitrust work was important to protecting Americans from abusive megacorporations and that such work was a central part of Trump's appeal to MAGA voters. He urged the courts to hold a Tunney hearing to get to the bottom of what had happened between Davis, Mizelle, and Woodward. "All it took to be fired were lobbyists exerting influence on my superiors to retaliate against me for protecting the rule of law against the rule of lobbyists," Alford said in his speech.

At the Justice Department, Alford's former boss Gail Slater tried to reassert her authority over Antitrust decisions and convince White House and Justice Department officials that this was no way to run a railroad—or a division of the Justice Department. The government's double reversal on the HPE deal was just one more example of the frequent chaos inside Justice in 2025. The HPE outcome could also be viewed as natural in an administration that believed above all else in cutting deals and where deals were often struck within a clubby network of well-connected insiders. People like Mike Davis. Or Christopher Kise.

While the influence of Davis, and separately Kise, rose within the department, Slater, who actually ran a Justice Department division, saw her authority further weakened until, in early 2026, she was forced out of the administration. Davis, her former friend, took a public victory lap over her ouster. "These sanctimonious federal prosecutors who don't think they are accountable to anyone drive me crazy," he told me. "President Trump learned his lesson from the first term. He's not going to put up with their bullshit this time." As Trump-style dealmaking in tax cases and corporate mergers set off alarm bells for Justice Department staffers, the administration also signaled a shift in the types of fraud cases it cared about. From Minnesota to California to Ohio, the Trump administration vowed to crack down on social services fraud. The White House even announced a new senior Justice Department position— which, officials said, would report directly to the White House—to pursue such investigations. But the same administration had taken steps to dial back corporate fraud investigations. Trump claimed that some types of white-collar crime enforcement, like foreign corporate bribery cases, hurt America's ability to compete for business overseas.

While the administration seemed eager to go after fraud in government spending, many current and former Justice Department lawyers worried that the second Trump administration heralded a new leniency with consumer fraud and corporate executives lining their own pockets. White House officials talked about the second Trump term as a "golden age" in America, but more than one Justice Department lawyer privately predicted a golden age of white-collar crime.

CHAPTER 16

The Library Strikes Back

Emily Austin, a twenty-three-year-old conservative social media influencer, stood in a black dress outside the West Wing of the White House. Austin—whose previous political activity included launching a group called Hot Girls for Cuomo, to support the former New York State Governor Andrew Cuomo in his unsuccessful effort to become New York City mayor—was excited and proud.

It was the afternoon of February 27, 2025, and Austin had just emerged from the West Wing, where she and roughly a dozen social media influencers had met with President Trump, Secretary of State Marco Rubio, Attorney General Pam Bondi, and FBI Director Kash Patel.

Austin proudly held a large white binder. Red letters on the cover read THE EPSTEIN FILES: PHASE 1. Splashed diagonally across the cover, in huge gray type, was the word DECLASSIFIED.

Days earlier, Bondi had been asked on Fox News about a supposed "client list" of Jeffrey Epstein's. "It's sitting on my desk right now," she said, ramping up public expectations that damning revelations were about to break.

In a video posted to her Instagram account, Austin triumphantly tapped the side of the heavy binder. "Look at what we got today. The Epstein files, baby!" she crowed.

When Austin and the other influencers walked out of the White House, a group of photographers happened to be standing nearby, waiting to take pictures of British Prime Minister Keir Starmer, who had come to discuss the war in Ukraine. The photographers turned their lenses to snap photos of the influencers displaying their binders like trophies they had won. Some influencers smiled and laughed.

Wearing a cowboy hat, the conservative political commentator Chad Prather called his binder a "souvenir" of his White House visit. "The Trump DOJ has EVERYTHING," he wrote on social media.

Rogan O'Handley, a forty-year-old right-wing commentator who went by the social media handle "DC Draino," sternly raised a binder above his head and held it there dramatically. O'Handley later admitted that they were "giddy" about having gotten the binders from Bondi. "I realized the enormity of this document," he said later, "or at least what we thought was in there."

The binders' contents were a waste of office supplies. Each binder contained four tabs, marked A, B, C, and D, and the contents were no more classified or declassified than the letters of the alphabet. They included flight logs made public years earlier, during a trial, and an address book that belonged to Jeffrey Epstein and had been circulating on the internet for years.

The binder was a bust, one that even Republicans denounced as a dumb publicity stunt. Bondi's love of props at her public events had created a huge headache not just for her and the eager-to-please influencers, but also for the president and his administration. A tsunami of online mockery put the influencers on the defensive. Seeking to convince her followers that she was not a fool, Austin argued that the binders were proof of how FBI agents and prosecutors had tried to trick Bondi. "If there's anyone to be mad at, it's the deep state," she insisted in a video stream later that day.

The fight over the Epstein files—a poorly understood, frequently misused term—would metastasize into the largest self-inflicted crisis of President Trump's first year, a major setback for him that was fueled in large part by Bondi and Patel's enthusiastic embrace of the speculation and suspicion that surrounded the disgraced and long-dead financier.

The "Epstein files" was the shorthand name for decades' worth of FBI documents, emails, photographs, and videos gathered over multiple investigations of Jeffrey Epstein for sex trafficking and of his sudden jail cell death in 2019.

Epstein, a millionaire financier who partied with the rich and powerful in Manhattan and Palm Beach, Florida, had for years used his staff to recruit high school girls to come to his home and give him massages, which he then turned into sexual abuse. The girls were generally paid two or three hundred dollars for each "massage."

An investigation by Florida officials and the FBI led to Epstein pleading guilty in 2008 to state charges of soliciting prostitution from a minor. But the terms of his plea deal proved incredibly lenient, allowing him to come and go from the jail where he resided for all of thirteen months. As part of the deal, the U.S. attorney in Florida agreed to forgo federal charges against him that could have meant decades in prison.

In 2018, a series of reports by the *Miami Herald* refocused public attention on how Epstein had used his money and connections to escape more serious punishment for his crimes. The following year, Manhattan federal prosecutors filed new charges against him. Epstein was arrested and held without bail while awaiting trial.

On August 10, 2019, barely a month after his arrest, jail guards found him dead in his cell, hanging by a bedsheet. Subsequent investigations presented compelling evidence to conclude he had killed himself, but many portions of the public were not convinced. Epstein's death would fuel years of speculation that he had been killed to cover up the sins of his powerful and famous friends.

The conspiracy theories around Epstein often fell along political lines. Many Republicans suspected Bill Clinton was a co-conspirator. Democrats thought Epstein's yearslong, well-documented friendship with Trump, which apparently ended in the early 2000s, meant the president had to know what his friend had done.

Everyone who had a theory about Epstein generally agreed on one thing: The FBI knew who knew about Epstein. The answers they wanted were sitting somewhere in FBI servers, and public demands for those answers only grew in the years after Epstein's death.

In creating the FBI, Hoover had envisioned not just a professional workforce of sharp-eyed investigators, but also a vast library of the information those investigators collected—information that could be effectively searched for proverbial needles in a haystack that would solve crimes all over the country. For close to a half century as FBI director, Hoover had zealously guarded that library of files as his domain.

During the 2024 presidential campaign, many of Trump's backers had vowed to throw open the doors to that library and give Congress and the public access to files about everything, ranging from the January 6, 2021, riot at the U.S. Capitol to the JFK assassination and Jeffrey Epstein.

Kash Patel was so eager to fulfill that mission that one of his first acts as director was to order a massive review of the Epstein files in early 2025. Most of the FBI agents and analysts thrown at the task lacked the experience to know how to examine that material and redact information about victims or other innocent people. The small cadre of FBI employees who normally reviewed internal documents for public release are given extensive training and then learn the process from more experienced peers. The Epstein document reviewers, by contrast, were given a quick tutorial, an angry pep talk, and an enormous task.

They repeatedly made mistakes. Then they were told to do it again.

"We have no idea what we're doing," said one person assigned to the work. "The people telling us what to do know even less."

Through the spring of 2025, the Epstein file review overseen by Patel and his deputy Dan Bongino was widely considered a disaster by the rank-and-file agents, a feedback loop of rushed instructions, failed execution, and then orders to start over.

In May, Bondi and her deputy, Todd Blanche, held a meeting with the president to discuss several Justice Department issues. In that meeting, Bondi told the president that his name appeared in some of the still-secret Epstein documents, along with those of other high-profile people. It wasn't entirely a surprise: Trump's name had surfaced in previous documents. But the embarrassing detail soon leaked out due to an ugly fight the president had with billionaire Elon Musk.

Their breakup came over Trump's "Big Beautiful Bill," a massive piece of legislation that would accomplish a number of Trump policy objectives but drive up the national debt in the process. Musk hated it. "Time to drop the really big bomb," he wrote on social media. Trump, he said, "is in the Epstein files. That is the real reason they have not been made public. Have a nice day, DJT!" In another post, Musk added, "It's a cover up (obviously)."

Asked by a reporter if he had been told he was in the Epstein files, the president denied it.

Then, in July, after Bondi, Patel, and Bongino had spent months raising expectations that shocking Epstein documents would soon be released, the Trump administration completely reversed itself. In a July 7 statement that no one at the Justice Department or FBI was willing to put their name on, officials said there would be no further releases of Epstein documents.

"As part of our commitment to transparency," the memo began, and then went on to describe a "systematic review" that revealed there was no "incriminating 'client list.'" The memo said there was "no credible evidence found that Epstein blackmailed prominent individuals as part of his actions. We did not uncover evidence that could predicate an investigation against uncharged third parties."

In trying to end the speculation, the Trump administration only further inflamed it. Along with the July memo, the Justice Department released security video from the hallway outside Epstein's jail cell on the night he died, to show that no one was seen moving toward or away from the cell in the critical period.

Reporters then pointed out to the administration that there appeared to be a missing minute in the video, at precisely midnight. Officials scrambled to explain that there was nothing suspicious about that,

that it was just the result of the security system resetting every twenty-four hours. But even that answer fell apart under closer scrutiny—it was later revealed that the video released by the Justice Department had actually been stitched together from two separate recordings after the original recording had been destroyed as unnecessary evidence. Inside the FBI, technical experts theorized that when the two periods were stitched together, they failed to cover precisely one minute of the recording, which could not be recovered.

Such answers were deeply unsatisfying to the public and the slice of social media that had spent years speculating about who had done what with Epstein. For years, those investigators had privately bemoaned to me the seemingly unkillable conspiracy theories that gained new life after Epstein's death. The Epstein issue was the latest in a string of dark conspiratorial fantasies—from QAnon to claims that Venezuelan software stole the 2020 election to arguments that the January 6 riot was secretly orchestrated by FBI agents—that motivated and animated segments of Trump supporters.

By July 2025, the belief that the government was hiding the truth about Epstein was not something Trump could just order people to ignore. But he tried. "Nobody cares" about Epstein, he declared angrily as he tried to tamp down the anger over the announcement that no more files would be released.

The president complained on social media that his supporters are "all going after Attorney General Pam Bondi, who is doing a FANTASTIC JOB! We're on one Team, MAGA, and I don't like what's happening." But whatever he said, his followers still wanted to look inside the FBI's library of secrets.

The fallout from the July announcement that no more files would be released was severe among the very social media swarms the administration had counted as their biggest allies. Bondi in particular lost a tremendous amount of credibility inside and outside the administration. Under pressure from influencers, podcasters, and social media bots, senior law enforcement officials began blaming one another.

FBI Deputy Director Dan Bongino accused Bondi of raising public expectations for the files with talk of a client list that would never be produced. At a White House meeting, a furious Bondi accused Bongino of leaking details to the press, something he denied. For a few days, it seemed Bongino might quit in disgust.

Nine days after shutting down the review of Epstein documents, the Trump administration fired Assistant U.S. Attorney Maurene Comey, the federal prosecutor in New York who had worked on the Epstein case and who had won the 2022 conviction of Ghislaine Maxwell, Epstein's former aide who recruited many of his victims.

Maurene Comey was an accomplished prosecutor in her own right, but she was also the daughter of James Comey, the former FBI director Trump had long despised. Within the Justice Department, her firing was viewed as further evidence that the president's revenge campaign was expanding. And no one in the Justice Department's top ranks, it seemed, was going to stand in Trump's way.

In a farewell letter, Comey warned her colleagues not to give in to the fear the Trump administration was trying to spread through the ranks of the Justice Department. "If a career prosecutor can be fired without reason, fear may seep into the decisions of those who remain. Do not let that happen. Fear is the tool of a tyrant, wielded to suppress independent thought," she wrote. "Instead of fear, let this moment fuel the fire that already burns at the heart of this place. A fire of righteous indignation at abuses of power. Of commitment to seek justice for victims. Of dedication to truth above all else."

Even if her firing was more about her father than her cases, the dismissal of Maurene Comey only brought more public attention to how strangely the Trump administration behaved when it came to anything related to Epstein.

A day after Comey was dismissed, *The Wall Street Journal* reported that Trump had once contributed to a book of birthday messages for Epstein, and Trump's entry featured a hand-drawn outline of a naked woman, with his signature placed where the pubic hair would be. Written inside the curves of the woman's body was a conversation between Epstein and Trump.

Voice Over: There must be more to life than having everything

Donald: Yes, there is, but I won't tell you what it is.

Jeffrey: Nor will I, since I also know what it is.

Donald: We have certain things in common, Jeffrey.

Jeffrey: Yes, we do, come to think of it.

Donald: Enigmas never age, have you noticed that?

Jeffrey: As a matter of fact, it was clear to me the last time I saw you.

Donald: A pal is a wonderful thing. Happy Birthday—and may every day be another wonderful secret.

Trump denied he'd ever written or drawn such a thing. "I don't draw pictures," he declared, and he sued the *Journal*.

A week later, Deputy Attorney General Todd Blanche flew to Florida to interview Ghislaine Maxwell, who had a long way to go to finish her twenty-year prison sentence. Interviewing Maxwell came with significant political and legal risks. Maxwell had had numerous opportunities earlier in her case to cooperate, and she had not. Now any information she might offer could fairly be seen as a ploy by a criminal seeking a pardon or a reduction in her sentence.

What was particularly unusual, however, was Blanche's decision to conduct the interview himself. No one I spoke to at the Justice Department could recall anything comparable, when the second-most-powerful official personally investigated and interviewed a prison inmate. If Justice Department leaders wanted to interview Maxwell, the far more rational choice to do so would have been the prosecutor who had put her in prison—but Maurene Comey had been fired days earlier.

Trump's approach to the Maxwell case had been strange from the start. When Maxwell was indicted in 2020, he spoke sympathetically of his old friend. "I haven't really been following it too much. I just wish her well, frankly," he told reporters. "I've met her numerous times over the years, especially since I lived in Palm Beach and I guess they lived in Palm Beach." Whatever the case was about, he added, "I wish her well."

Blanche's interview with Maxwell stretched over two days. She said she had no incriminating evidence against Trump. "I never witnessed the president in any inappropriate setting in any way," she said. "In the times that I was with him, he was a gentleman in all respects"—a statement that echoed what Virginia Giuffre, one of Epstein's most out-spoken victims, had also said about Trump. Maxwell also denied the basic charges against Epstein and said those who had been friends and associates of his had been unfairly smeared just for being close to him. "Some are in your cabinet, who you value as coworkers," she said, with-out specifying whom she meant.

Blanche quickly moved on to another topic. It wasn't the only time in the interview he seemed to veer away from obvious and necessary follow-up questions.

One of the most popular conspiracy theories surrounding Epstein was that he was a secret agent or an asset of Mossad, the Israeli intelli-gence agency, and that the reason his crimes were allowed to go on for so long was because intelligence agencies had shielded him.

Maxwell denied that, but her answers seemed to open a door that Blanche did not want to pass through.

When he asked if she had ever had contact with a Mossad agent, she replied, "Well, not deliberately."

"Pardon me?" Blanche asked.

"Not deliberately," Maxwell repeatedly coolly.

Blanche did not ask her what she meant.

Within days of the interview, Maxwell was transferred to a prison camp in Texas with less security and better living conditions, even though prison regulations call for sex offenders not to be placed in such facilities. Blanche later told NBC that Maxwell was moved for security reasons. "She was suffering numerous and numerous threats against her life," he said.

The Maxwell interview did little to slow the momentum building in Congress for legislation that would force the Justice Department to re-lease the Epstein files. In November, that effort only got stronger when congressional Democrats released emails from Epstein's estate that sug-gested Trump had known about Epstein's behavior.

An April 2, 2011, email from Epstein to Maxwell read, "I want you to realize that that dog that hasn't barked is Trump." One victim, Epstein wrote, "spent hours at my house with him, he has never once been mentioned. Police chief, etc. im [*sic*] 75% there," he wrote.

Maxwell replied, "I have been thinking about that . . ."

While maddeningly vague, the emails were damning in that the villain's own words indicated that there was more to know about Trump's dealings with him.

In 2019, as Epstein faced renewed public attention over his past crimes and lenient plea deal, he emailed someone else, saying that Trump "said he asked me to resign" from the Mar-a-Lago club, but Epstein insisted that he was "never a member ever." The financier added, "Of course he knew about the girls as he asked Ghislaine to stop."

The emails made it increasingly inevitable that Congress would force the administration to release the files. Representative Lauren Boebert, a Colorado Republican, was summoned to a meeting at the White House Situation Room with senior administration officials, including the attorney general and the FBI director. The meeting was the capstone to a monthslong pressure campaign by Trump and his allies to get Boebert to drop her support for the legislation that would force the Justice Department to review and release any files about Epstein that did not compromise national security or victim identities. Boebert refused to back down.

Shortly before Thanksgiving, the House passed the Epstein Files Transparency Act, in a vote of 427–1, followed by easy passage in the Senate. The supposedly razor-thin margin lawmakers had spent months fighting over had given way to nearly universal support. Acknowledging defeat, the president quickly signed it. The law gave the Justice Department thirty days to produce the files.

For years, Trump had used his political strengths to overcome legal dangers. After the defeat on the Epstein legislation, he tried to use the levers of the criminal justice system to save himself from a political setback. Days before the vote, he ordered the Justice Department to open a criminal investigation into Epstein's "involvement and relationship" with Democrats, including Bill Clinton. The Epstein issue was a "hoax involving Democrats, not Republicans," Trump declared. Asked by reporters if it was right for him to be ordering up criminal investigations, he said, "I'm the chief law enforcement officer of the country. I'm allowed to do it."

The president had taken the finer points of the Supreme Court's 2024 immunity decision to heart and declared himself in charge of prosecutions. The investigation he ordered was assigned to Jay Clayton, the head of the Manhattan federal prosecutor's office. In December, about a month after taking the Trump assignment, Clayton golfed with the president in Florida, according to people familiar with the matter.

Inside the Justice Department, the new law meant another crisis. Nearly two hundred lawyers in the National Security Division—almost every lawyer who worked there—was assigned to start reviewing Epstein documents in order to comply with the transparency act, which gave the administration until December 19 to release them. The Justice Department decided that the multiple reviews that had been conducted by FBI personnel in the spring were such a mess, they would have to start over again.

Some of the department's National Security lawyers were sent to Secure Compartmented Information Facilities, or SCIFs, to review files. To many Justice Department staff unlucky enough to get the assignment, the reason for sending them to SCIFs seemed obvious—secrecy. Phones are not allowed in SCIFs, so employees could not take a picture of any documents even if they wanted to.

Other lawyers were allowed to work on some of the material at their office or remotely, but the sprawling document review, which included at least one unverified and possibly false tip to the FBI about sexual misconduct by Trump against a minor, left many lawyers suspicious about how many of the documents they reviewed would eventually see the light of day.

A week before Christmas, the department released roughly one hundred thousand pages of Epstein documents, including many pictures. Trump aides pointed reporters to the photos of Bill Clinton, trying to turn the political debacle for Trump into, if not a win, then at least a draw.

Representative Thomas Massie, a Kentucky Republican, who had pushed for months to release the documents, said the administration had failed to comply with the law by not supplying all the files and by heavily redacting many of them. In one instance, a photo of a credenza in Epstein's house, on which sat a photo of Trump, was posted on the Justice Department website. Hours later, the photo was removed from the department's online collection, raising fresh suspicions that the DOJ was trying to minimize the political harm to the president while playing up the photos of Clinton. Officials put the Trump photo back up online, saying they had taken it down only out of temporary concern it might show victims.

"We are not redacting information about President Trump," Blanche pledged publicly on December 21, saying there were roughly a million pages to sort through.

Less than two weeks later, sources shared with me a new, alarming estimate: There were roughly 5.2 million pages of Epstein file documents, and more lawyers would be drafted into the effort to review them all. Nearly a year into the Trump administration's effort to review and release Epstein documents, the people running the department seemed still not to know how many documents they were talking about.

About 125 lawyers from the U.S. Attorney's Office in Manhattan were assigned to the Epstein document review. That was more than half the attorneys employed by the most consequential federal prosecutor's office in the country.

But the effort, as with other efforts throughout the tortured year, moved slowly. Justice Department leaders seemed flummoxed running such a large enterprise. Blanche had largely taken over the public and private management of the issue from Bondi. He did not make the same kind of embarrassing public flubs as Bondi, but he and his staff still struggled.

"It is a grind," Justice Department official Tysen Duva admitted to Criminal Division lawyers at the start of 2026. "We are not where we need to be overall," he wrote in an email. While Blanche had enlisted a horde of Justice Department lawyers in the effort, the individual output varied wildly. Senior officials tried to get the lawyers to review 1,000 pages a day. One lawyer reviewed 13,426 pages in three days—a staggering amount that made some coworkers wonder how closely the lawyer was reading the material. Other lawyers reviewed no pages in the same time frame.

In late December, Blanche said the department would release pages in "rolling production," tranche by tranche of documents. They issued nearly 30,000 more pages, including a purported suicide letter from Epstein that was almost certainly fake. The letter, in handwriting that looked very different from Epstein's, suggested that he and Trump shared the same attraction to minor females. The envelope it was sent in also suggested it was a fraud—there were no prisoner inmate numbers, which is standard for prison mail, and the return address was wrong.

The year 2026 began with more than four hundred Justice Department lawyers working on reviewing Epstein files, and only about 3 percent of the total pages had been vetted for release, I was told. Blanche missed his own January deadline, pushing the Epstein disclosures deeper into a congressional election year.

When the bulk of the files were finally released publicly later that month, the reputational blast radius was immense. Emails showed that Trump's Commerce Secretary, Howard Lutnick, had maintained a friendly relationship with Epstein for years after his conviction, proving false Lutnick's past claims that he had cut all ties with the man.

In Britain, the former Prince Andrew was arrested on suspicion of misconduct in office, after emails from the Epstein files suggested he shared government information with Epstein. Also arrested was Britain's former ambassador to the U.S., Peter Mandelson—though in the UK legal system, an arrest does not mean a person will be charged with any crime.

The Epstein files also contained unconfirmed allegations of sexual abuse by Donald Trump. FBI files showed that one woman told them that in the mid-1980s, when she was a young teenager, Epstein introduced her to Donald Trump, and that Trump violently assaulted her. Curiously, the FBI documents detailing her multiple interviews with

FBI agents in 2019 were not released in the January dump of millions of pages—though some related summary documents were.

The great irony of Trump's failures around the Epstein files was that his political rise was fueled in no small part by his penchant for hurling baseless accusations against foes, rivals, or any convenient targets for his wrath. For Trump, the Epstein files were a dangerous dose of his own medicine—a raft of unverified information, anonymous accusations, and ugly inferences. Unlike with the Russia investigation, it was hard for the president to blame his Epstein problems on the Democrats, when the clamor for the files had begun within his own base and was fed by his own deputies, like Bondi, Patel, and Bongino. Democrats eventually joined the call for the releases, but it was Trump's supporters who had started the brushfire and his eager-to-please aides who had fed the blaze until it threatened to incinerate all their reputations. After the Epstein files were released, Bondi appeared before the House Judiciary Committee, where she struggled—angrily—to answer questions about the case. "The Dow right now is over fifty thousand dollars," she declared, while Representative Jamie Raskin, a Maryland Democrat, laughed at her. "Americans' 401(k)s and retirement savings are booming; that's what we should be talking about."

In 2025, nothing else hurt the credibility of Justice Department and FBI leaders like the Epstein files missteps, because the people most inclined to believe in cover-ups tended to be Trump's own supporters. Trump's chief of staff, Susie Wiles, told *Vanity Fair* that Bondi "completely whiffed on appreciating that there was the very targeted group that cared about this." The Epstein files were also a karmic comeuppance for Kash Patel. His love of conspiratorial fantasies was coming back to bite him and his boss.

Collecting valuable intelligence by necessity also means collecting a lot of bad intelligence, and plenty of embarrassing details about people's personal lives. For generations, J. Edgar Hoover and his successors had carefully guarded the FBI files, trying to keep a tight grip on the number of false accusations and the amount of bad information that spilled out.

Bondi, Patel, and others had taken their jobs promising to throw open the proverbial library doors to prove that their predecessors had been corrupt. But when given their own set of keys to that library, they created a scandal they couldn't control, one that weakened the president they were so desperate to please.

Included in the Epstein files was one particularly damning document. In 2019, Michael Reiter, the local police chief who had first investigated Epstein, told the FBI about a call he received from Donald Trump back in July 2006, shortly after news broke of the Epstein case. Reiter told the FBI that Trump called him and said, "Thank goodness you're stopping him, everyone has known he's been doing this."

The Epstein saga is more, though, than simply a story about a rich man whose horrible life and suspicious death became an indictment of elite class impunity. The Justice Department and the FBI have long operated as trusted keepers of secrets, given extensive investigative powers with the expectation that they would make necessary, and sometimes difficult, decisions about who should be charged with crimes, and who should not. In turn, the public, the courts, and Congress would generally trust federal law enforcement to keep lies and embarrassing secrets out of the public eye. The Epstein case, however, challenged the idea that the Justice Department could still be counted on to do the right thing. First, he was granted a very lenient sentence for a man who victimized so many girls. Then, he died under circumstances that only raised more suspicions about the elite circles in which he had thrived for so long.

No longer willing to trust the Justice Department, Congress—and, by extension, the public—opted for something far messier: a kind of informational free-for-all, in which three million pages were released without context or fact-checking. People would decide for themselves who was guilty, who was complicit, and who lied.

CHAPTER 17

Credit and Credibility

At the start of 2026, workers hung a giant blue banner of the president's face on the outside of the Justice Department, where FBI agents walking into and out of their building would see it. Floodlights positioned underneath the banner ensured that Trump's glowering expression was inescapable even at night. Within weeks, the lighting also exposed shoddy craftsmanship, as the fading blue paint gave way to giant white cracks.

Over the course of 2025, Trump and his deputy chief of staff Stephen Miller harnessed the broad might and resources of the FBI and the Justice Department to focus on immigration, street crime, and their perceived political enemies. Every administration makes policy choices about how to deploy personnel to fight different types of crime. Roughly halfway through Joe Biden's presidency, the Justice Department poured more federal resources into fighting street crime. Just as Biden officials took some credit for the falling crime that followed, Trump, Bondi, and Patel can reasonably take some of the credit for the decreases in crime that continued on their watch. In 2025, murders fell by roughly 20 percent, a record decline on top of the prior year's record.

But while Trump's law enforcement agencies poured energy into the kind of low-level arrests that police officers call "street rips," prosecutors and agents throughout the department described much less effort expended on the kinds of complex cases that only federal law enforcement can do.

So, with that in mind, the Trump administration can also take credit for cutting the number of new tax scheme investigations from ninety-two to just thirty-four in 2025. The administration can also take credit for an unprecedented downsizing of the Justice Department workforce. The department lost 8 percent of its employees between November 2024 and November 2025, according to data from the Office of Personnel Management.

U.S. attorney offices—the crime-fighting engines of the department—lost 14 percent of their head count. At some offices, one out of three desks were empty by the end of the year. The Justice Department's criminal division, which consisted of about one thousand people when the Trump administration began, lost nearly 1 in 5 of its workers.

Lengthy, complex organized crime investigations fight the problems of drugs and crime by ripping an entire gang, root and branch, out of a community all at once, the kind of case that takes years to build and whose positive effects also tend to last years. In Philadelphia in late 2025, Kash Patel joined prosecutors to announce the indictment of thirty-three members of a drug-dealing street gang. Considered a major success by law enforcement officials, the case had taken many years to investigate and indict. But the government's own data for 2025, and dozens of interviews conducted for this book, indicate that when it came to organized crime and other important parts of federal law enforcement, the Trump administration could take credit for significantly scaling back the number of complex, long-term investigations that are the Justice Department's specialty. Street crime and immigration were far from Trump's only targets. The president had declared himself "the hunter," and his administration invoked amorphous presidential power to fire more than two hundred Justice Department lawyers and FBI agents, particularly those who worked on cases involving the president or his supporters.

At least six thousand other Justice Department lawyers, analysts, agents, and other staff decided to quit. Once again, raw numbers tell only part of the story. Those fired in the administration's purge and those who fled in frustration were among the most experienced and influential figures in their respective agencies. Their replacements were less experienced, more malleable, and more fearful.

The Justice Department found it increasingly difficult to fill such jobs, because Trump's top deputies alarmed and alienated much of the nation's legal community by prioritizing outcomes over processes.

At the FBI, Patel can take credit for downgrading what it takes to become an FBI special agent, allowing law enforcement agents from other agencies to skip many weeks of traditional training at Quantico. He lowered the legal and factual standard for opening investigations of those targeted by the president or Stephen Miller, and he lowered the standard for firing agents who displeased him by simply having worked on cases they were assigned.

In their quest for retribution against the president's perceived enemies, Trump, Miller, Bondi, Blanche, and Patel have made drastic changes at the Justice Department and FBI. Over the course of reporting for this book, more than one hundred current and former law enforcement officials expressed the view that the Justice Department as they knew it was dead, or that the FBI as it had functioned for half a century no longer existed.

They have a point, but I don't believe it is the final word on the subject.

Some of the changes at the Justice Department are likely irreversible. The appointment of Patel, a fierce partisan who personally ordered investigations based on convoluted suspicions about his predecessors, makes it unlikely that any future administration will allow FBI directors to serve the full ten-year term that once helped insulate the FBI from politics. That insulation has been stripped away, and it is likely that every new president will pick his or her own new FBI director. Whether they serve for eight years or four years or less, those directors will likely have to be far more responsive to the demands, complaints, and wishes of the president, or the president's deputy chief of staff.

Some of what the Justice Department does only the Justice Department can do, and those areas have been among the most affected by Bondi, Blanche, and Bove.

There is no other part of the American legal system built to tackle corruption in local, state, and federal government like the now-comatose Public Integrity Section. As one of the castaways from that office put it, the work that section does makes enemies, not friends, but for a long time, everyone generally understood the need for it. The section helped prosecute the ABSCAM corruption scandal, the Jack Abramoff lobbying scandal, a New Jersey senator's stash of gold bars, and the outrageous lies of New York Congressman George Santos.

There was a striking moment in late 2025 that revealed just how difficult, perhaps impossible, it will be to restore something like an effective Public Integrity Section. After Congress subjected the country to the longest government shutdown in U.S. history, a deal was struck in November between Republicans and Democrats to turn the lights back on. One of the bills restarting full government functions included a peculiar provision: If the FBI were to take data, such as phone records, about U.S. senators without notifying them, those senators could sue for half a million dollars for each instance of data taken.

As strange as the provision was, it had a stranger backstory.

During Special Counsel Jack Smith's investigation into Trump's effort to block the results of the 2020 election, his investigators had, in late 2023, seized the phone records of eight Republican lawmakers, focusing on those who were reportedly the subject of pressure campaigns from Trump and his lawyer Rudy Giuliani. Investigators wanted the records to confirm that Trump figures had made these kinds of phone calls as had been described by witnesses or news articles, according to people familiar with the investigation. Republicans in Congress, including Senator Charles Grassley, the judiciary committee chairman, accused Smith and the FBI of spying on lawmakers for political reasons.

This new provision not only tried to prevent the FBI from ever doing such a thing again, but it also made the conditions retroactive to 2022, so the lawmakers whose phone records were taken by the FBI in 2023 were automatically eligible to sue for millions of dollars. And in case a jury did not embrace the idea of lawmakers effectively giving themselves piles of taxpayer dollars, the law also sharply limited the kinds of defenses government lawyers might try to make in fighting such a lawsuit.

Lindsey Graham, a South Carolina Republican, was one of those whose phone records were taken by the FBI. After even fellow lawmakers criticized the provision, Graham did not back down, saying he would "definitely" sue. "And if you think I am going to settle this thing for a million dollars? No. I want to make it so painful no one ever does this again."

Perhaps most remarkable about the multimillion-dollar payouts the Republicans sought for themselves was that the leader of the Senate Democrats, Charles Schumer of New York, had gone along with it. Congressional aides said Schumer decided the provision would protect Democratic senators from unjustified investigations by Bondi's Justice Department. It was a telling moment that showed how liberal politicians viewed the Justice Department in the age of Trump: It could not be trusted. If the senators could not get presidential immunity from investigation, they would settle for a little insurance.

In early 2026, a new must-pass spending bill including a provision canceling the payout provision to senators for having their phone records seized. The reversal enraged Senator Graham, who vowed that the fight was far from over.

Given the lack of political faith in the types of cases the Public Integrity Section once handled, it is increasingly difficult to envision some successive administration and Congress agreeing to rebuild it with the kind of authority it once had. Its work was far from perfect, but the section had long served a critical role in fighting corruption in Washington and state capitals around the country. That is gone. The Public Integrity Section started 2026 as little more than a name on a door. Within the Trump administration, some officials began the year hoping to revive it in a much-reduced form, perhaps with only a half dozen lawyers. Even if that effort is successful, its reach would by necessity be far smaller, and there is every reason to believe any prosecutors who work there would still face the same demands for absolute fealty to the wishes and wants of the president and the White House.

Another part of the Justice Department undergoing drastic changes is the Civil Rights Division. As I described in an earlier chapter, most of the lawyers who worked there left in 2025, and few of those empty positions have been filled. The lawyers who remain have been reassigned to entirely different types of cases, against universities, city governments, and state officials. Civil rights groups are still fighting in court on issues like voting rights and police misconduct, but there is no easy substitute in the American legal system for the Justice Department Civil Rights Division. The laws the division once enforced remain on the books, for now, but it would take a herculean effort for a future administration to re-create their effective enforcement.

The third part of the Justice Department that has been deeply affected by the Trump administration is the National Security Division, which was established in the wake of the 9/11 attacks to combat both terrorism and espionage. Many of the division's most experienced lawyers fled or were forced out in 2025—no small thing when it comes to the complex cases the division handles. The division ended the year in a special kind of bureaucratic hell: Nearly every one of its lawyers was assigned to review documents related to the Jeffrey Epstein case.

The consequences of the abuse and misuse of the National Security Division is hard to measure from outside the department. The number of espionage cases that drift aimlessly because the lawyers assigned to them keep leaving, one after another, is not a matter of public record, but it is significant. The biggest national security cases tend to stretch over years and continents, and the Trump administration has—by dint of constantly ordering its troops to run in one direction and then another, then another—proved an endless source of distraction for the people trying to do that work. The Civil Rights Division had helped prosecute the gunman who massacred innocent worshippers at a historic Black church in Charleston, South Carolina, and it helped prosecute the police officer who killed George Floyd. When an ICE agent in Minneapolis shot and killed Renee Good, a local mother of three, in January 2026, senior Justice Department officials sharply limited investigations into her death. Two weeks later, DHS agents shot and killed another protester, Alex Pretti, a nurse at a Veterans Affairs hospital.

These four areas—FBI leadership, public corruption, civil rights, and national security—are the ones where Trump's changes at the Justice Department will be hardest to undo. A number of ex-Biden administration officials have already begun discussing how a subsequent Democratic administration might restore the long-standing professional areas, practices, and policies the Trump administration discarded.

But the enormity of the problem facing the Justice Department can't simply be solved by a fresh set of attorney general memos reversing a prior set of memos, or by hiring back a number of people fired without cause. Since the 2016 election, marked by the Hillary Clinton email investigation and the Russia election-interference investigation, the Justice Department has been skidding like a car on a snowy road, fishtailing back and forth as it tries to regain stability and direction.

When Edward Levi took over the Justice Department in the wake of Watergate, he had a gargantuan task of rebuilding both the department and the public's trust in it. Levi decried what he called "corrosive skepticism and cynicism concerning the administration of justice." In a 1976 speech, he described the challenge of running a democracy when the next crop of political leaders want payback for the perceived excesses of the prior administration. "We are in such a period of cyclical reaction today, justifying what we do now as a kind of getting even with the events of prior years. This in itself is another form of the game of victims and losers. We are adversaries not only with ourselves, but also with the past."

Jack Smith, the most important prosecutor in the department during the Biden years because of whom he was prosecuting, proved himself to be more of a legal tactician than a strategic thinker. Smith could have made different choices, and those choices might have led to different outcomes.

For instance, if the January 6 case about the president was important primarily for showing the country what Trump had done, Smith could have indicted any one of the president's uncharged co-conspirators, such as Rudy Giuliani, and sidestepped many of the difficult legal questions about presidential immunity that delayed and ultimately killed the case. Or if Smith had charged the classified documents case in Washington instead of Florida, he could have similarly avoided an ugly, endless fight with Judge Aileen M. Cannon.

Even if he felt that for jurisdictional reasons he had no choice but to file the documents case in Florida, he could have included in that indictment details of the conflicts over the search warrant that had already involved Judge Cannon, which would have effectively ruled her out as a potential trial judge for the case. Smith's moves were designed to win in court, not in the political arena, but they didn't succeed even there.

Smith and Attorney General Merrick Garland were the kind of government lawyers who loved process to a fault. But any attorney general, and any special counsel, would be hard-pressed to succeed in the political environment of the 2020s, when public distrust of institutions, elites, and the government runs very high.

The Justice Department and the FBI operate largely in private, but they need public trust to function effectively. Prosecutors and federal agents generally cannot talk about the vast majority of what they do, because talking would compromise investigations or violate a defendant's rights. Public trials can dispel some, but not all, doubts about the integrity of federal law enforcement officials, and the agencies count on the public's faith in them to do the rest.

But in an age of growing public distrust and voter skepticism, when the approval ratings for most public institutions (including the press, it should be said) have fallen precipitously, it is harder for the Justice Department and the FBI to succeed. Attacks on the DOJ and the Bureau are now effective political weapons. For nearly a decade, Trump has gone after agents and prosecutors as part of the "deep state," his term for a liberal, bureaucratic conspiracy that he claims wants to kneecap his political career. Democrats, in turn, frequently compare him to Russian

President Vladimir Putin, calling Trump an aspiring autocrat seeking to end the rule of law and the "norms" that protect them. Both arguments help explain the Justice Department's weakened present condition and its precarious future.

Trump's use of the term *deep state* is important, given its history. The phrase comes from Turkey, where it is called *derin devlet*, describing a secret, far-reaching criminal conspiracy among organized crime, military, and police figures. The general concept has long existed in Turkish society, which has a penchant for conspiratorial thinking, but it gained new life in 1996, after a seemingly innocuous event: a car crashing into a truck.

When first responders arrived at the scene of the accident in northwestern Turkey, they were startled that the damaged car contained a Mafia boss, a police chief, a Kurdish official, and a beauty queen. The incident seemed to confirm the suspicions of many Turks that mysterious networks of influential people secretly pulled the strings inside government for their own benefit.

In the early 2000s, Turkish politics became a battle between a secular, urban-focused ruling class and a growing opposition who criticized the old guard as selfish, out-of-touch elites focused on preserving their own power. That clash helped propel Recep Tayyip Erdoğan, who described himself as the true voice of the people, into the presidency. As president, he continued to campaign against the government he now ran, blaming the "bureaucratic oligarchy" for obstructing him and his goals by clogging up agencies and the judiciary.

In 2013, a corruption scandal nearly toppled Erdoğan, after tapes were leaked in which he and his son appeared to discuss what to do with millions of euros in cash inside a house. In response, Erdoğan attacked the investigators, calling their eavesdropping a "judicial coup" and a "dirty conspiracy" by law enforcement officials. "If we let it go on," he said of the wiretapping, "there will be no privacy for families, nor for the state in this country." Erdoğan carried out a sweeping purge of judges, police chiefs, and prosecutors involved in the case.

In 2016, elements of Turkey's military launched a real coup against him. The coup failed, however, and led to his cracking down further not just on government agencies and officials, but also on other facets of Turkish life.

The comparison of Trump and Erdoğan offers a different way of understanding Trump's "deep state" accusations. One of the earliest and loudest American voices against the deep state has been Kash Patel, but when Patel has been pressed to explain how the deep state actually works, he often stumbles and retreats to sweeping generalities. As the FBI director in 2025, with the vast power that job conveys, Patel tried and largely failed to turn the deep-state argument into a criminal case against former FBI leaders. The burn bags investigation in Western Virginia was closed without charges, and the indictment of James Comey in Eastern Virginia was short-lived, ending in a humiliation for the prosecutors who brought it.

Patel and Trump are still trying. The prosecution theory that law enforcement officials sometimes derisively refer to as "the Grand Conspiracy" has been transferred to the Southern District of Florida, where it may get a boost from Judge Aileen Cannon, who in 2024 ruled that Jack Smith was not a valid special prosecutor and who dismissed Smith's indictment against Trump for allegedly mishandling classified documents.

Patel's fishing expedition—not for evidence, but for a prosecutor willing to bring charges based on his deep-state theories—continues. After those efforts failed with Todd Gilbert and Erik Siebert in Virginia, Patel's new hope lay with Jason Reding Quinones, the U.S. attorney in Miami.

The FBI director's initial inability to turn his deep-state theories into indictments is not because the former law enforcement and intelligence officials he is hunting are so deviously clever. It's because the deep state works better as an ideology of resentment than as an organizational chart. At its core, the talk of deep-state sabotage is an appeal to the growing distrust of elites, experts, bureaucrats, and institutions, particularly law enforcement authorities. When those institutions pose a risk to politicians, the deep state is invoked to try to fend off the danger. But a nation that embraces conspiratorial thinking and rejects reality is one bound to punish the innocent as well as the guilty.

And that is where the rule of law comes in. Since 2017, many lawyers and liberals have argued that the rule of law naturally takes primacy over every other form of government power, including the power of a president. After multiple special counsels, two impeachments, and four indictments against Trump, the Supreme Court in 2024 weighed in, with the conservative majority ruling that presidents have far-reaching immunity for official acts.

The highest court in the land concluded that the rule of law contains a special carve-out for what happens in the White House. In ruling so enthusiastically for Trump, the conservative justices had clearly come to distrust the views of anti-corruption prosecutors at the Justice Department—not just Jack Smith, but an entire generation of Smith's colleagues and predecessors. In charging Trump, Smith gambled that the High Court would view investigating a president as not altogether different from investigating a senator. He lost that bet, and the cascade of consequences will make it harder for all of Smith's would-be successors to investigate even a senator.

The Democratic argument for the rule of law and the preservation of "norms"—a vague term for traditional decision-making processes at the Justice Department—proved exceptionally fragile in the face of the second Trump administration. The defense of "norms" often boils down to a sales pitch for the preservation of the status quo for its own sake. Not only has that argument proved ineffective with voters, but it may actually have driven them away.

In some ways, the department was uniquely vulnerable to the kind of sweeping changes made by Trump, Bondi, Blanche, Bove, and Patel. Lawyers and agents trained over a lifetime to carefully follow rules and regulations were poorly equipped against leaders willing to fire anyone who said no to them. And as long as the courts take years to decide whether the nation's civil service laws are still relevant, those civil servants go to work every day at the mercy of those leaders.

Trump, Miller, and his team want specific results (like firing an FBI agent who investigated January 6 or indicting Senator Adam Schiff on weak allegations about his mortgage), and throughout 2025, the Trump administration repeatedly deprioritized process (like determining if there was cause to fire people or whether there was sufficient evidence to support an indictment).

The core of the work of an attorney, and of the law itself, is process—finding facts and applying those facts to the case law. Senior Trump officials, however, often treat process as an obstacle or an excuse, a nerdy card trick played by liberals, academics, and elites to thwart others.

Jack Smith, the former special counsel, brought a January 6 case against the president that pushed legal boundaries and took major risks with the Justice Department's credibility and authority, for which the department paid dearly in the form of a Supreme Court decision that granted sweeping new immunity and authority to Trump and every president who succeeded him. But Smith at least followed a process to reach that outcome. In sharp contrast, when the Trump administration found the process did not give them what they wanted (say, an indictment of James Comey or a dismissal of charges against New York City's mayor), they simply fired people until they got the desired result.

When Emil Bove arrived at the Justice Department and began firing people in early 2025, the agents and prosecutors in his sights were understandably afraid and unsure of what to do. James Dennehy, then the head of the FBI's New York office, wrote an email to his staff comparing the situation to his time as a young marine digging foxholes. "The foxhole provided me with the protection I needed for the battle that was to come, and when the bullets flew, it was worth the effort," Dennehy wrote. "Today, we find ourselves in the middle of a battle of our own, as good people are being walked out of the FBI and others are being targeted because they did their jobs in accordance with the law and FBI policy." Dennehy said he understood if agents resigned, but he wanted them to know he was staying "to defend you, your work, your families, and this team." It was time, he said, to "dig in."

His email was publicly championed as a declaration of resistance or a refusal to bend the knee to the partisan demands of the new administration. People in the administration thought so, too because Dennehy was fired not long after writing it.

But many others I know in the FBI and the Justice Department took Dennehy's words differently—as an exhortation to others to show the courage of soldiers who do not cower but who quietly wait, weapons in hand.

By the end of 2025, many honorable people had been fired or forced out of the Justice Department and FBI, while others chose to leave rather than do something that violated their moral code. A not-insignificant number of lawyers chose to embrace the new administration's goals, out of either an actual belief in those changes or a personal ambition that eclipsed their sense of right and wrong.

The largest grouping of Justice Department employees, however, fell into a third category. They were the agents, lawyers, paralegals, analysts, and other staff who continued to do their job, largely out of view of the department's political leadership. Even with the constant turmoil of Trump's first year in office, many people at the department were able to continue doing good, important work on behalf of the country, as with the indictment of dozens of gang suspects in Philadelphia that took years to bring to fruition.

"We are mole people now," joked one. "And someday we will pop back into the light."

The efforts by Trump and Stephen Miller to take absolute control of the FBI and Justice Department were faster and more successful than many Justice Department insiders would have guessed in the days after the 2024 election. For that reason, it is difficult to predict how much more change there will be in the remaining years of the administration, particularly when the Supreme Court has yet to engage on some key issues.

In 2026, there are two areas in which the Trump administration seems determined to act aggressively. The first is elections. As a congressional election nears in which Democrats appear to have a decent chance to retake the House of Representatives, Trump and his allies have revived claims of fraud and deception surrounding voting, and

Trump has publicly promised arrests. Harmeet Dhillon, the head of the Civil Rights Division, seems primed for a confrontation, having already sued half the states in the country, seeking access to their voter rolls.

The other area of greater potential conflict is civil rights. The Trump administration is intensely focused on protests against his policies. Since the 2020 protests for racial justice in the wake of George Floyd's murder by a Minneapolis police officer, Trump and his aides have grown increasingly angry over the very existence of protests. Stephen Miller, in particular, argues that protests have become a kind of cover story for leftist violence against the government and conservatives.

It was startling how often the reporting for this book uncovered instances of senior officials enraged by the mere presence of protesters, both on America's streets and online. As public demonstrations will likely intensify in an election year, the Justice Department's role will be critically important, as the administration puts the sweeping investigative power of National Security Presidential Memorandum 7 into action.

Two things are already clear from what happened at the department in 2025: The president's desire for revenge is deep-seated and seemingly inexhaustible and will continue to reverberate through federal law enforcement. The jerry-rigged indictments in Virginia against James Comey and Letitia James collapsed under the weight of their own malice. Justice Department leaders did not give up, transferring to federal prosecutors in Florida the Trump administration's effort to investigate Comey, former president Barack Obama, and a large cast of former Obama administration officials for supposedly conspiring to create fake investigations of Trump.

In his second term in office, President Trump declared himself to be a hunter, and he made the Justice Department and the FBI his hunting dogs. In 2025, those efforts largely focused on foes from Trump's past, such as Comey, James, and Schiff. In 2026, the department seemed to be expanding its list of revenge targets to include Jack Smith and others.

But the second year is also showing signs of change. Trump's energies have increasingly turned to new targets, like Jerome Powell, the head of the Federal Reserve Board. Trump wanted Powell out because he didn't like the way the Fed set interest rates. The U.S. attorney in Washington, Jeanine Pirro, opened a criminal investigation into Powell's oversight of a renovation of the Federal Reserve headquarters, though officials denied that she was ordered to do so by the administration.

With the case against Powell and federal investigations of state and local officials in Minnesota over their response to an aggressive immigration crackdown, the Trump administration has expanded the reach of his revenge campaign, using federal law enforcement not just to settle old scores, but also to pursue fresh prey.

Already, a host of blinking red lights across the American legal system show the tremendous damage done to the credibility of the Justice Department. The courts are not perfect, but they are a reality-based enterprise increasingly at odds with a presidency that often seeks to redefine the law. Since a senior Justice official declared the administration owns "the doors to the courtroom," the department's clashes with judges have only intensified.

In Minnesota, the top federal judge, a Republican appointee, said in early 2026 he had found more than two hundred instances of the Trump administration defying court orders in recent months.

"The court is not aware of another occasion in the history of the United States in which a federal court has had to threaten contempt—again and again and again—to force the *United States government* to comply with court orders," wrote Judge Patrick Schiltz, part of a growing chorus of federal judges furious over the administration's intransigence and sloppiness.

In Chicago and Los Angeles, juries repeatedly rejected hyped-up charges of impeding or assaulting federal agents engaged in Trump's immigration crackdown. In Washington, a local community group launched monthly classes teaching the principles of jury nullification—educating everyday citizens about how, if they become jurors, they can vote to acquit defendants in court if they don't like how agents and prosecutors conduct themselves.

In early 2026, a DC grand jury refused prosecutors' efforts to indict a half dozen Democratic lawmakers for making a video reminding military and intelligence agency personnel that they had an obligation to refuse illegal orders. Trump had pushed hard for the lawmakers to be investigated and prosecuted, but the anonymous grand jury of DC residents overwhelmingly rejected the premise of the charges against the lawmakers.

As the administration loses public confidence for the steps it is taking, it also risks losing even more credibility for the steps it isn't taking. For all the frenetic activity pushing the FBI to open cases against Democrats, or protesters, or officials who are simply deemed insufficiently obedient, the Trump Justice Department is marked by a kind of eerie quiet when it comes to investigating crimes by anyone in the Trump administration, or anyone with good friends in the administration.

The investigations of border czar Tom Homan and former New York City Mayor Eric Adams were snuffed out quickly. When the Defense Secretary, Pete Hegseth, shared seemingly classified military details in a Signal chat that accidentally included a reporter, Bondi quickly declared there was nothing to investigate. As long as Trump is the president, federal criminal investigations into his allies will likely never even begin.

These are not small consequences. The credibility of the Justice Department and the FBI is essential to maintaining a free, safe, and just society. They are immensely powerful institutions, but that wasn't always the case. When the Justice Department was created after the Civil War, it was so small, it didn't even have its own building, and its lawyers worked in offices above a bank in downtown Washington (a bank which later collapsed in scandal under the literal noses of the Justice Department lawyers). As America grew, the country's expectations of the federal government grew with it, and Congress passed more laws for the Justice Department to enforce. The department grew in power, reach, and responsibility because the country's political leadership agreed that such growth was good and such enforcement was needed. They also generally agreed about what types of misconduct constituted crimes.

In 2026, Democrats and Republicans increasingly disagree on what corruption is, and that poses tremendous challenges for the future of the Justice Department. If the Justice Department's slide toward tribalism and political scalp-taking is to be stopped, or reversed, the other arms of government will likely be needed to reach some kind of baseline agreement about what the department's mission is, particularly when it comes to politically consequential investigations. And the department will also need a new and decidedly faster approach to prosecutions and investigations, one that tackles head-on the growing distrust of authority, expertise, and elites of any kind.

The institutionalists and Democrats who hope to eventually rebuild the Justice Department to the independence it had in the early 2020s want the department to be two contradictory things—protected and defended by the political leadership of the country and also with ultimate authority over that leadership to investigate and prosecute criminal conduct by powerful politicians. That is a tall order and one not likely to come from a return to "norms," a milquetoast word for traditions without the muscle to back them up. If the Justice Department is to become effective again at fighting crime within the country's political class, it will likely need some of those norms to be turned into laws punishing misconduct inside the Justice Department. To be effective, those laws would likely need to come with meaningful criminal penalties. The Justice Department's Tax Division was killed in 2025, but the law protecting the misuse of taxpayer information lives on. That offers a model for the rest of the department to operate under a more forceful and permanent set of laws to prevent the corrosive misuse of arrest, investigative, and prosecutorial power. Passing such laws would require Congress to rise from the grave for the purpose of strengthening rather than weakening the department. In 2025, the two most significant laws passed involving the Justice Department were both votes of no confidence in federal law enforcement. One law ordered the department to make public nearly all its investigative files related to Epstein. Another promised senators personal payments of millions of dollars if the Justice Department ever seized the lawmakers' phone records without notifying them. A restoration of Justice Department independence requires a consensus in Congress that it is necessary. It's also hard to imagine effective federal law enforcement without the nation's higher courts affirming the basic protections of civil service laws, putting an end to the political purges inside the FBI and Justice Department.

The responsibility to do better lies not only with Congress and the courts. Since 2016 at least, too many American voters have come to see the FBI and the Justice Department primarily as axes to be wielded in political combat. The Justice Department is named after an ideal—and its success depends on the public generally having faith that the ideal is worth pursuing, even if it is never fully achieved. To bemoan the weaponization of the Justice Department and the FBI for their own sakes is to miss the point entirely. Better to lose the Justice Department than lose the principles of justice. Better to lose the FBI than lose our nation's fidelity to facts. It is those principles, far more than any building or badge, that Americans of all persuasions should defend and strengthen.

These are no small tasks, but the greatest hurdle to restoring prosecutorial discretion and Justice Department independence probably lies in the White House. Trump has grabbed for himself a tremendous amount of new power to torment his enemies, critics, and other targets with the machinery of the criminal justice system. Once a president gains new power, it is rare for his successors to abandon it, and a post-Trump Justice Department may find itself still trapped in Levi's cycle of "getting even with the events of prior years."

Finally, federal law enforcement officials have too often behaved as cloistered monks who expect to be protected by others from the ill winds of politics. But the carvings on the walls of Justice Department headquarters show the Greek gods of wind blowing the spirit of justice out to the four corners of the country. A newly successful Justice Department will have to learn how to speak more plainly, act more cautiously, and argue more convincingly about the true meaning of justice.

Until then, America's top law enforcement agency is likely to remain the Department of Revenge.

Acknowledgments

The people who deserve the deepest thanks for this book would suffer the most for being listed here. Instead of names, I will acknowledge the character of those who gave this work meaning.

They are Americans who took an oath to support and defend the Constitution against all enemies, foreign and domestic.

They are Americans who know that being an officer of the court demands honesty, integrity, and ethical conduct, not only when it is easy but when it is hard.

They are Americans who disagree on many things, but who share a belief that the way to resolve disputes is not through lies, threats, or self-serving backroom deals.

Many of those people never considered, until 2025, that their oath to "bear true faith and allegiance" to their country might mean risking their livelihoods. Nevertheless, when confronted with difficult moral choices (and some that were not difficult), they made sacrifices to defend principles that protect the American people. Even more than the "rule of law" or "norms," two concepts that probably don't poll well or get many clicks, they stood up for basic human decency and common sense. Thank you.

I am grateful to Priscilla Painton for believing in this project and making it so much better. As always, I am indebted to Larry Weissman and Sascha Alper for believing in me. Researcher Julie Tate has my deep thanks for deft fact-checking.

I started working on this book shortly before joining *The New York Times*, where my editors Richard Stevenson, Matea Gold, and Margaret Ho provided tremendous support and guidance at all hours of the day and night. Covering the Justice Department in 2025 is a busload of work, and I am grateful to be on that bus alongside the *Times* reporters Glenn Thrush, Alan Feuer, Charlie Savage, Adam Goldman, Jonah Bromwich, William K. Rashbaum, Eileen Sullivan, and Michael Schmidt. All my colleagues at the *Times* have been incredibly kind and welcoming to a middle-aged Mountain Dew addict who throws a neon Nerf football around the office, especially Tyler Pager, Hamed Aleaziz, Robert Draper, Zolan Kanno-Youngs, Michael Bender, Shawn Mc-Creesh, Theodore Schleifer, Adam Liptak, Abbie VanSickle, and Ann Marimow. Heartfelt thanks go as well to my former colleagues at *The Washington Post*, particularly Perry Stein, Shayna Jacobs, Derek Hawkins, Rachel Weiner, Spencer Hsu, Mark Berman, Josh Dawsey, Rosalind Helderman, Shane Harris, and Matt Zapotosky. And I am forever grateful to my fellow reporters covering the Justice Department, for their fidelity to truth, the American way, and snacks.

The last and deepest thanks go to my wife and sons, who since 2015 have rolled their eyes every time I've said, "Work is a little crazy right now but should calm down soon." The truth is they are my calm, my comfort, and my comedy. Let's go home.

Notes

PROLOGUE

2   *"We own"*: Interviews with sources. Granting anonymity to discuss sensitive internal discussions at the Justice Department and the FBI is not a step taken lightly, but it's sometimes necessary to explain what happened inside these extremely powerful institutions, where strict secrecy is a job requirement. Wherever possible, I have sought to interview people on the record about their knowledge of events.

CHAPTER 1: DAY ONE

8   *"The issuance of"*: Colleen Long and Zeke Miller, "Biden Pardons Fauci, Milley, and the Jan. 6 Panel," Associated Press, January 20, 2025, https://apnews.com /article/biden-trump-fauci-milley-pardons-january-6-3cba287f89051513fb 48d7ae700ae747.

8   *Justice Department headquarters*: Luther A. Huston, *The Department of Justice* (Frederick A. Praeger, 1967), 54.

9   *In the post-9/11 era*: Scott Shane and David Johnston, "U.S. Lawyers Agreed on Legality of Brutal Tactic," *New York Times*, June 6, 2009, https://www.nytimes .com/2009/06/07/us/politics/07lawyers.html.

9   *In 1995*: Kristina Sgueglia, "Murder Conviction of Ex-FBI Agent Linked to Whitey Bulger Overturned," CNN, May 29, 2014, https://www.cnn.com /2014/05/28/justice/bulger-connolly-fbi-conviction-overturned.

9 *In the twentieth century*: Beverly Gage, "What an Uncensored Letter to M.L.K. Reveals," *New York Times*, November 11, 2014, https://www.nytimes.com /2014/11/16/magazine/what-an-uncensored-letter-to-mlk-reveals.html.

10 *In 1999*: Eric Lichtblau, "Political Leanings Were Always Factor in Tobacco Suit," *New York Times*, June 19, 2005, https://www.nytimes.com/2005/06/19 /politics/political-leanings-were-always-factor-in-tobacco-suit.html.

11 *Four senior officials*: Hamed Aleaziz, "Trump Administration Fires Immigration Court Officials as Crackdown Begins," *New York Times*, January 20, 2025, https://www.nytimes.com/2025/01/20/us/politics/trump-administration -fires-immigration-judges.html.

11 *Simultaneously, about ten*: Interviews with sources.

12 *Within an hour*: Interviews with sources.

13 *"We both know"*: Interviews with sources.

13 *The senior prosecutors*: Interviews with sources.

13 *In December 2024*: Interviews with sources.

14 *The late-afternoon meeting*: Interviews with sources.

14 *Of the ten lawyers*: Interviews with sources.

15 *The bureaucratic process*: Interviews with sources.

15 *Nevertheless, the federal*: Robert Downen, "Houston Man Pardoned by Trump Arrested on Child Sex Charge," *Texas Tribune*, February 6, 2025.

15 *Ingrassia hadn't waited*: Brian J. Driscoll Jr. et al. v. Kashyap P. Patel, *Complaint*, U.S. District Court for the District of Columbia, September 10, 2025, 25-cv- 03109, 18–22.

15 *Awkwardly, Driscoll got*: Interviews with sources.

CHAPTER 2: THE WORST LAWYERS MONEY CAN BUY

19 *"Honor of a lifetime"*: "John Giordano Sworn in as 64th U.S. Attorney For District of New Jersey," press release, U.S. Department of Justice, March 5, 2025, https://www.justice.gov/usao-nj/pr/john-giordano-sworn-64th-us -attorney-district-new-jersey.

19 *"Somebody said to me"*: Patrick Bet-David, "Donald Trump's Legal Issues," in *PBD Podcast*, Episode 345, January 4, 2024, 23:40, https://www.youtube.com /watch?v=h2UkMRm2Ei0.

20 *"You are on"*: Larry Neumeister and Jake Offenhartz, "Trump Walks Out of Court During Closing Arguments of E. Jean Carroll Defamation Trial," Associated Press, January 26, 2024, https://www.pbs.org/newshour/politics/lawyers- have-final-say-in-e-jean-carroll-defamation-trial-a-day-after-trump-testifies.

20 *"I understand you"*: Aaron Katersky et al., "Trump Butts Heads with Judge in Heated Courtroom Exchanges During E. Jean Carroll Case," ABC News, January 17, 2024, https://abcnews.go.com/US/trump-butts-heads-judge -heated-courtroom-exchanges-jean/story?id=106452547.

22 *Sigal Chattah had*: Interviews with sources.

24 *Blanche answered to*: Interviews with sources.

24 *So, in late July*: Interviews with sources.

24 *The same data*: Interviews with sources.

26 *In 2022, she*: Bill Dentzler, "AG Candidate, in Feud with Former Ally, Says Text Not Racist, Leaked to Damage Her," *Las Vegas Review-Journal*, February 11, 2022, https://www.reviewjournal.com/news/politics-and-government /nevada/ag-candidate-in-feud-with-former-ally-says-text-not-racist-leaked-to -damage-her-2528181/.

26 *In another administration*: Interviews with sources.

28 *Donald Trump and*: Interviews with sources.

30 *"Wow, what a disappointment"*: Devlin Barrett, Hamed Aleaziz, and Adam Goldman, "Across Justice Dept., Fear, Anxiety, and Angry Bosses," *New York Times*, January 28, 2025, https://www.nytimes.com/2025/01/28/us/politics /justice-department-trump.html.

30 *He sent menacing letters*: Rob Stein, "Medical Journals Hit with Threatening Letters from Justice Department," NPR, May 2, 2025, https://www.npr.org /sections/shots-health-news/2025/05/02/nx-s1-5374993/medical-journals -hit-with-threatening-letters-from-justice-department.

32 *Martin had little patience*: Interviews with sources.

33 *In their memo to Martin*: Interviews with sources.

36 *Sometimes, he would*: Interviews with sources.

36 *"I think anybody"*: Jordain Carney and Hailey Fuchs, "Tillis Says He'll Oppose Ed Martin, Dealing Grave Blow to Trump's DC Prosecutor Pick," *Politico*, May 5, 2025, https://www.politico.com/live-updates/2025/05/06/congress /thom-tillis-opposes-ed-martin-00330664.

37 *The Trump administration had forced*: Interviews with sources.

37 *Gibson had lost*: Devlin Barrett, "Justice Dept. Official Says She Was Fired After Opposing Restoring Mel Gibson's Gun Rights," *New York Times*, March 10, 2025, https://www.nytimes.com/2025/03/10/us/politics/justice-depart- ment-mel-gibson.html.

37 *Justice Department officials*: Interviews with sources.

38 *Even the State*: Interviews with sources.

CHAPTER 3: PIN DROP

41 *Adams had won*: "New York City Mayor Eric Adams Charged with Bribery and Campaign Finance Offenses," press release, U.S. Attorney's Office, Southern District of New York, September 26, 2024.

43 *"I know what"*: Emma G. Fitzsimmons, "Trump Defends Adams, Arguing Both Are Being 'Persecuted,'" *New York Times*, October 18, 2024.

44 *"When a person"*: Interview with source.

44 *"I was wrong"*: "Dr. Phil Sits Down with Tom Homan Incoming Border Czar," Facebook video, n.d., https://www.facebook.com/watch /?v=535474536156950.

44 *"I think he"*: Emma G. Fitzsimmons, "Trump Says He Would Consider Pardoning Eric Adams," *New York Times*, December 16, 2024.

45 *"President Trump has made clear"*: Michael S. Schmidt et al., "How the Justice Dept. Helped Sink Its Own Case Against Eric Adams," *New York Times*, February 13, 2025.

47 *That same day*: Emil Bove, "Terminations," internal memo, PDF, U.S. Department of Justice, January 31, 2025, memochrome-extension://efaidnbmnnnib pcajpcglclefindmkaj/https://www.warner.senate.gov/public/_cache/files/8/5 /8590fa4b-e135-4ea5-b76f-0f13c097a489/57173F5183F4632CC51D21798D 2BEB945EE70C717140FA62CABC283B83D628A9.memorandum-from-the -acting-deputy-attorney-general-01.31.25.pdf.

47 *The following week*: Emil Bove, "Dismissal Without Prejudice of Prosecution of Mayor Eric Adams," internal memo, PDF, U.S. Department of Justice, February 10, 2025, chrome-extension://efaidnbmnnnibpcajpcglclefindmkaj/https://www .law.nyu.edu/sites/default/files/Bove%20to%20Sassoon_FILE_9882.pdf.

49 *"If she were"*: Interview with source.

49 *Sassoon stood her*: Letter from Danielle Sassoon, U.S. Department of Justice, February 12, 2025.

50 *"First, your resignation"*: Letter from Emil Bove, U.S. Department of Justice, February 13, 2025, https://www.nytimes.com/interactive/2025/02/13/ny region/memo-from-bove-1.html.

51 *"I am entirely"*: Letter from Hagan Scotten, U.S. Department of Justice, February 14, 2025, https://www.presidency.ucsb.edu/documents/resignation -letter-from-assistant-united-states-attorney-for-the-southern-district-new.

53 *"Yesterday was a hard day"*: Interviews with sources.

54 *With only thirty*: Interviews with sources.

55 *"Toni is one"*: Devlin Barrett et al., "In Moving to Stop Adams Case, Career Lawyer Sought to Stave Off Deeper Crisis," *New York Times*, February 16, 2025.

56 *Bacon entered*: Interviews with sources.

CHAPTER 4: FIND OUT

57 *When Alina Habba*: Interviews with sources.

58 *On her first day*: Interviews with sources.

59 *Sitting in a conference room*: Interviews with sources.

59 *"We could turn"*: Jack Posobiec, *Human Events* podcast, 17:02, March 27, 2025, https://www.iheart.com/podcast/1119-real-americas-voice-232242864 /episode/human-events-with-jack-posobiec-march-27th-2025-271166519.

59 *But before Habba*: Interviews with sources.

60 *Bove, in the spring*: Interviews with sources.

61 *The members of Congress*: "Newark Mayor Arrested Outside Delaney Hall in ICE Protest," NJ Spotlight News, May 9, https://www.youtube.com/watch?v=t-kEcQm4QJ0.

61 *In Washington, Deputy*: Interviews with sources.

62 *Within days*: Interviews with sources.

63 *Habba planned*: Interviews with sources.

64 *At one point*: Interviews with sources.

CHAPTER 5: STREET JUSTICE

67 *When Ed Martin*: Interviews with sources.

68 *Fox News ultimately*: David Bauder et al., "Fox, Dominion Reach $787M Settlement over Election Claims," Associated Press, April 18, 2023, https://apnews.com/article/fox-news-dominion-lawsuit-trial-trump-2020-0ac71f75acfacc52ea80b3e747fb0afe.

69 *On the night*: Interviews with sources.

70 *There were 274*: Emily Davies et al., "2023 was District's Deadliest Year in More than Two Decades," *Washington Post*, January 1, 2024, https://www.washingtonpost.com/dc-md-va/interactive/2024/dc-crime-homicide-victims-shooting-violence/.

71 *In 1991 alone*: Washington, DC, "A Report on Homicide in the District of Columbia, 2001–2004," PDF, n.d., https://mpdc.dc.gov/sites/default/files/dc/sites/mpdc/publication/attachments/homicidereport_2005.pdf.

71 *Small groups*: Perry Stein et al., "FBI Dispatching Agents to D.C. Streets as Trump Weighs Calling National Guard," *Washington Post*, August 10, 2025, https://www.washingtonpost.com/dc-md-va/2025/08/10/dc-crime-trump-crackdown/.

72 *But their colleagues*: Interviews with sources.

72 *Those agents used*: Teo Armas et al., "ICE Is Joining D.C. Police Patrols. Moped Drivers Are Getting Detained," *Washington Post*, August 21, 2025, https://www.washingtonpost.com/dc-md-va/2025/08/21/dc-police-ice-moped-crackdown-delivery-drivers/.

73 *In the first six*: Hamed Aleaziz et al., "How Washington Became a Testing Ground for ICE," *New York Times*, October 1, 2025, https://www.nytimes.com/2025/10/01/us/politics/washington-dc-ice.html.

73 *It wasn't just*: *José Escobar Molina v. U.S. Department of Homeland Security*, 25-CV-3417, U.S. District Court for the District of Columbia.

75 *Walking across the station's*: Irie Sentner, "Vance's Trip for Burgers Crashes into Trump's DC Takeover," *Politico*, August 20, 2025, https://www.politico.com/news/2025/08/20/jd-vance-protests-trump-washington-takeover-00516596.

76 *"They don't care"*: Interviews with sources.

77 *Waiting for the clerk*: Devlin Barrett, "In Washington Crackdown, Making a Federal Case Out of Low-Level Arrests," *New York Times*, August 24, 2025, https://www.nytimes.com/2025/08/24/us/politics/trump-dc-crime-takeover-federal-court.html.

82 *"These catch-and-release"*: Minho Kim, "Arrested by Federal Agents, Some D.C. Residents Languished in Jail for Days," September 8, 2025, https://www.nytimes.com/2025/09/08/us/politics/dc-jail-arrests-pirro-trump.html.

82 *In August and September*: Alan Feuer, "Trump's Retribution Campaign Leaves D.C. Prosecutor's Office in Crisis," *New York Times*, November 2, 2025, https://www.nytimes.com/2025/11/02/us/politics/trump-pirro-washington-prosecutors.html.

83 *Gregory Lairmore*: Salvador Rizzo, "Jury Finds D.C. 'Sandwich Guy' Not Guilty of Assaulting Officer," *Washington Post*, November 6, 2025, https://www.washingtonpost.com/dc-md-va/2025/11/06/dc-sandwich-guy-trial-trump-federal-takeover/.

85 *"We're supposed to be"*: Ashley Parker, "Inside the Sandwich Guy's Jury Deliberations," *The Atlantic*, November 12, 2025, https://www.theatlantic.com/politics/2025/11/dc-sandwich-guy-jury-trump/684898/.

85 *While agents*: Brad Heath, "Federal Drug Prosecutions Fall to Lowest Level in Decades as Trump Shifts Focus to Deportations," Reuters, September 29, 2025, https://www.reuters.com/legal/government/federal-drug-prosecutions-fall-lowest-level-decades-trump-shifts-focus-2025-09-29/.

86 *Within the FBI*: Interviews with sources.

CHAPTER 6: BODIES IN MOTION

87 *"This is so"*: Interviews with sources.

90 *Soon after Trump*: "Protected Whistleblower Disclosure of Erez Reuveni," June 24, 2025, Letter to Senate Judiciary Committee, https://www.judiciary.senate.gov/imo/media/doc/06-24-2025_-_Protected_Whistleblower_Disclosure_of_Erez_Reuveni_Redacted.pdf.

90 *Trump signed the document*: Interviews with sources.

92 *In 2022*: Mike Stobbe and Geoff Mulvihill, "US Overdose Deaths Fell 27% Last Year, the Largest One-Year Decline Ever Seen," Associated Press, May 14, 2025, https://apnews.com/article/us-overdose-deaths-opioids-1561a9f-189255ad60c533462f10490a2.

92 *The highly potent*: Devlin Barrett, "Poison Pill: How Fentanyl Killed a 17-Year-Old," *Washington Post*, November 30, 2022, https://www.washingtonpost.com/national-security/2022/11/30/fentanyl-fake-pills-social-media/.

93 *The president was*: Interviews with sources.

94 *"Oh shit"*: Devlin Barrett, "Justice Dept. Whistle-Blower Warns of Administration's Assault on the Law," *New York Times*, July 10, 2025, https://www.nytimes.com/2025/07/10/us/politics/trump-bove-reuveni-whistleblower-doj-deportations.html.

99   *In late March*: Interview with Erez Reuveni.

99   *"I don't know"*: Jeff Zeleny and Kit Maher, "Trump Says He Didn't Sign Proclamation Invoking Alien Enemies Act," CNN, March 22, 2025, https://www.cnn.com/2025/03/21/politics/trump-signature-alien-enemies-act-proclamation.

100   *The Trump administration's*: Alan Feuer, "U.S. Tied Migrants to Gang Based Largely on Clothes or Tattoos, Papers Show," *New York Times*, March 31, 2025, https://www.nytimes.com/2025/03/31/us/politics/us-deportations-tren-de-aragua-deportation-guidance.html.

101   *Friday, March 28*: "Addendum to June 24, 2025, Protected Whistleblower Disclosure of Mr. Erez Reuveni," press release, July 7, 2025, https://www.judiciary.senate.gov/press/dem/releases/durbin-releases-documents-corroborating-justice-department-whistleblowers-allegations-against-embattled-trump-judicial-pick-emil-bove.

105   *"This was an illegal"*: Joel Rose and Sergio Martinez-Beltran, "Judge Orders the Trump Administration to Return Man Who Was Mistakenly Deported," NPR, April 4, https://www.npr.org/2025/04/04/nx-s1-5352448/judge-orders-the-trump-administration-to-return-man-who-was-mistakenly-deported-el-salvador.

108   *Rob McGuire*: Alan Feuer, "Justice Dept. Leaders Pushed to Charge Abrego Garcia, Emails Show," *New York Times*, December 30, 2025, https://www.nytimes.com/2025/12/30/nyregion/abrego-garcia-charges-doj.html.

CHAPTER 7: THE CORPSE OF CONGRESS

111   *Inside the DOJ*: Interviews with sources.

114   *In early May*: Interviews with sources.

115   *"Nothing was happening"*: Interviews with sources.

116   The Washington Post: Perry Stein et al., "Whistleblower: Emil Bove Misled Lawmakers About Case of NYC Mayor Eric Adams," *Washington Post*, July 28, 2025, https://www.washingtonpost.com/national-security/2025/07/28/emil-bove-nomination-judge-mislead/.

116   *The Justice Department inspector general*: Interviews with sources.

116   *"It's very frustrating"*: Interviews with sources.

118   *Trump demanded and got*: Annie Karni, "Keeping the House Absent, Johnson Marginalizes Congress and Himself," *New York Times*, October 28, 2025, https://www.nytimes.com/2025/10/25/us/politics/mike-johnson-speaker-congress.html.

CHAPTER 8: THE LIBRARY OF SECRETS

120   *Patel had never*: Kash Pramod Patel, *Government Gangsters: The Deep State, the Truth, and the Battle for Our Democracy* (Post Hill Press, 2023).

120   *Former coworkers recalled*: Interviews with sources.

121 *Throughout Trump's first*: Interviews with sources.

123 *"You gotta get"*: Interviews with sources.

125 *To pay for*: Cheryl Lederle, "J. Edgar Hoover: The Crimebuster and the Catalogers," Library of Congress Blogs, March 27, 2012, https://blogs.loc.gov /teachers/2012/03/j-edgar-hoover-the-crimebuster-and-the-catalogers/.

126 *Once in charge*: Interviews with sources.

127 *Even some conservatives*: Interviews with sources.

127 *Just before Halloween*: Glenn Thrush and Devlin Barrett, "Eager for Center Stage, Patel Casts Aside Caution in Statements as F.B.I. Leader," *New York Times*, December 15, 2025, https://www.nytimes.com/2025/12/15/us/politics /kash-patel-fbi.html.

128 *The FBI director*: Glenn Thrush et al., "Scrutiny Mounts of F.B.I. Under Patel as Kirk's Killer Remains at Large," *New York Times*, September 11, 2025, https://www.nytimes.com/2025/09/11/us/politics/fbi-patel-kirk-shooting .html.

CHAPTER 9: BURN BAG

131 *Room 9582*: Court filings, *U.S. v. James B. Comey*, 25-cr-272, Eastern District of Virginia.

131 *In June 2025*: Joe Rogan, *The Joe Rogan Experience*, June 6, 2025, 28:50, https://www.youtube.com/watch?v=C81bFx8CSA8.

133 *"In my heart"*: "C. Todd Gilbert Sworn in as United States Attorney for the Western District of Virginia," press release, U.S. Department of Justice, July 15, 2025, https://www.justice.gov/usao-wdva/pr/c-todd-gilbert-sworn-united -states-attorney-western-district-virginia.

135 *A week after*: Court filings, *U.S. v. James B. Comey*, 25-cr-272, Eastern District of Virginia.

138 *Many U.S. attorneys*: Interviews with sources.

138 *The FBI director*: Interviews with sources.

139 *Tracci had worked*: Interviews with sources.

140 *Prosecutors on the burn bag*: Interviews with sources.

143 *In July, Blanche*: Interviews with sources.

144 *Siebert was handed*: Interviews with sources.

CHAPTER 10: WEAPONS DRAWN

150 *Blanche, through his deputies*: Interviews with sources.

151 *The next day*: Katherine Faulders et al., "Trump Poised to Fire US Attorney for Resisting Effort to Charge NY AG Letitia James: Sources," ABC News, September 19, 2025, https://abcnews.go.com/US/trump-poised-fire-us-attorney -resisting-effort-charge/story?id=125700904.

153 *Halligan told*: Maura Judkis, "She Told Trump the Smithsonian Needs Changing. He's Ordered Her to Do It," *Washington Post*, April 21, 2025, https://www.washingtonpost.com/style/power/2025/04/21/lindsey-halligan-smithsonian-executive-order/.

158 *Days later*: Alan Feuer, "Judge Says Justice Dept. May Have Committed Misconduct in Comey Case," *New York Times*, November 17, 2025, https://www.nytimes.com/2025/11/17/us/politics/comey-justice-department-misconduct.html.

165 *In early December*: Devlin Barrett and Jonah E. Bromwich, "Grand Jury Said to Decline to Reindict Letitia James," *New York Times*, December 4, 2025, https://www.nytimes.com/2025/12/04/us/politics/letitia-james-indict-trump.html.

166 *Desperate for a win*: Jonah E. Bromwich et al., "A Grand Jury Again Declines to Reindict Letitia James," *New York Times*, December 11, 2025, https://www.nytimes.com/2025/12/11/us/politics/grand-jury-letitia-james.html.

CHAPTER 11: ETHICS, SCHMETHICS

167 *In 2015*: Stephanie Clifford and Matt Apuzzo, "After Indicting 14 Soccer Officials, U.S. Vows to End Graft in FIFA," *New York Times*, May 27, 2015, https://www.nytimes.com/2015/05/28/sports/soccer/fifa-officials-arrested-on-corruption-charges-blatter-isnt-among-them.html.

168 *One consequence*: Sam Borden, "FIFA Approves Plan to Fast-Track 2026 World Cup Host Bidding Process," ESPN, May 11, 2017, https://www.espn.com/soccer/story/_/id/37521706/fifa-approves-plan-fast-track-2026-world-cup-host-bidding-process.

170 *"I figured I"*: Interview with Joseph Tirrell.

170 *In late 2023*: Devlin Barrett and Tyler Pager, "Trump Said to Demand Justice Dept. Pay Him $230 Million for Past Cases," *New York Times*, October 21, 2025, https://www.nytimes.com/2025/10/21/us/politics/trump-justice-department-compensation.html.

175 *Like FBI director*: Interviews with sources.

176 *Trump's remarks*: Interviews with sources.

178 *There was another, unspoken reason*: Interviews with sources.

CHAPTER 12: MESSAGE IN A BULLET

183 *Days after Kirk's death*: "Vice President JD Vance Remembers Charlie Kirk," YouTube video, September 15, 2025, https://www.youtube.com/live/ngofqx9EfcM.

183 *In January 2024*: Dominique Moody, "Pro-Palestinian Caravan Near Blinken's Home After Encampment Cleared Out," NBC 4 Washington, July 27, 2024,

https://www.nbcwashington.com/news/local/pro-palestinian-caravan-near
-blinkens-home-after-encampment-cleared-out/3676812/.

185 *The next morning*: Devlin Barrett, "The Battle in Virginia Over an Activist
Who Protested Stephen Miller," *New York Times*, November 3, 2025, https://
www.nytimes.com/2025/11/03/us/politics/stephen-miller-activist-battle-free
-speech.html.

185 *The Millers wanted*: Interviews with sources.

188 *Two weeks after*: Devlin Barrett, "Justice Dept. Official Pushes Prosecutors
to Investigate George Soros's Foundation," *New York Times*, September 25,
2025, https://www.nytimes.com/2025/09/25/us/politics/justice-trump-george
-soros-foundation.html.

189 *He also issued*: National Security Presidential Memorandum 7, "Counter-
ing Domestic Terrorism and Organized Political Violence," White House,
September 25, 2025, https://www.whitehouse.gov/presidential-actions/2025
/09/countering-domestic-terrorism-and-organized-political-violence/.

190 *Schools, hospitals*: Devlin Barrett, "New Figures Show Surge in Threat Cases
Throughout American Life," *Washington Post*, January 12, 2024, https://www
.washingtonpost.com/national-security/2024/01/12/threats-swatting-fbi
-justice-prosecutions/.

CHAPTER 13: OUR RIGHTS VERSUS THEIR RIGHTS

194 *Stacey Young*: Interview with Stacey Young.

195 *In early 2025*: Interviews with sources.

195 *Trump put it*: Erica L. Green, "Trump Says Civil Rights Led to White People
Being 'Very Badly Treated,'" *New York Times*, January 11, 2025.

196 *"The responsibilities"*: Pam Bondi, "General Policy Regarding Zealous Advocacy
on Behalf of the United States," Memorandum for All Department Employees,
U.S. Department of Justice, February 5, 2025, https://www.justice.gov/ag
/media/1388521/dl?inline.

197 *In early March*: Devlin Barrett, "Orders to Investigate Columbia Protesters
Raised Alarms in Justice Dept.," *New York Times*, May 1, 2025, https://www
.nytimes.com/2025/05/01/us/politics/columbia-protests-justice-department
.html.

199 *"We already have"*: Lou Dobbs, *Lou Dobbs Tonight*, Fox Business News,
November 10, 2020, https://www.dhillonlaw.com/dhillon-on-2020-election
-litigation/.

200 *In the spring*: Jacey Fortin et al., "Justice Dept. to End Oversight of Local
Police Accused of Abuses," *New York Times*, May 21, 2025, https://www
.nytimes.com/2025/05/21/us/trump-police-consent-decrees.html.

201 *"That turns the process"*: Interview with Ejaz Baluch Jr.

203   *The new kind*: Devlin Barrett, "Trump Recasts Mission of Justice Dept.'s Civil Rights Office, Prompting 'Exodus,'" *New York Times*, April 28, 2025, https://www.nytimes.com/2025/04/28/us/politics/trump-doj-civil-rights.html.

203   *That sense of purpose*: Perry Stein, "Justice Department Struggles as Thousands Exit—and Few Are Replaced," *Washington Post*, November 10, 2025, https://www.washingtonpost.com/national-security/2025/11/10/justice-department-hiring-stalled/.

CHAPTER 14: ELECTION DAZE

208   *"Thank you to all"*: Interviews with sources.

211   *While Trump*: Jessica Taylor, "Trump Dissolves Controversial Election Commission," NPR, January 3, 2018, https://www.npr.org/2018/01/03/575524512/trump-dissolves-controversial-election-commission.

211   *"No Republican administration"*: "Harmeet Dhillon Is Suing and Cleaning Up the Voter Roles in These Key States," YouTube video, January 3, 2026, 1:30, https://www.youtube.com/watch?v=H9WO69gCFaQ.

212   *The criminal charges*: Eric Leonard, "LA County to Pay $5 Million to Settle Alleged Baseless Prosecution of Voting Software Provider," NBC 4 Los Angeles, January 23, 2024, https://www.nbclosangeles.com/investigations/la-county-pays-5-million-to-settle-alleged-baseless-prosecution-of-voting-software-provider/3319783/.

213   *The* Los Angeles Times: James Queally, "Trump's DOJ Hires Voting Rights Lawyer Behind L.A. Case Cited by Conspiracy Theorists," *Los Angeles Times*, January 3, 2026, https://www.latimes.com/california/story/2026-01-03/eric-neff-department-of-justice-la-election-lawsuit.

213   *"It was a rigged"*: Cheyanne M. Daniels, "Trump Says Individuals Will Soon Be Prosecuted for 2020 Election," *Politico*, January 21, 2026, https://www.politico.com/news/2026/01/21/trump-2020-election-prosecutions-00738778.

213   *A week after*: Interviews with sources.

CHAPTER 15: PLAYING FAVORITES

216   *In 2002*: "San Jose, California Man Pleads Guilty to Selling Explosives on eBay," press release, U.S. Department of Justice, May 2, 2002, https://www.justice.gov/archive/criminal/cybercrime/press-releases/2002/verPlea.htm.

216   *He was charged*: "Early Bitcoin Investor Charged with Tax Fraud," press release, U.S. Department of Justice, April 30, 2024, https://www.justice.gov/archives/opa/pr/early-bitcoin-investor-charged-tax-fraud.

216   *Ketan Bhirud*: Interviews with sources.

217 *In the spring*: Devlin Barrett and Glenn Thrush, "Justice Dept. Considers Merging Drug and Gun Agencies in Broader Reorganization," *New York Times*, March 27, 2025, https://www.nytimes.com/2025/03/27/us/trump-dea-atf.html.

219 *Aaron Henricks*: Interviews with sources.

220 *President Richard Nixon*: Tape Number 002, "White House Tapes: Sound Recordings of Meetings and Telephone Conversations of the Nixon Administration, 1971–1973," Richard Nixon Presidential Library and Museum, https://www.nixonlibrary.gov/white-house-tapes/002/conversation-002-002.

222 *Since its creation*: Luther A. Huston, *The Department of Justice* (Frederick A. Praeger, 1967).

223 *About a month*: Interviews with sources.

226 *In the spring*: Interviews with sources.

CHAPTER 16: THE LIBRARY STRIKES BACK

232 *"We have no idea"*: Interviews with sources.

233 *"Time to drop"*: Will Steakin, "It's a Cover Up:' Musk Floods X with Posts Attacking Trump over Epstein," ABC News, July 17, 2025, https://abcnews.com/US/cover-musk-floods-posts-attacking-trump-epstein/story?id=123836343.

233 *In a July 7 statement*: U.S. Department of Justice and Federal Bureau of Investigation, memo, DOJ and FBI, July 7, 2025, https://www.justice.gov/opa/media/1407001/dl?inline.

233 *In trying to tamp*: Daniel Ruetenik, "What the 'Missing Minute' in the Jeffrey Epstein Jail Video Shows," CBS News, September 3, 2025, https://www.cbsnews.com/news/jeffrey-epstein-missing-minute-jail-video-shows/.

234 *FBI Deputy Director*: Marc Caputo, "Scoop: FBI's Dan Bongino Clashes with AG Bondi over Handling of Epstein Files," *Axios*, July 11, 2025, https://www.axios.com/2025/07/11/epstein-files-dan-bongino-pam-bondi-trump.

235 *"If a career"*: William K. Rashbaum et al., "Prosecutor Fired by Trump Calls Fear the 'Tool of a Tyrant,'" *New York Times*, July 17, 2025, https://www.nytimes.com/2025/07/17/nyregion/maurene-comey-fired-trump.html.

235 *A day after*: Khadeeja Safdar and Joe Palazzolo, "Jeffrey Epstein's Friends Sent Him Bawdy Letters for a 50th Birthday Album. One Was From Donald Trump," *Wall Street Journal*, July 17, 2025, https://www.wsj.com/politics/trump-jeffrey-epstein-birthday-letter-we-have-certain-things-in-common-f918d796.

236 *"I never witnessed"*: Transcript of Ghislaine Maxwell interview, U.S. Department of Justice, July 24, 2025, https://www.justice.gov/maxwell-interview.

237 *Within days*: Hollie McKay and Daniel Edward Rosen, "A Reward for Cooperation: Ghislaine Maxwell's Covert Transfer to Cushy Prison in Texas Suggests Special Treatment," *New York Sun*, August 1, 2025, https://www.nysun.com

/article/a-reward-for-cooperation-ghislaine-maxwells-covert-transfer-to-cushy
-prison-in-texas-reeks-of-special-treatment.

238 *Representative Lauren Boebert*: Annie Karni et al., "Trump Ramps Up Pressure
on G.O.P. to Thwart Epstein Vote," *New York Times*, November 12, 2025,
https://www.nytimes.com/2025/11/12/us/politics/trump-epstein-vote-boebert
.html.

239 *Nearly two hundred lawyers*: Devlin Barrett and Michael Gold, "A Million
More Epstein Documents Have Been Found, Justice Dept. Says," *New York
Times*, December 24, 2025, https://www.nytimes.com/2025/12/24/us/politics
/epstein-files-documents-doj.html.

239 *Other lawyers were allowed*: Interviews with sources.

240 *Less than two*: Interviews with sources.

240 *"It is a grind"*: Interviews with sources.

CHAPTER 17: CREDIT AND CREDIBILITY

246 *In Philadelphia in*: "33 Alleged Members of Violent Kensington Drug Trafficking Organization Charged in 41-Count Indictment," press release, U.S.
Department of Justice, October 24, 2025, https://www.justice.gov/usao-edpa
/pr/33-alleged-members-violent-kensington-drug-trafficking-organiza-
tion-charged-41-count.

248 *One of the bills*: Devlin Barrett, "Spending Bill Would Pave Way for Senators
to Sue Over Phone Searches," *New York Times*, November 10, 2025, https://
www.nytimes.com/2025/11/10/us/politics/senators-shutdown-smith-phone
-searches.html

248 *Investigators wanted the records*: Interviews with sources.

249 *Lindsey Graham*: Ian Kayanja, "'Far More than That!': Graham Plans to Sue
DOJ over Phone Records in Jan. 6 Investigation," ABC 15 News, November 19,
2025, https://wpde.com/news/local/far-more-than-that-graham-plans-to-sue
-doj-over-phone-records-in-jan-6-investigation.

253 *The phrase comes*: Matthew Wills, "The Turkish Origins of the 'Deep State,'"
JSTOR, April 10, 2017, https://daily.jstor.org/the-unacknowledged-origins-of
-the-deep-state/.

253 *In 2013*: Soner Cagaptay, *The New Sultan: Erdogan and the Crisis of Modernity*
(I.B. Tauris, 2017).

256 *"The foxhole provided"*: Adam Goldman et al., "Top F.B.I. Agent in New York
Vows to 'Dig In' After Removals at Agency," *New York Times*, February 2,
2025, https://www.nytimes.com/2025/02/02/us/politics/fbi-new-york-email
-trump.html.

Index

About the Author

Devlin Barrett has covered federal law enforcement for more than twenty-five years. He writes about the Justice Department and the FBI for *The New York Times*, and he previously worked for *The Washington Post*, *The Wall Street Journal*, the Associated Press, and the *New York Post*. In the past decade, he has been part of three Pulitzer Prize–winning reporting teams—for Public Service, for National Reporting, and for Breaking News Reporting—and was a cofinalist for Pulitzer Prizes for International Reporting and Feature Writing. He is also the author of *October Surprise: How the FBI Tried to Save Itself and Crashed an Election*, an account of the FBI's role in the 2016 presidential election. Barrett lives in Virginia with his wife and children.